LAND OF THE CAUVERY TO THE LAND OF BRAHMAPUTRA

"Reminiscences of S. Manoharan, an erstwhile civil servant, on his memorable and lively experiences."

S.Manoharan

ISBN
Paperback 979-8-89588-646-5
Hardcase 979-8-89610-979-2

Dedicated to Dr. Kalarani Manoharan ('Raanimaa')

My Beloved Wife

Contents

M. Gopalakrishna
I.A.S. (Retd.)

"Bhramara" 12-2-823A/23
Santoshnagar, Mehdipatnam
Hyderabad – 500 028
Tel. No." 23513420
Fax: 23525322
E-mail: gopalkm2006@rediffmail.com

F O R E W O R D

The book "Land of the Cauvery to the land of the Brahmaputra" is the memoir and vivid recollection of events of his life by Shri S. Manoharan, an IAS Officer (1975) of the Assam-Meghalaya cadre.

It is a frank and fascinating chronicle of his work in Assam, Chennai, and in Delhi during the different phases of his career over 35 years. The varied nature of jobs he held till his retirement as Special Secretary to the Government of India in the Ministry of Water Resources in 2010 reveals his versatility and uncanny foresight to handle difficult situations with the cooperation of colleagues.

His account is reflective, recalling incidents and events which makes for delightful reading about the conditions and travails in Assam, relations with Ministers and politicians, and the prevailing environment. The forthright description of events and action taken shows him as a sensitive, sensible, humble, and development-oriented civil servant.

His tenure as DC in two Hills Districts, Chief Electoral Officer, Joint Chief Commissioner of Imports and Exports at Madras, Secretary Health, Commissioner Plains Division, Resident Commissioner in Delhi and as Joint Secretary in the Ministry of Steel and as Additional and Special Secretary in Ministry of Water Resources reveal his repertoire of skills and versatility in tackling and difficult situations.

Recalled from Andhra Pradesh as Home Commissioner in Assam in 1982-83 to conduct Elections under President's Rule in difficult conditions and total non-cooperation of staff and public, I chose Manoharan as the Joint Secretary (Home) who more than justified his selection. That association with him and his wife Kala Rani and son Rajkumar is continuing for over 40 years.

The book delineates conditions in Assam and recapitulates the travails and troubles that Civil servants have to take to improve administration and provide good governance at grass-roots level.

Readers will surely appreciate the nature of jobs and conditions under which Civil servants function and the need for ethics, values and morals in life and in performing one's duty. The book should find a place in Training Institutions and libraries in Assam and all over India and help aspiring Civil servants to know the nuances of administration.

Sri M. Gopalakrishna, IAS (Retd.)
Former Assam & A.P Cadre Officer

September 20, 2024

Introduction

CHAPTER
01

I started writing my memoirs as a former civil servant in the year 2023, 13 years after my superannuation. When I began this work, I wondered whether I would have the capability to write my reminiscences in chronological order without the benefit of written notes about various interesting events or anecdotes in a cogent and coherent manner. I had to literally depend on my memory to illustrate the important events and interesting anecdotes during my professional career spread over an approximate period of 35 years. I daresay, without exaggeration, that I was compelled to recall pleasant and memorable experiences as an officer belonging to the 1975 I.A.S. batch, based singularly on my memory and also through the encouragement and motivation from some of my batchmates, cadre mates, friends, and well-wishers that included my close family members as well.

I was rather sceptical as to whether I would do justice to this overwhelming task of publishing this maiden endeavour in a successful manner and if it would be of any interest to the reader to know about my varied experiences as an erstwhile civil servant of the Assam – Meghalaya cadre. The raison d'être of attempting to write proper and truthful reminiscences of my civil service years, 13 years after my superannuation, was not only to apprise the reader about the opportunities and challenges I came across as a civil servant but also as a personal challenge at trying my best to recollect the important events that were spread over more than a period of 3 decades during my varied assignments in 3 different states of the country.

In hindsight, I had an apprehension whether I would be able to get into the Indian Administrative Service due to lack of any private education or a civil service background of my parents or close relatives. Getting into the I.A.S. was my cherished dream during my postgraduation studies, as I was not interested in teaching or any other professional assignments.

It was my very first attempt after my postgraduation in a science subject from Annamalai University in the year 1973. To realise my cherished dream, I prepared thoroughly and diligently worked hard with steadfast perseverance for one-year. However, by God's grace, I got through the Civil Service Examinations held by the UPSC in October 1974 in my very first attempt. I considered this to be a godsent opportunity for me to serve the people of our country to the best of my ability. At the same time, during my initial training days, I was shocked to receive the information, which was like a bolt from the blue, that I was allotted the Assam-Meghalaya cadre and not my home state, Tamil Nadu. Hailing as I did from Tamil Nadu, it was an extremely challenging assignment to work in a faraway North Eastern state like Assam, where the language, culture, and traditions etc are totally different. But this did not deter me from adapting myself to the new environment in my first field assignment as Assistant Commissioner under training at Silchar, the Headquarters of Cachar District in Assam and to get along and serve the people of that district as a very young I.A.S. officer trainee. In my assignments in the succeeding years, I had worked with a great sense of responsibility and diligence not only in the State of Assam but also on Central Government deputation assignments at erstwhile Madras and New Delhi.

I strongly believe in the dictum 'Service to Humanity is Service to God Almighty'. The opportunity to relate to this powerful message was provided by my entry into the I.A.S. And I feel that I was able to acquit myself in this regard with impeccable integrity, selfless service and utmost concern for the welfare of the people of the state in each and every assignment throughout my career. Serving far from one's home nearly 3,000 km away was a daunting task. There were hardships along the way, but converting the challenge to serve the people of the region did provide comfort and solace. And I was able to ensure that I served the country with utmost commitment, diligence, dedication, hard work and integrity without any fear or favour.

In my view, the I.A.S. is perhaps the only service which provides abundant, enviable, and excellent opportunities to any member of the civil service towards ensuring adaptability, interactions with varied sections of the people in the rural and urban areas of the country, with an objective assessment of the needs of the people and to come up to their expectations in the best possible manner. At the same time, one would get the job satisfaction provided one did his or her level best for providing not only selfless service but also with utmost competence and efficiency as per the expectations of the people in general and the poorest of the poor in particular. I would like to mention here that as a civil servant, I had to come up to people's expectations, especially when a villager who is illiterate or semi-literate comes to the office of the Sub-Divisional Officer or Deputy Commissioner of the district to solve his issues. He was aware of the limitations and constraints faced by the Deputy Commissioner or the head of the District Administration. However, his personal issues were apparent and of utmost importance in his mind.

In Assam, the Deputy Commissioner is called *Upa Ayukta*. If a Deputy Commissioner, when confronted by a villager to address his issues, pleaded helplessness and mentioned that he was unable to provide any immediate solution, the smart villager countered that since the Deputy Commissioner was the Upa Ayukta, it was his foremost duty and responsibility to find out an *Upai* as an answer or solution to the issues brought forth by the villager. Or else, there was no noteworthy purpose in his title of Upa Ayukta. If you dispassionately looked at the villagers' candid assertion, it was full of common sense reflecting on the fact that as it was the duty of a civil servant to come to the aid of the villager when he came to meet the Deputy Commissioner with the fond hope of finding a solution to his problem.

Throughout my civil service career in Assam over many assignments, I had many **interesting experiences**. I would attempt to recall pleasant memories of my initial stay as Sub-Divisional Officer of Golaghat Sub-division of the then Sibsagar district and interactions with the villagers in addition to details of my many visits to interior places. These experiences were further enriched by my tenure as a field officer in the 2 hills districts of Assam, as Deputy Commissioner. Of course, apart from working in the field as a Sub-divisional officer and the Deputy Commissioner of the 2 hills districts, I did try to make significant contributions during assignments at various levels in the State Secretariat. These postings were helpful in shaping up the career of a budding civil servant and learning in detail the processes and procedures contributing to the system of administration at the state and Union levels. It also allowed me an opportunity to interact with senior officers of the Government of India and those in senior positions of various public Sector Undertakings. And beyond this, the opportunity to attend various conferences within the country and abroad, including those in certain international organisations, allowed me to widen the scope of my knowledge in new areas in the implementation of government policies in the cause of the larger good of public service.

I always considered working in the civil service provided tremendous opportunities for a member of the service to not only get exposure to various issues and problems but also provided for his or her refinement and continuous learning process. Despite the fact that one might sometimes fail in the expectations of the people or his colleagues and supervisory officers, who would be the best judge about the performance of a civil servant.

To learn and to adapt oneself to difficult situations in life was always part and parcel of the civil service. Learning, I mean, not only through books or rules and regulations governing the service conditions, but also learning by way of interactions with the people of various sections of society, colleagues, and supervisory officers in order to help them if one could give some kind of solace to their issues whenever there were occasions that demanded or wherever there were opportunities to help the people during one's assignment in different areas.

For instance, in the field-level assignments, like Sub-Divisional Officer or Deputy Commissioner, during the difficult law and order situations, there might be instances where one could do their level best to save somebody's life at stake. I did, of course, save the lives of some people when there were very serious law and order situations when I happened to be the Sub-Divisional Officer of Golaghat Sub-division. I did not want to narrate the issues like what were the reasons for such numerous losses of lives or untoward incidents and suffice it to say that, by God's grace, I could rescue some people during such difficult law and order situations involving conflicts between various sections of society. That kind of experience gave me the satisfaction that I did the best possible help in such extremely difficult circumstances.

I did not want to write elaborately about my tasks in the introduction chapter itself, as the reader could ascertain after going through various chapters in this book whether, as a civil servant, I did justice to my assignments.. I did come out with certain hilarious anecdotes and also certain serious incidents wherein one even risked one's own life; after all, taking a risk is a part and parcel of the life of a civil servant.

My primary objective is that if the reader finds it interesting to go through the contents of the book and whether he would appreciate the sincerity with which I did my level best to give an exposure of what I did for a period of 35 years in the service of the people, I will be delighted to say the least. In addition to spending about 35 years in the civil service, I did contribute my mite in certain post-superannuation part-time assignments in the Government of India and Central Public Sector Undertakings as well for a period of 10 years. When I exited the conference hall of the Ministry of Water Resources on the 31st May 2010, after a long fulfilling career of almost 35 years in the civil service and especially as the then Special Secretary to the Government of India in the Ministry of Water Resources, as my last assignment, I did state the following. I consider that it would be appropriate to end my introduction as below:

"I served the Nation and the people for several decades, and it was a great privilege and honour for me, by God's divine grace, to work in different assignments in the State of Assam and in the States of Tamil Nadu and Delhi on Government of India deputation assignments. I had unequivocally stated with my sense of pride on that day of my farewell meeting that I would exit that hall holding my head very high with dignity and, of course, humility, and last but not least with utmost satisfaction of serving the people with my commitment, compassion, dedication, dynamism, and sincerity to the hilt. I would also like to add without any blemish throughout my civil service career in different assignments, I had discharged my duties and responsibilities as expected of me as a conscientious and sincere civil servant for the welfare of the people of our country." I felt very proud and said so amongst the officers and staff who had assembled on that day to bid me a warm farewell with love and affection.

When I looked back even today about my joining the I.A.S. on 13th July 1975 and my superannuation on 31st May 2010, I vividly recall various incidents in my official career in 3 different States of the country with my crystal clear objectivity of ensuring transparency and efficiency with commitment and compassion, with a motto of serving the people with politeness, dignity, and humility in whichever assignments I did hold during my service period.

It may not be out of place to mention here that I tried to recount my experiences and encounters without indulging in self-praise on one side or being critical of others. I have made an effort to present an honest, sincere, and objective assessment in what I think was a self-fulfilling and satisfactory role as a civil servant.

Initial Years of Training at the Lal Bahadur Shastri National Academy of Administration (LBSNAA) at Mussoorie.

Before one got used to travel by Boeing or Airbus jet flights after several years of service, on official duties or otherwise, like any student who just passed out after postgraduation from a university, one was expected to travel in a second-class train compartment, no matter whether one travelled from the Deccan plateau or from the western or northern states or from the North eastern regions. Naturally, like other fellow probationers (that is how a new recruit to the I.A.S. or any other member of the All India Services or other Class I Central Services was called during the training till he or she was confirmed in service), the writer also travelled from his hometown by a long-distance train in a second-class compartment. Once I reached Delhi, the next mode of transport was either by bus or train from Delhi to Dehradun.

I preferred to travel by train. In the same compartment, I noticed 2 more fellow travellers from my part of the country. However, they neither exchanged pleasantries nor tried to make friends with me. I also did not venture to do so. The egoistic self-important assumption that you were heaven-born, unlike not so privileged mortals, after making it to the most prestigious I.A.S. was evident and writ large on one's face. Of course, both of them became my great friends later in the academy itself after we were formally introduced to each other. Our close friendship continues even now after more than 4 decades, without any friction whatsoever. Thankfully, we have not fallen to the charms of typical rivalry that one sees among batchmates. One of the fellow officers is Mr. K. S. Sripathi who became the Chief Secretary to the Government of Tamil Nadu, and the other gentleman is Mr. T. Srinivasan who became the Chief Secretary to the Government of the State of Rajasthan.

The friendship nurtured with love, affection, and warmth at the academy continues until this day, even though 4 decades have passed and we have no bloated sense of ego at all as of today, even though each one of us had excelled in many ways in our civil service career and that too, in 3 different states.

From day one onwards, one developed an enormous sense of smugness and perhaps felt as to why there was a need for one to make the first move. All 3 of us were aware that the destination was Mussoorie only, as there was more than enough of the heavy luggage like the big steel trunk boxes and big suitcases everyone carried as their personal belongings. You may wonder whether there was a dire need for carrying so much heavy luggage on the part of officer trainees (or rather the neither sophisticated nor praiseworthy terminology, i.e., the 'probationers'). The officer trainees had to stay for the next 9 months, and hence the requisite paraphernalia was warranted.

The journey from Dehradun Railway station to Mussoorie was a wonderful and unforgettable one with the taxi driver haggling for fare. He was more interested in dumping as many human beings inside the car as he liked, as he would dump as much baggage not only in the boot but also on our lap and onto the top of the car. Anyway, I did not attempt to bargain not due to a lack of my bravado but due to my inability to converse in the local language, called 'Hindi'. One of the important tenets for a successful civil servant i.e., 'discretion is better than valour' has been ingrained in me, as I did not want to argue with the taxi driver. I meekly accepted his demand, in view of my very little knowledge of the language and to avoid the prospect of being mercilessly offloaded along with my luggage from the ramshackle vehicle by the rude taxi driver. I was more interested in reaching the destination first, as I was already exhausted due to 2 long-distance journeys undertaken on not-so-fantastic trains, unlike the 'Rajdhani ' and 'Vande Bharat ' trains of our modern era.

After reaching Mussoorie, I met a tough-looking but handsome guy in the administration. He informed me that the formal allotment of a room would only happen the next day and that it would typically be on a sharing basis with another member of the civil service. However, on that very first day, I was given a room temporarily on the campus to be shared by a fellow probationer in the civil service. Lo and behold, when I entered the room with my heavy luggage to occupy a bed, as I was in a terrible hurry to rest, a stern-looking person welcomed me in chaste local language which was not even used in common parlance, nor could I understand heads or tails of it. I politely gave my identity in English and even more politely informed him that he would be better off conversing in English, which would make it easier for me to respond correctly to his mundane questions. It seemed like he had never come across anyone from a state other than his own ilk in his life. Perhaps, he assumed that every citizen in every corner of the country could easily understand and was obligated to speak only in his own lingo fluently.

It was virtually a kind of interview conducted by him, although I believed my interview was already over with UPSC clearing me in my very first attempt to enter the Indian Administrative Service. I compensated for my lack of ability to respond to him in his chaste lingo by offering him large portions of pastries, cakes, and coconut cookies, which were diligently packed by my beloved and gracious mother. I also had an ulterior motive, as I wanted to sleep peacefully that night. Furthermore, I did not want to listen to a continuous harangue from him about the dire necessity on my part to learn the local language. The poor fellow did not know or realise at that time that it would take a minimum of one or two decades for him to speak, read, and write in my mother tongue, called 'Tamil'. How I wished that night or cursed him that he should be sent on formal assignment to serve in a state south of the Vindyachal Mountains for the remainder of his civil service career.

But God the Almighty did not answer my prayers that way, and he was lucky to be posted in his own home state where he might have excelled in his various assignments for the next 3 decades or so. However, destiny willed otherwise for me. Instead of my home state, I was allotted a faraway state, and there could not probably be any state further from my hometown. I had to learn and pass not only one language of that state but 2 languages in addition to Hindi. The reader might be knowledgeable about double jeopardy, but in my case, it was triple jeopardy, as I had to be proficient in 3 languages in addition to, of course, my mother tongue and English.

After a few months in the academy, I did learn to converse comfortably to the extent possible and to read and write in Hindi.

On the very next day, i.e., on 13th July 1975, I formally joined the I.A.S. and took an oath of affirmation to the Constitution of India. On that day, I was allotted a room at the Happy Valley Annexe wherein my roommate happened to be an Indian Foreign Service (IFS) probationer. Generally, the principle of allotting 2 gentlemen in one room during the Foundational Course was always that one from the I.A.S. and another from the Central Service and that too, from different regions to ensure the proper mingling of the officer trainees.

However, in my case, it turned out to be a blessing in disguise in the sense that a Tamil gentleman was allotted as my roommate. It so happened because my name was spelt as Mancharan and my roommate's name was spelt as Gangapathi. In other words, I was considered a gentleman from the northern part of the country, and my roommate, by his name itself, revealed that he was from the southern part of the country. The Administrative Officer might have allotted 2 Tamil gentlemen in the same room due to the misspelling of our names and his poor appreciation or knowledge about south Indian names. My roommate's name was actually Mr. M. Ganapathi, an officer trainee from the other premier, privileged service, the IFS. Fortunately for me, he studied in the northern states due to his father's postings in different places in the North. He was quite knowledgeable in Hindi. Apart from being a roommate, he was my Hindi teacher as well. The friendship I developed with him as a roommate is unforgettable and long-lasting. We treat each other as brothers. He is extremely kind-hearted and one of my outstanding well-wishers with excellent qualities of head and heart. After serving as an Ambassador of India to some countries, he retired as Secretary in the Ministry of External Affairs. It might be worthwhile to add that just before the printing of this book, and around almost fifty years since we first met, it has been Mr. Ganapathi who has painstakingly reviewed and edited this book!

Recollection of my experiences as an I.A.S. Trainee at the Lal Bahadur Shastri National Academy of Administration in Mussoorie from 13th July 1975 until March 1976 during the first phase and from April 1977 to June 1977 during the second phase of Traineeship.

I will attempt to recollect my lasting memories of our interactions as officer trainees, which were more often than not, filled with unbridled banter and boisterous laughter.

To begin with, it took some time for all the trainees of the 1975 batch to break the ice and come to know one another as there were four hundred or so officer trainees from not only the I.A.S., but also from other All India Services and other Class I Services. All of us attended the Foundational Course for 4 months beginning from July 1975. Thereafter, the officer trainees of the I.A.S. batch alone spent about another 5 at the Lal Bahadur Shastri National Academy of Administration at Mussoorie during the first phase of the professional course of the I.A.S. The officer trainees from the other services went off to their respective training academies. I deliberately avoided mentioning the term 'I.A.S. Probationers', though that was the so-called designation officially given to us at that time. I am rather wary of mentioning that term now in view of the fact that a probationer might also mean 'an offender on probation'. The term probationer was used during our training period until after completion of our training period, which included one-year of field training in the district of the state of allotment and thereafter, for another period of 3 months or so for the second phase of the professional course at the academy at Mussoorie.

During the training period of the first phase and second phase of the professional course, I do recall our various programmes viz. Physical training exercises, horse riding lessons, classroom sessions, formal dinners, other social get-togethers and the many festive occasions wherein, we as trainees had participated with joy and abandon. But I must narrate one particular incident about which many of our friends and I vividly remember and cherish all these years with reference to our dinner on the day the cadre allotment was announced.

Our friends could be broadly classified into 2 categories, viz., one group of officer trainees who got the state of their choice or preference or their own home state and another group of officer trainees who were not as fortunate as the former group and were allotted states simply based on some type of lot system that was prevalent at that time, i.e. totally unexpected and/or far away state cadres that were not so much preferred. For the uninformed, this mattered a lot to the officers as the allotted state becomes home for the officers for most of the next 35 years or so, unless they are specifically deputed for time-bound postings outside their cadre state.

On that unforgettable night, each and every officer trainee who came to know about his or her cadre allotment, after dinner and of course, even before that, were highly spirited. After dinner as well, they continued to imbibe more and more appetisers depending on one's capacity and capability, leading to virtual banter, merry-making, and ruckus on that night. The raison d'etre was that one group of our friends was extremely delighted and felt exuberant after getting to know of the cadre allotment of one's own choice and so happily imbibed more appetisers for the celebration of one's sheer and utmost bliss to spend the rest of his professional career in their state of choice or liking. Another group of our friends was extremely dejected and depressed after getting to know of the cadre allotment, which was certainly not their choice. This latter group also got thoroughly sozzled due to more than adequate appetisers and became very highly spirited just to forget their disappointment, disgust, frustration, misfortune, and sorrow.

In other words, both groups of our friends started dancing to the tunes of the music played and indulged in revelry and merry-making, continuing to imbibe spirits in more than adequate quantities. God only knows who imbibed more or less or more than adequate. That kind of uncontrolled celebration and revelry went on and on much beyond midnight. Later on, as I got rather dizzy, perhaps, I felt sleepy and leaned on one of the sofas in our very big and beautiful lounge and slept. Suddenly, my ebullient and effervescent friend, who was perhaps a little more sober than me, literally woke me up by shouting "*Thalaiver*, get up immediately as some fumes were coming out of your head." (Incidentally, some of my friends started addressing me like that irrespective of whether I was worth being called a leader). The reason for the fumes coming out of my head or the thick growth of luxurious hair on my head was that someone who was a smoker threw the burning cigarette butt without putting it out. Due to his careless attitude, the sofa cover caught fire, and smoke started coming out. As I rested my head on that portion of the sofa, my very dear friend thought that something was amiss, and my hair caught fire. As a very good Samaritan, he took pity on me and woke me up. Adequate water was poured on the sofa, and the fumes were put out. It is another matter that some saner counsel prevailed upon some of us, as we were jolted out of our height of unbridled madness and revelry due to the unexpected turn of events on that night.

During the first phase of our training period at Mussoorie, I had come across many of my batchmates from various regions and different Class One Services. It was a wonderful opportunity for me that I met them during the first phase of our training period. However, after the Foundational Course, I would have hardly met any of the officer trainees of Class One Services.

Nevertheless, after the Foundational Course, as our professional course continued, I had made excellent friendships with many of my batch mates which remained throughout my service period and after my superannuation as well.

During our professional course, we had to attend classes for different subjects that were taught and at the end of the course, sit for examinations as well. By and large, the classes were held only in the morning between 9 am to 1 pm. After the lunch recess in the afternoon, there were only classes for officers like me who were allotted cadres other than their own home states to learn the language of the state of allotment. In my case, I had to learn the Assamese language that was for one hour. The teacher, Tharani Kanta Rabha, who taught me was a wonderful human being. I and some of my friends from Assam visited his house as well. It was not like a student-teacher relationship but more of a warm friendship between 2 grown-up gentlemen. He was very polite and courteous. Later on, the same gentleman suddenly came one day and met me after more than 2 decades at Guwahati when I happened to be the Commissioner of Lower Assam Division. I was delighted to meet him and spend some time with him. Because of my position as Divisional Commissioner, he started addressing me as 'Sir'. I prevented him from calling me 'Sir'. I told him that I was his student and he was my teacher at the academy, but beyond that we were more like friends. He felt so delighted and interacted with me for quite some time. I asked him pointedly whether he needed any help from me to which he responded that he made a visit only to meet me for courtesy, nothing more and nothing less.

During the professional course, I had to attend Hindi classes between 4 to 5 pm. I had to learn Hindi and pass an examination in the language at the end of the first phase of the professional course while writing examinations in other subjects. I had learnt Hindi in school, which I had not put to any use since that time. The Hindi teacher was very kind-hearted and taught me and some other officers who were from the southern states. In the case of officer trainees who were allotted to their own home state, there were no afternoon classes at all for attending language classes. In a way, the afternoons were free for them. I felt rather bad as I had to spend all the afternoons attending the language classes.

In addition to attending regular classes, very often, there were guest lectures and interactions among the officer trainees. In other words, the entire curriculum at the academy was like another course in a college. Besides attending regular classes, we used to spend evenings participating in outdoor and indoor sports and games. I learnt billiards and sometimes played badminton. Unfortunately, I was not a regular player in any of the games.

There were also opportunities to play musical instruments at the academy. Sometimes, I used to join my friends who were playing the guitar and used to play drums, etc.

Interestingly, we had horse riding classes in the early hours of the day, i.e., from 6 am to 7 am on some days, and physical exercises on some other days. These were compulsory, so one had to attend whether one liked it or not. During the horse riding classes, there was one difficult task that one had to learn. While sitting on the horse and holding the bridle, the horse would jump over a hurdle. It was a challenging task because the horse found it easy to jump the hurdle, but one had to be careful and hold the bridle very tight; otherwise, one would fall off the horse's back, which might lead to a serious injury. Although some of us might have enjoyed horse riding very much, some officer trainees found it to be a less welcome exercise, considering the need to control the horse to the desired extent. There were several stages in proper horse riding that were taught by the *Syce* (trainer).

I vividly remember a hilarious incident when we went horse riding to a nearby open field, which was a rather big ground. In such places, one could go rather fast, which was called cantering. In such cases, the rider had to hold the bridle very tight so that he was safe on the horseback. When it started running, perhaps, I was rather scared and started holding the bridle and also the neck of the horse rather tight. Then the horse started running faster, and the trainer at a distance started shouting at me that I should have held the bridle very tight and should not have held his neck to control the speed of the horse because the horse might be scared and started running fast. That was the only day I was afraid. At this instance, I would also like to mention that like attending examinations on the subjects taught to us, we had to pass the horse-riding test also. The horse trainer only would decide whether one had the ability to control the horse, and one got properly trained in riding the horse as different stages of riding were taught by him. One of the important criteria for passing the horse riding test was whether one could sit stable on the back of the horse without fear and with proper control when the horse jumps over the hurdle. Fortunately, I had passed the horse riding test like passing other examinations, including the languages taught to me.

As mentioned in the foregoing paragraphs, there were several cultural events and social get-togethers, and hence, we got an opportunity to familiarise ourselves with the cultures of various states. All festivals were celebrated at the academy, and many of our friends participated in such cultural events. There used to be debates on many subjects, and I had participated in one or 2 debates as well. I would like to conclude my training period at the academy as an unforgettable one with many episodes; one had come across in view of the first time exposure to a wonderful hill station and stay at the beautiful academy where we spent the first 9 months of our training programme. Due to space constraints, I would just like to mention that in addition to my participation in many cultural events, social get-together dinners organised at the academy, I could say that for me it was a stage of transformation from that of an officer trainee to a knowledgeable civil servant with the requisite qualities of head and heart to serve the people and, of course, with a sense of fair play and justice in the later years. Moreover, the training period provided a great opportunity to develop friendship with many of my batch mates hailing from different parts of the country. The friendship and bonhomie developed during those months of training continue to be cherished as pleasant memories and have enabled me to keep in touch with them even after 4 decades.

During the second phase of my training period from April 1977 to June 1977, I could not reach the academy in time due to my personal hardships. I fell ill and had to be admitted to the hospital in Madras for some minor surgery. So, I arrived at the academy 3 weeks late and hardly spent just over 2 months from the end of April 1977 to June 1977. During the second phase, the faculty members from the Indian Institute of Management, Ahmedabad, conducted classes on management lessons. During the second phase, it was also necessary for officer trainees to share their experiences as field officers during the one-year training period in their assigned state. For instance, I had to give a talk on my own experience as a trainee officer, i.e. as an Assistant Commissioner under training at the Office of the Deputy Commissioner, Cachar District in the State of Assam. This included my experiences in field training, visits to villages, and police stations, etc. In order to understand the entire gamut of district administration, the one-year field training involved attachments with the Office of the Superintendent of Police, the Office of the Block Development Officer, the Office of the Tahsildar, and other field-level functionaries. I also received training on the duties of an Executive Magistrate as outlined in the Criminal Procedure Code (CrPC). I functioned as an Executive Magistrate and carried out my duties as stipulated in the various provisions of the CrPC. Apart from participating in training at the Office of the Deputy Commissioner, one had to attend a one-week training programme at the Office of the Superintendent of Police in the District Headquarters.

After I joined as an Assistant Commissioner under training for the period April 1976 to March 1977, I accompanied the Deputy Commissioner on his tours and also visited many villages along with the Tahsildar and Block Development Officer. Within a couple of months after I joined, there were floods and the entire town of Silchar was flooded to a great extent, in addition to many parts of the district. I had a very rare experience of travelling in a helicopter which had loads of rice, wheat, and other items to be dropped to marooned villages in the district. In a nutshell, during the second phase of the training period, I had to narrate my experiences, observations, and the lessons I had learnt during the period of one-year spent in the district. I had to respond to the questions raised by my fellow colleagues in the class. Likewise, each and every trainee officer had to narrate his or her experiences. In a way, the second phase provided an opportunity for me to interact with my friends from other states and to appreciate their field experiences in their States of allotment. I could compare my experience with theirs' and one could derive more knowledge from the experiences and interactions that the others had..

Training as Assistant Commissioner at Silchar, Cachar District from April 1976 to March 1977 in the State of Assam

My first day of arrival in the State of Assam, my allotted cadre, started on a hilarious note. I was posted to the Cachar district for training after the cadre allotment. I reached the District Headquarters town, Silchar, after a little more than an hour's flight from Calcutta, now renamed Kolkata. Incidentally, it was my first-ever air journey and that too, in a vintage model aircraft, the 'Fokker Friendship' of Indian Airlines, which is no longer in use now.

I must now admit from memory dating back to more than 4 decades ago that the air journey was comfortable and the air hostess was a charming and gracious person with pleasing manners and genuine care and concern, unlike some of the unfriendly crew with plastic smiles on their faces in the modern era. The breakfast offered with due courtesy was 2 *idlis* and 2 vadas with chutney and sambar, and they were steaming hot. I was pleasantly surprised to eat *idlis* up above in the sky on my very first flight to an unknown and unfamiliar destination, with the subconscious apprehension in my mind.

Coming back to the interesting experience I had on the very first day, as soon as I got down from the aircraft, I was jostling with the not-so-disciplined crowd to locate my 2 big suitcases among the many pieces of luggage of other passengers which were dumped on some stone slabs or on the dirty floor of the arrival hall of the small airport. The airport was located at a distance of approximately 25 km or so from the town. I had to stay in the District Headquarters town for one-year to get fully acquainted with the multidimensional aspects of the art of governance as a field-level functionary under the guidance of the head of the District Administration, the Deputy Commissioner. Moreover, I had better learnt the nuances of district administration as a young probationer by withstanding all sorts of odds, obstacles, and difficulties that might come in my way in my future official career.

I was at a distance of more than 2800 km from my hometown and imagine my plight of landing in an alien atmosphere like 'Alice in Wonderland' in the company of altogether unknown people in an unknown place with the people of that area speaking in a language which I could not decipher at all, as I had to depend only on my knowledge of English with a modicum of understanding of Hindi. Coming back to the arrival hall hauling my 2 big suitcases with much difficulty, I expected a chauffeur-driven government vehicle to take me to the Circuit House, i.e., how the government guest house is christened in the District Headquarters all over India. To my utter disappointment and dismay, I did not see a vehicle belonging to the district administration despite my formal request communicated to the district head of the administration by a formal letter followed by a telegram more than a fortnight preceding my arrival.

With no other alternative available to leave the airport for my intended place of stay, I had to hire a taxi with much cajoling and persuasion to make the taxi driver understand and appreciate my plight as a young proud civil servant posted to his 'big city'. My entreaties were of no avail as he flatly refused to take me alone in the ramshackle and the typical vintage black and yellow coloured ambassador taxi and instead he had dumped half a dozen or more passengers, fortunately with small pieces of luggage, along with my luggage as well. He started driving in a callous and rash manner, totally unmindful of the comforts of the passengers in the vehicle on the dusty and bumpy road ahead. Throughout my journey from the airport to the district headquarter town, I had to put up with not only the bumpy road and the dust in ample measure but also to tolerate the noise and pollution from my fellow passengers in the taxi who did not stop talking even for a second.

I had categorically instructed the taxi driver that I must be dropped at the Circuit House only, and it was a deal he had agreed to at the airport before our departure. But before half a kilometre or so between the Circuit

House and the main road, he decided to abruptly stop and asked me mercilessly to get down with my luggage despite my vehement protests. He was least bothered about the assurance he had given regarding dropping me at the correct destination despite my vociferous arguments in broken Hindi, which was the lingua franca between him and me. He just did not care a bit about my self-acclaimed status nor showed the least consideration that I was absolutely new to his town, who neither understood the local language nor dialect and a helpless citizen to his most cherished city or town, as the case may be. It was my 'sheer good luck' if I may say so that I was destined to get trained there by the sleight hand of destiny.

In a way, it turned out to be a good omen for me, though I was fretting and fuming that I was left in the lurch in the middle of the road, totally uncared for except by the Divine Grace of God the Almighty. As a matter of fact, I wondered what was in store for me for the next year and how I would face the odds, obstacles, and difficulties that might come my way to reach my goal of shaping myself as a civilised, humane, and sincere civil servant in the service of the nation. I was yet to get familiarised with the harsh realities of the life of a future civil servant, which was and would never be a bed of roses.

If the reader thinks over my plight in a rather critical and sarcastic manner, I can only pity him and wish that he had landed in a similar situation to realise the hard facts narrated by me without the least exaggeration. The driver took the fare from me without, of course, haggling for change or asking me for tips or more than the agreed fare. He offered me, though, an unsolicited advice after seeing my plight of not knowing how to reach the Circuit House, as obviously, I could not afford to walk with 2 big suitcases even though the distance to be covered was less than one km. As advised by the taxi driver, I had to hire a cycle rickshaw, popularly called '*rishka*' instead of '*rickshaw*' in the local language.

I had to swallow my bloated ego on that very day itself, and in a way, the incident helped me ensure that I had better learnt the hardest lesson in my life that 'sooner you discard your bloated ego, the better it is for your future peace of mind and happiness'. Here, I would like to humbly make the distinction between what is 'sense of pride and what is a 'sense of bloated ego'. I always had my sense of pride that I was one amongst the

126 candidates selected in my coveted civil service called the I.A.S., out of a total of more than 1,60,000 or so ladies and gentlemen who competed at that time and that too, in my very first attempt in the year 1975. After completion of my postgraduation at Annamalai University and without taking up any other government or public or private sector assignment, I straightaway joined the I.A.S., of course, with an absolute sense of pride after my thorough preparation for the I.A.S. examination for one-year with concentration, commitment, dedication, and devotion. Till date, I continue to cherish my sense of pride as I never surrendered my conscience nor my self-respect, for the sake of any ill-gotten wealth as well as have maintained a total disregard for unscrupulous norms of behaviour and conduct. I decided that I would continue to serve the people with commitment, compassion, dedication, humility, and sincerity throughout my civil service career till my superannuation and thereafter, for 10 more years as well in several important part-time assignments under the Government of India and in the Public Sector Undertakings.

But whatever little sense of bloated ego perhaps I had, as a privileged human being in view of my civil service status, I honestly admit that from the day of my arrival at Silchar for my district training and onwards, I started shedding my ego gradually. By the time I got posted as the District Magistrate (or District Collector or Deputy Commissioner) within the next few years, the process was complete. It is not an exaggeration if I may say so, as of late, you would come across scores of civil or uncivil or servile civil servants even during their service or several years after their superannuation, reduced to simple ordinary senior citizens' status, yet to give up their so-called bloated ego or, if I may say, their self-proclaimed or assumed status consciousness for no rhyme or reason.

Sub-Divisional Officer of Golaghat Sub-division from July 1977 to February 1979

My pleasant memories of taking over my first independent charge assignment as Sub-Divisional Officer of Golaghat Sub-division with Headquarters at Golaghat and my continuance as the head of the Sub-divisional administration are narrated below.

In the month of July 1977, after I took over as Sub-Divisional Officer of Golaghat Sub-division at Golaghat of Sibsagar District with its headquarters at Jorhat, I was delighted to occupy the official residence of S. D. O. which was a very old British-era structure. I was given to understand and appreciate that it was more than 95 years old at that time; basically a very strong huge wooden structure supported by big-sized bamboo/wooden stilts beneath the bungalow, and covered with a thatched roof.

The bungalow was a huge one with a residential office chamber and a staff room, etc., in addition to the usual paraphernalia. The kitchen was located on the ground floor at the rear side. One could approach the kitchen from the residence through a wooden staircase from the second bedroom. Just beneath the bungalow, in between the stilts, 3 vehicles were parked. One was a pretty old original Land Rover vehicle, which had been lying there unused for several years and was beyond redemption. Another jeep was also parked. That was a Willy's Jeep with a left-hand steering facility. In addition, there was a very old Ambassador car parked as well. For a bachelor like me at that time, it was a great luxury, as the residence was fully furnished.

Moreover, the bungalow had a big front veranda with an antique-type longish 'easy chair'; it was a broad one with 2 long arms wherein one can rest their arms and relax to the maximum extent possible. The house had a huge compound with a big lawn in front with flower-bearing trees. Behind the residence within the premises, one could organise a vegetable garden as well. There were staff quarters in addition to the bungalow within the premises of the residence. Two drivers, namely, Mr. Tahir Ali and Mr. Mansoor Ali Khan, were living with their families. The bungalow peon or the cook, Mr. Parameshwar, was an interesting and clever gentleman, with a facade that looked like an innocent person, similar to the 2 very clever drivers. In addition, the staff consisted of a gardener who was rather physically emaciated due to his bad drinking habit and another staff member called a chainman for taking care of the lawn and backyard of the residence of the Sub-divisional officer.

Fortunately or unfortunately, I had no other alternative except to depend on such interesting characters for my stay at the residence, as they were expected to take care of the premises of the bungalow during my presence as well as absence frequently on my tours within the sub-division and outside. I was only 26 years old when I took over my very first independent assignment in my administrative service career. At that young age, I had learnt a very big lesson in my life, i.e. 'Face is certainly not the index of the mind.' Or in other words, if I may say so, perhaps, sometimes, appearance is deceptive and one should always be very careful and cautious in dealing with people. After all, as an administrator, over the next more than three decades in service, I had to invariably know the art of human resource management, various aspects of public relations, and dealing with varied types of people in multifarious assignments in three different states, as luck would have it and of course, by God's divine grace.

I would be failing in my duty if I failed to mention about the excellent care and precautions taken by my predecessor for my reception and my stay at the Circuit House for a few days. Mr. Tahir Ali, the driver, received me at the Furkating railway junction after I reached that station, which is a nearby railway station to Golaghat town, and took me to the Circuit House at Golaghat, where I was expected to stay for a few days. My predecessor hardly stayed at the bungalow after I joined in his place and bequeathed, literally, the house in a very good shape, the cook, and the cow as well in a few days' time. No doubt, my predecessor's wife had trained the cook exceedingly well, and for me being a bachelor, it was like a welcome change, like getting home-cooked food prepared by the cook. He was a very good cook undoubtedly, but he was a clever and a cunning guy and not so dependable, as I had realised his propensity for mischief much later. In the succeeding paragraphs, I will narrate some interesting issues created by him in view of his capacity for doing mischief by keeping an image or facade or whatever one may call as innocence par excellence at its face value.

When my predecessor Mr. S.K. Tewari handed over the charge of the assignment of the head of the administration of that sub-division to me and left for his promotional posting at the State Secretariat, he had informed me that there was a police constable who had requested him to keep his cow within the premises, as it was a milch cow. My predecessor made monthly payments for the milk consumed by him and his wife to that police constable. The police constable was a very clever guy and was happy to let the cow feed on the grass grown on the lawns and backyard, etc. Although I was wary of keeping the cow as a non-speaking companion in addition to multiple members of the household staff on the premises, I respected the sentiments and request of my predecessor who was living with his wife. The police constable was very much delighted that he had smoothly and successfully handed over the custody of his movable property, i.e., a white-coloured beautiful cow from my predecessor to me, bereft of tortuous negotiations.

The fundamental exposition, if I may say so, was that my predecessor and the police constable, whose name I don't recollect now, were of the view that as long as I stayed, I would get reasonably priced and unadulterated milk. Like the transfer of temporary ownership of the cow to me, my predecessor had emphasised the advantages of retaining his old bungalow peon or cook called Parameshwar, who would take care of my boarding arrangements and housekeeping, etc., in the best possible manner. My predecessor and his devoted wife were giving enough hints to me that being a total stranger to the place and that too, very far away from my hometown, I could depend on the cooking abilities and integrity on the part of Mr. Parameshwar, who had worked with him during his stay as the then S. D. O. Golaghat for about nearly 2 years.

Most importantly, I did notice that the police constable and the cook were country cousins in the sense that they hailed from the same state. As my knowledge of the local language, i.e. Assamese, was not-so-good and as

I was equally not very well acquainted with the language, i.e. Hindi, spoken by my predecessor and his cook, I thought that it would be better to abide by the saner counsel of my predecessor, as it would be a futile exercise to search for a new bungalow peon or cook. On hindsight, if I may say so, the cook and the household staff took maximum advantage of my lack of attention to cooking aspects, the expenditure incurred, and housekeeping arrangements, etc. It is not an exaggeration in view of my busy schedule of official engagements and frequent tours, etc, on my part.

After a few days of my joining, I started residing in the prestigious more than 95-year-old bungalow with a thatched roof occupied by my predecessors who were former I.C.S. and I.A.S. officers. I started residing in that bungalow in the middle of July 1977, as the head of the administration of the wonderful sub-division of Golaghat. I had lived there for about 20 months. I could have completed a little more than 2 years but for my transfer to another important assignment due to some necessity as informed by the then Chief Secretary, Assam.

The official residence of the Sub-divisional Officer, Golaghat, had a big compound with 2 large gates, i.e. entrance and exit, though only one gate was used for both entry and exit. The other exit gate was permanently closed. My next-door neighbour was the Sub-divisional Police Officer. His government quarter was a typical Assam-type building, unlike the S. D. O.'s sprawling residence. There was a driveway to enter from the main road in front through the entrance gate to the S. D. O.'s residence. Most interestingly, just opposite my residence beyond the main road, there was a huge playground or a large open space which was used as a multipurpose facility, for holding public meetings and for children to use as a playground. More significantly, the Independence Day and Republic Day flag-hoisting ceremonies were held there at the Sub-divisional headquarters.

During my almost 2 years of stay at the residence in Golaghat, it was a great pastime for me to take a morning cup of tea sitting on the wide veranda with its wooden floor of the house, as if sitting on the mezzanine floor or on the first floor balcony of a house overlooking a big public open space and watching the children playing in the field and people going about their normal routine purchases of vegetables, provisions, etc. in the market or carrying on their daily livelihood activities.

After a fortnight of joining the office, the driver Mr. Tahir Ali enquired about my driving ability. I said candidly that I did not know and ascertained from him whether it would be possible for him to teach me the art of driving. He responded that he had taught driving lessons to many predecessors of mine and he would be able to make me drive a vehicle in the quickest possible time. I was reassured by him that within the next week after I settled down in my assignment, he would start his driving lessons with the Willy's Jeep available at the residence. It was, of course, a left-hand drive, as the steering wheel was on the left side contrary to the steering wheel on the right side in the majority of vehicles by and large, including the very old ambassador car kept for official use.

So when my driver, Mr. Tahir Ali, suggested one fine morning that I start my driving lessons, I asked him to let me know if I could begin learning the art of driving with absolute precautions on the playground in front of the residence. He promptly said, "Sir, yes, of course, it is your prerogative undoubtedly." He further stated that it was the best place to start driving lessons on my part without any hesitation or apprehension of a beginner's first day of learning, as he would carefully restrict my driving lessons to one side of the open space, as it was a huge one, without causing inconvenience to the children or anyone using that playground for their recreation.

After the requisite clarification of my doubts and apprehensions, he drove the old Willy's Jeep with a left-hand drive from the residence on one fine morning, and I sat on his right side next to the driver's seat. We reached the playground in just a couple of minutes. The moment we had reached the playground, my driver got down from the vehicle and requested me to sit on the left side in front of the steering wheel. He started explaining the basic features of the vehicle for the driving purpose with absolute clarity in Hindi as well as Assamese languages, and I carefully listened to him intensively, as an obedient student with rapt attention to the lessons of a learnt teacher. After he made sure that I had somewhat understood his way of teaching, considering my lack of adequate understanding of the Assamese language and slightly better understanding of the Hindi language at that time, he advised me to start the engine, apply the first gear, slowly release the gear, and put gentle pressure on the accelerator with the help of my right foot.

He again and again reassured me that nothing would go wrong as he had taught driving lessons to many predecessors of mine without the slightest hitch. Therefore, in the open space of the playground around 8 am, I started driving only with the first and second gears. After some time, he taught me how to change into the third and fourth gears and application of the brake. Like a studious and sincere student very keen to learn the driving process carefully bereft of any lacunae, I listened to him intently and drove the vehicle on the left, right, and straight across with a limited speed in the vastly open space of the big playground or public place without much disturbance or apprehension that I might cause an accident inadvertently.

Mr. Tahir Ali, my driver, emphasised that I should concentrate only on the direction in front of the vehicle, even though there was no obstacle or roadblocks on the playground, as a matter of abundant caution and as the fundamental necessity for a successful completion of my learning process. He was a very good teacher, no doubt, for a beginner like me who was keen on learning to drive a vehicle with much enthusiasm, energy, and indomitable spirit. He taught me after about half an hour how to change into reverse gear as well. Thereafter, he told me that the lessons of that day were over. So, I had spent an hour learning on the first day of my driving initiative. We would start the driving lessons again the next day.

On the next day, at about 8 am, he drove the Willy's Jeep from my residence to the playground across the road. Again, the same rigmarole continued for an hour or so. On the second day, of course, he asked me to sit in the driver's seat and start driving the vehicle. For a change, he said to me that he would not hold the steering wheel along with me, and I should have the confidence to start the engine and shift the vehicle into first gear, then slowly change to second and third gear. He advised me to start and drive the vehicle in different directions without fear as there were not many people except a few boys playing at a distance. Of course, Mr. Tahir Ali, my driver and teacher rolled into one personality, was a very good teacher and a pleasant personality. As I happened to be his boss, he couldn't scold me if I committed any mistakes. As a beginner taking driving lessons for the first time, I was rather nervous and changed gears frequently and applied the brake wrongly at times. I must say that he was extremely patient with me in going through the lessons.

After the second day of my lessons, at around 10 am, when I got ready to go to my office, i.e. the office of Sub-Divisional Officer of Golaghat Sub-division, of which I was the head of the office, he parked the vehicle in front of the Bungalow on the ground floor. When I came down the stairs from my residence, which is a very big British-era old wooden structure supported by very strong bamboo poles or stilts, as one might recall, Mr. Tahir Ali coolly asked me to sit in front of the steering wheel of the Willy's Jeep and start driving to go to the office through the main road, and he sat next to me. For the time being on that day roles were reversed! I was his driver in a comic sense if I may say so. Jokes apart, I was a bit scared and hesitated for a short while. The distance between my residence and office was approximately one kilometre only. It was morning time, and people were on the road visiting offices and shops, etc.

But my driver, Mr. Tahir Ali, said when I hesitated to drive the vehicle on my own with my apprehension that I might hit someone either by accident or wrong driving while taking some turns, as I was a new learner without even a learner's licence, Mr. Tahir Ali boldly uttered in his mother tongue, i.e. Assamese language, "Sir, *Bolok, Appunni Mahakumaadhipati Mahoday. Kunhe ki kobo. Bhayakoribonaalaaghe. Moi assu nohoi. Moi saithakkim Appunni gaadhi solabo. Appunni kibaa bhool kori le moi xahai korim. Appunni aaraamot solaauk.*" In other words, it means, "Sir. Come on, you are Sub-divisional officer. Who can say anything? Please don't be afraid. I am here with you. If you commit any mistakes, I will come to your rescue. Please relax and start driving with ease."

If I look back on hindsight, today after about 46 years, it appears to me that like Lord Shri Krishna who was otherwise known as Paarthasaarathi i.e. Arjuna's Driver giving lessons of Karma and life itself, my enthusiastic driver and my teacher was there for imparting knowledge of the fundamentals of the art of driving to me with tremendous confidence and words of encouragement to drive the vehicle on my own on the second day of learning to my office without fear and with utmost confidence. Lo and behold, I did drive the vehicle without committing any mistakes or minor accidents with absolute confidence and of course, with the physical and moral support of my driver who on that day was my teacher.

Fortunately, I drove with confidence and based on the motivation, physical and moral support of my Guru Mr. Tahir Ali, I not only successfully drove the vehicle to the office, but also drove back the vehicle to my residence in the afternoon for lunch. Since both my drivers with their families were also living in the staff quarters within the compound of the S. D. O.'s residence, Mr. Tahir Ali had to take food at his residence. This is the usual practice whenever I was in the headquarters and I was not on official tours. After an hour or so, I went back to the office again driving the vehicle along with the driver sitting on my right side, as it was a left-hand drive. In the evening around 6 pm, I returned to my residence again myself in charge of the steering wheel and my driver was like my boss sitting on my right side overseeing my driving ability.

This rigmarole continued for a week or so. When I came back one day in the evening around 6 pm or so, as I was driving the vehicle, an interesting incident happened. Suddenly, as a cycle rickshaw came very close to my vehicle, despite my sincere efforts to avoid the cycle rickshaw puller and his vehicle getting damaged, I hit the cycle rickshaw slightly. I was driving very slowly and cautiously due to my first day experience of driving on the road with thrill and enthusiasm, so I felt very bad.

I stopped the vehicle for a while and advised my driver to get down and check for himself whether there was any major damage to the cycle rickshaw. Of course, there was not much damage and the cycle rickshaw puller also did not create any fuss. But my Guru, Mr. Tahir Ali, made a profound statement: "Sir, *koonbha beya sokku logai dile hoi to, etiya ek dam theek hoi gol.*" In other words, it means that whosoever had cast his evil eyes on your driving ability, it didn't matter, as after this minor hit by me on the cycle rickshaw, it was like purification of its ills on its own. I didn't have to worry too much.

The story of my driving lessons and my driver's certificate, like the vaccination certificate, that you are fully competent to drive a car as well came after a month or so. In the meantime, I had taken the Willy's Jeep with my driver outside my headquarters as well on tour on quite a few days. Fortunately, for me, as I was trying to get a new Ambassador Car, a status symbol of those yesteryears to boast around your stamp of authority, my efforts had borne fruit in an unexpected manner. Not that the government sanctioned me an Ambassador Car immediately, as it required on my part to condemn the existing old jeep and then only it was possible to get a new car.

In Assam, we have an elected local body at the level of sub-division, which is called '*Mahakuma Parishad*', entrusted with the development works of the sub-division. In those years, there was a three-tier Panchayat Raj system prevalent in the State of Assam. There were Gram Panchayats, i.e. local self-government institutions, an elected body of people's representatives headed by a president and members of the Gram Panchayat at the village level. At the Taluk level, i.e. for a combination of several villages and rural areas, an elected body functioned, which was called '*Anchalik Panchayat*', and it had its president and various elected representatives of several areas, etc. At the Sub-divisional level, the '*Mahakuma Parishad*' functioned. It was headed by a Chief Executive Counsellor and comprised several elected Counsellors representing various parts of the sub-division or a group of villages represented by their elected representatives. This is the local self-government setup.

Immediately after a few months of my joining as Sub-divisional Officer, the elected body at the level of sub-division was dissolved, and I was asked to take over the functions of *Mahakuma Parishad* as an administrator for a few months, until alternative arrangements were made or until the newly elected body came into being.

As the then-elected body of *Mahakuma Parishad* was dissolved and as per the directions of the government, I took over as the administrator of that particular assignment in addition to my regular duties and responsibilities as Sub-divisional officer at Golaghat. The office of the *Mahakuma Parishad* was very near the office of the Sub-divisional officer, Golaghat. Therefore, I went and took charge as Administrator in the Office of the **Chief Executive Counsellor (CEC)**, *Mahakuma Parishad*. The then Chief Executive Counsellor was Mr. Jiten Barua. Of course, he was a thorough gentleman and he was very pleasant in handing over the charge of his assignment to me as the administrator without any heartburns. The vehicle belonging to CEC was an Ambassador Car, and he handed over the car keys to me. Incidentally, I got an Ambassador Car as luck would have it without resorting to condemnation of Willys jeep at that time.

As a consequence, I had to undertake certain tours within the sub-division as an administrator as well as the Sub-Divisional Officer of the Golaghat Sub-Division. As the head of Sub-Divisional Administration, in addition to being in the headquarters for many days in a month, at least for a minimum of 10 days or so, I had to undertake tours to different parts of the sub-division in addition to meetings conducted by the Deputy Commissioner of the district. Of course, Shri Tahir Ali, my driver, drove the vehicle throughout my journeys. Occasionally, he used to hand over the car keys to me so that I could drive the car on the National Highways, and very often it so happened that he encouraged me to drive at a particular speed. Very rarely, I used to drive at a higher speed as well just to test the vehicle as well as my driving ability.

On one such tour, I had to proceed hurriedly to a neighbouring Taluk which was about 25 km away as there was an accident, and people were admitted to the local hospital at that time. So, I was in a great hurry to go to the hospital to take care of the injured persons as well as to look after their comforts. In fact, the vehicle the passengers travelled in was a big bus. They were tourists from Maharashtra, and fortunately, none were killed; some of them were injured to some extent but not of a very serious nature. The bus incidentally fell into a nearby ditch, and ultimately, we had to take enough measures to rescue not only the bus but also to organise transport for the passengers who had recovered after some minor treatment and were sent back to their destination from where they had come.

Here I would like to narrate a small incident. Since I was in a great hurry to visit that particular hospital on the way, suddenly when I was driving a little faster speed, a hen crossed the road; so I could not apply the brake in time and as a consequence the hen came under the wheel. When I got down from the vehicle to see what had happened, it was already dead. At that particular point of time, with a bit of sense of humour and timing, the driver told me, "Sir, now your driving lessons were absolutely complete as whatever the evil eyes that were cast on you, they were all over with this kind of sacrifice of a hen at the cost of your wonderful learning ability of driving with skills within a short period. So please don't worry. Let us go to our destination." This is what the driver at that time told me. I still remembered that particular incident. At this point of time, I would like to conclude that the art of driving lessons taken by the driver was very helpful in my later years as an erstwhile civil servant and occasionally only, I used to drive the vehicle and once it so happened I had taken the vehicle straight up to the State Headquarters at least to a distance of more than 250 kms but after some distance of course, I handed over the vehicle to the driver himself and I continued my journey.

The bond established with the driver Shri Tahir Ali continued in later years, and occasionally he used to come to the State Headquarters to meet me and my family. He was a wonderful human being with enough care and caution whenever he drove me to different parts of the sub-division, the District Headquarters, or to the state capital, i.e., Dispur (Guwahati). I am very grateful to him not only for teaching me as a Guru, the art of driving in the early stages of my life but also because not even one accident ever happened when he was driving the vehicle with me to various parts of this sub-division or to the District Headquarters, and also occasionally to the State Headquarters. I am grateful to him for his kindness, love, and affection to date.

Incidentally, the Sub-Divisional Officer of the Sub-division in Assam is called SDO (Civil). This is to distinguish several SDOs of various technical departments like SDO-PWD, SDO-Public Health Engineering Department, SDO-Agriculture, SDO Flood Control, SDO-National Highway, SDO-Health and Medical, etc. SDO-Civil is the head of the Sub-divisional administration, and all other SDOs of technical departments by and large report to the SDO-Civil and seek guidance or instructions wherever necessary. Moreover, as a Sub-divisional officer-Civil, I was expected to travel on tour to many places in the sub-division to supervise the works of the technical departments, in my capacity as head of the administration of the entire sub-division and also to attend to complaints, if any, received from the members of the public such as about the bad maintenance of roads or inadequate water supply or any agricultural issues.

There was an Officers' Club which functioned as a recreation centre at the dak bungalow, for which I was the President, in my capacity as the SDO. There was a Circuit House as well. By and large, the visiting officers normally stay in the Circuit House. The Dak Bungalows in Assam were established several decades ago, initially as inspection bungalows for touring officers. Over a period of time, many of the technical departments have established their own inspection bungalows in certain parts of the sub-division. Consequently, a few rooms in the dak bungalow by and large were occupied by officers of the lower ranks temporarily in case of absence of official accommodation. In the Officers' Club there were not many recreational activities except table tennis or playing cards, etc., in the drawing & dining room in the Dak Bungalow. I used to go to meet the officers at the club sometimes in the evenings.

Incidentally, I was the youngest officer in the group even though I was the Head of the Officers' Club. I was very friendly with them, which was reciprocated by the technical officers and colleagues who were quite cordial and interacted with me in a pleasant manner. I made it a point that whenever I visited the Officers Club, I would never broach any issues of administration or technical matters, as the club was meant for recreational purposes only.

On one of the late evenings, I remember the date vividly, the 4th of November 1977, I happened to be at the club. As I was chatting with some of the other members, the officer-in-charge of the Police Station at Golaghat came in hurriedly to meet me. I went out to know what exactly the urgency was. He whispered to me that he had received a wireless message that I should immediately contact the Deputy Commissioner (DC) at Jorhat. I rushed to my residence to talk to the Deputy Commissioner on the phone. In any case, the distance between the club and my residence was less than a kilometre. Mr. S K Chakravarti, the then Deputy Commissioner, who always used to treat me like his younger brother, informed me that there was a matter of some seriousness and concern. He said that he and senior officers were waiting at Jorhat airport on that evening to receive the then Hon'ble Prime Minister Mr. Morarji Desai, and the airplane did not arrive. Therefore, there was a tremendous apprehension that the plane might have lost its way in view of the very heavy rainfall, with the worst possible fear being that it might have crash-landed nearby. He informed me that since the matter was extremely serious, I should not disclose the matter to anyone and take over a few vehicles from the technical department officers and hand them to the officer-in-charge of the Golaghat police station. The DC also told me that the Superintendent of Police had already sent several police personnel in vehicles to search for the places wherein the plane might have landed during that inclement weather. He also informed me that there was an apprehension that the plane might have crash-landed somewhere in the forested areas near Golaghat. So it was a very serious issue, and I immediately rushed to the Officers' Club and requested my colleagues to hand over their vehicles to me for an emergency without disclosing why I needed their vehicles. Of course, I told them that the vehicles would be returned after a few hours.

Hence, a few vehicles with the drivers were handed over to the officer-in-charge of Golaghat police station by me for the search purpose. In the meanwhile, the officer-in-charge had already received instructions from the police headquarters. I also directed him to immediately send search parties with torchlights, etc., to ascertain whether the Prime Minister's aircraft had landed somewhere near the forest areas of Golaghat Sub-Division. Since it was a very sensitive matter, I advised him to be very careful and undertake the operations with utmost secrecy. I even told him that I had simply collected the vehicles from the technical department SDOs without disclosing the reasons as to why I had done so. After that, I left for my residence and informed the DC about sending search parties from Golghat town to nearby forest areas of the sub-division. I was also anxiously waiting to get any further information either from the DC or from the Police search parties whom we had sent to various parts of the sub-division. Later in the night, I ascertained from the DC that the plane had crash-landed not very far from Jorhat town, maybe about less than 10 km on a paddy field. The entire course of events is retraced below.

The aircraft could have deviated from its original flight path in view of the poor visibility due to the very heavy downpour. It was raining heavily, and the pilot could not somehow land at the airport where the DC and SP and other security personnel were waiting to receive the then Hon'ble Prime Minister. They, of course, noticed the aircraft hovering in the sky, but then it suddenly disappeared.

The entire district administration and police personnel were extremely anxious and seriously concerned about the fate of the VVIP aircraft. Search parties were immediately dispatched with wireless sets to locate the aircraft in case it landed anywhere in the forest or nearby areas. Later, after a few hours and late into the night, it was brought to the notice of the district administration that the plane had landed in a nearby paddy field, which was very slushy and muddy due to the heavy downpour.

I would like to pay tribute to the greatest sacrifice made by the pilot and the co-pilot, in addition to the other crew members, of the Indian Air Force

(IAF) aircraft. In true IAF tradition, with its priority of Service before Self and Security, the pilot, co-pilot, and crew members made sure that the nose cone landed on the field so that there was no threat to the life of the Prime Minister. The Prime Minister was seated along with his son Kantibhai Desai in the rear part of the aircraft and hence their lives were saved, though they suffered minor bruises and injuries. The training and experience of the pilots ensured that the aircraft landed on its nose down. The maximum impact was thus felt on the cockpit and the front of the aircraft. It was the supreme and ultimate sacrifice by the brave aircrew which saved the life of the Prime Minister. In the bargain, they gave up their lives in the service of the nation. An action that was most commendable and noteworthy. Besides, the incessant rains and slushy field ensured that the aircraft fortunately did not catch fire. As the aircraft had crash-landed on a paddy field, which was muddy and full of slush, the Prime Minister got out of the plane with great difficulty. After walking for some distance in the field, he noticed a lamp in a hut nearby and he went straight to that hut. There he disclosed to the residents of the hut that he was the Prime Minister of India. Since that villager was a helpful samaritan, he immediately offered the Prime Minister and his son water and tea, etc., and he tried to inform the nearby people about that incident. Of course, within the next few minutes or so, this news was received by the police personnel and district administration. I came to know later about this incident from the DC that 5 crew members were killed but the Prime Minister was alive. It was late in the night and despite the downpour, slushy and muddy field, the Prime Minister, despite his age and with his tremendous willpower and God's will, somehow reached the villager's hut on foot.

Later on, of course, that villager was invited to New Delhi and was honoured. Prime Minister Desai was also gracious in recognising the villager's effort. The airmen were also honoured. What was more gratifying to note here is that on the next day, the villagers during sunlight could see that the rear portion of that plane was damaged and, of course, the cockpit got stuck up in the paddy field only with the 5 dead bodies of aircrew members. It was so touching for me and other senior officers of the district administration that the villagers of that area organised a 'shraad' ceremony for the departed souls the next week in order to pay their obeisance to the air force warriors who sacrificed their lives to save the then PM of India. It was such an attitude of gratitude, and the villagers organised the 'shraad' ceremony in a very, very sincere and organised manner as though they had lost their own kith and kin.

For that ceremony, the DC, DIG of Police, SP and sub-divisional of Golaghat and Sibsagar sub-divisions, Sub-Divisional Police officers and the Director of the Regional Research Laboratory, Jorhat assembled there during the 'shraad' ceremony and participated in the rituals including the prayers of the villagers for the departed souls to rest in peace. It was a solemn occasion in which the entire top echelons of the district administration along with the local villagers participated to pay respects to the departed souls. They organised a simple vegetarian feast where we all assembled on the ground and took the food by sitting along with them on the ground not only as a mark of respect to the departed souls but also as a matter of thanksgiving to God Almighty and the local villagers.

When I visited the site after a couple of days, I could see the paddy field was literally cut across by the wings of the aircraft as though they were cut in the middle before the harvest. It was an unforgettable incident for me, and one could always appreciate the tremendous guts, fortitude, along with the determination to survive on the part of the octogenarian Prime Minister.

The incidents of the crash landing of the IAF aircraft with the VVIP on a paddy field at a distance of less than 10 km from the District Headquarters and the organisation of the memorable 'shraad' ceremony organised by the villagers to respect the greatest sacrifice made by the air force crew personnel for saving the life of the Hon'ble PM at the cost of their own life had been etched in my mind, and hence this episode.

HILARIOUS, INTERESTING AND UNFORGETTABLE EPISODE - EXPERIENCE OF INTERACTIONS WITH THE VILLAGERS WHO HAD BROUGHT A ROYAL BENGAL TIGER IN AN IMPROVISED CAGE TO THE OFFICE OF SUB-DIVISIONAL OFFICER, GOLAGHAT.

As the Sub-divisional officer of Golaghat, in the years 1977-79, I had to handle 2 difficult situations on 2 different days within a couple of months successively. Once, when a huge Royal Bengal Tiger on a particular day and another time, a very big black panther were brought inside improvised cages along with a trailer tractor from a nearby village about 15 km or so by a small group of villagers to my office.

The villagers literally wanted to gift me the animals out of sheer disgust, despair, and disappointment as they had previously wished to hand over the same on 2 different occasions to the then Assistant Conservator of Forests (ACF), Golaghat only to be rebuked and rebuffed by him for causing unnecessary and unwarranted difficulties for him. He didn't care to listen to their grievances as to how and why they had brought the animals to his office. Hence, their admirable and adorable presentation of the animals to my humble self, as I was their '*Mahakumaadhipati*', and it was only my sheer duty and responsibility to come to their rescue to tide over the crisis, as the head of the administration of Sub-division of Golaghat.

Frankly speaking, they threw their hands and asked me to take the animals on 2 different occasions and keep them at my office, as they felt extremely offended by the not-so-pleasant attitude, behaviour, and conduct of the then ACF Golaghat.

It is another story as to how I handled both situations and made sure that the animals did not break the cage and pounce on the people who gathered in very large numbers to witness the live spectacle of the fuming, fretting, and roaring of the poor hapless animals out of sheer anger, angst, and agony experienced by them in such a terrible environment. Fantastic and fascinating days of my memorable early months of my posting as S. D. O. Golaghat more than 45 years ago!

I have described the narrative as below based on my memory. It was, of course, an unforgettable and once-in-a-lifetime experience, say, twice in my life, at my age of around 27 years. Perhaps, I was destined to handle that peculiar and unforeseen situation then adroitly, as probably, God the Almighty willed that way so that in the future years, I might have to handle many more difficult situations occasionally confronting despicable, disgusting, recalcitrant, undesirable, and unscrupulous persons in politics and bureaucracy for more than 3 decades of service in the future, with commitment, dedication, and determination, indomitable willpower, and wielding authority to the hilt as and when necessary and of course, with compassion, due diligence, and sincerity.

Those were the early months of my stay at Golaghat, and my knowledge of the Assamese language was limited. I had to manage my understanding and appreciation of the local language based on day-to-day interactions with my personal peon, Mr. R. Bora, who was my Guru or teacher in the translation of words and sentences spoken by the people, (who used to come to meet me day in and day out to voice their requests or grievances) from Assamese to broken Hindi. Mr. R. Bora, my personal peon, was knowledgeable only in the Assamese language, being his mother tongue. However, his knowledge of Hindi was rather limited, as was mine.

So when there was some commotion outside my chamber on that day, I advised him to go and verify and let me know what the cause of such commotion was. I had made it a point very strictly that no one was allowed to enter my office chamber without my permission. He came back and uttered only 3 words, "Sir, *Bagh! Bagh!*" I thought that the word *Bagh* also means 'Run'. So I mistook him and asked him instead as to why I should run out of my office. For a while, there was a communication bottleneck between me and Mr. R. Bora, my faithful grade IV staff. He clearly understood my predicament and then requested me to come out of my chamber through sign language to see for myself, almost imploring me. I could see the terrible anxiety and anguish in his eyes and slight trembling of his voice.

When I came out, lo and behold, I could see that more than a hundred people had already assembled in front of my office outside the compound, and the Royal Bengal Tiger was pacing up and down with anger and anxiety, accompanied by his fuming, fretting, and roaring sounds within the improvised cage with restricted movements, of course, due to its huge size and the limitations of space in the cage. The cage was fitted on a tractor trailer, and I could see it when I came out of my office chamber.

Presence of mind made me come inside my office chamber immediately to get in touch with the officer-in-charge of Golaghat Police Station, who happened to be one Mr. B.C. Konwar (if I remember his name and initials correctly) and directed him to come immediately within 15 minutes and that too, with sufficient police personnel, as the situation might get out of control to handle the huge crowd which had assembled out of curiosity to know what would be the next move of the tiger if it succeeds in breaking the cage.

Fortunately, the tiger didn't attempt to break it. Probably, he was also apprehensive after seeing the huge crowd that it would be better to stay inside the cage by fuming and fretting instead of attempting to come out of the cage lest he may be bodily harmed. After all, he might have also used his sixth sense (!), which the crowd and I might not have guessed correctly. Like an intelligent human being, he might have also thought that discretion was the better part of valour at that point in time in view of his rather enviable position.

After I called the officer-in-charge of the Police Station and made sure that he had reached in 15 minutes positively to report to me, I gave clear directions to him that under no circumstances, the assembled crowd of perhaps more than a few hundred people should be allowed to take the law into their hands. He should take utmost care so that the people would not be allowed to pelt stones or any such object to further infuriate the tiger who was not in a sober mood.

Incidentally, Mr. B. C. Konwar, the Officer-in-charge of Golaghat Police Station, had a gigantic physique. Later on, I came to know that he was a champion wrestler. His very presence intimidated the unruly crowd, and he made sure, by his presence and with the help of other police personnel, that no one was allowed to do any kind of mischief. They were instructed to keep quiet or leave the place without creating any kind of nuisance or disturbance, either to the tiger or to the usual working of the officers and staff of the office of S. D. O. He carried out my directions in letter and spirit wholeheartedly in this regard.

Thereafter, after making the arrangements for proper safety and security of the animal and the people who had assembled, I asked my personal staff member to call the people who brought the tiger in the cage on a tractor trailer from their village inside my office chamber for a discussion. There were about 20 villagers who were exasperated already and wanted to get rid of the tiger. They requested me to keep the tiger in my office. I requested them to sit comfortably first and then listened to their version of what exactly had happened. Of course, I told them that with my meagre salary of less than one thousand rupees a month, I couldn't afford to provide sufficient meals for the big tiger even for a couple of days.

Moreover, I informed them that though I would have been literally happier to keep him chained properly outside at the entrance of my chamber to prevent undesirable and unscrupulous elements from coming to meet me with unwarranted issues and create problems for me, the maintenance costs of the tiger would be very high, and I could not afford it. Of course, my lingua franca with them was with my modest knowledge of broken Assamese along with a smattering of broken Hindi. The villagers and I understood each other with the help of my Assamese language Guru and interpreter, Mr. R. Bora, who was standing next to me on my left-hand side, too willing to help me at that critical juncture.

To cut the story short, I ascertained from the villagers regarding their travails and tribulations after offering them water, tea, and some snacks. After assuaging their hurt sentiments by the Assistant Conservator of Forests, Golaghat, I gradually determined the cause of the transportation of the 'Big Cat' or the Royal Bengal Tiger to my office.

They informed me that the depredations of the rogue tiger continued for quite some time in the past and that the stealthy animal regularly stole their goats and chickens every now and then during the dead of night, causing untold miseries to them. Therefore, the villagers had met and complained to the then ACF on several occasions in the past and requested him to somehow help them in tracking the tiger and wean him away from the nearby jungles. According to them, neither the ACF bothered to come to their rescue nor could they extract any retribution from the tiger that caused such frequent depredations.

Therefore, they decided to teach an important lesson to the ACF and the tiger both! Hence, they had fabricated an improvised cage and taken the animal, after it was captured first, only to the office of the Assistant Conservator of Forests. They requested him to take the animal and leave it wherever he wanted to as he was the senior-most Forest Officer at Golaghat. They also insisted that he should be their saviour in such an unenviable situation. Instead of listening to their grievances and taking immediate steps for their redressal, he admonished them very badly and literally threw them out of the office along with the caged animal by informing them that it was none of his business to respond to their request.

Hence, after getting offended by his disgusting, despicable, and recalcitrant attitude, with impolite conduct, they thought that only S. D. O. Golaghat would be their saviour and provide succour to them to overcome their unfortunate plight on that day. From the office of ACF, thereafter, they brought the tractor trailer and the tiger in the cage fitted onto the trailer to the office of S. D. O. for ventilating their grievances and for the resolution of their unfortunate plight on that day.

When I heard their pathetic plight, I immediately called the Assistant Conservator of Forests, stationed at Golaghat on the phone and literally lambasted him in English, with a warning that if he did not come to my office within the quickest possible time (as I was more apprehensive that the tiger may get more and more restless as he had become the object of an unseemly and unwarranted spectacle and his self-esteem took a beating), I would immediately get in touch with the Chief Conservator of Forests and the Chief Secretary of Assam in no time. He would be taken to task, and he may even be suspended forthwith for causing so much commotion and turmoil outside my office due to his couldn't-care-less attitude and defiance of the directions of the authority of the Mahakumaadhipati, i.e. myself.

He literally rushed to my office within 10 minutes after I had abruptly disconnected the phone. When I looked at him, I felt pity for him, as he might be more than 50 years of age and may have very few years left before superannuation. He looked as though a person so harassed and had lost all his energy to work any further, eagerly awaiting his superannuation without much hassle during his remaining years of service. I talked to him courteously and politely considering his age and appearance, unlike my tough talk on the phone. I made sure that I spoke to him in a dignified manner, unlike my angry outbursts on the phone, so that his self-esteem was not lowered at any cost in the presence of the villagers. After all, he was also a public servant like me. He looked so haggard and apprehensive that I might take steps for the strongest possible disciplinary action by his superiors considering my no-nonsense and tough talk to him on the phone. Somehow, I was unable to recollect the name of the Assistant Conservator of Forests, Golaghat.

Though I was very curt and authoritative on the phone, when he came inside my office chamber, I immediately offered him a chair and provided water, tea, and snacks. I made him comfortable and made sure that I would be happy if he took charge of the caged animal and made arrangements for the transhipment of the tiger to Guwahati Zoo or took custody of the same to be left in faraway jungles and preferably in the distant Kaziranga National Park to the greatest relief and happiness of the harassed and fatigued villagers. I had also made sure that the ACF did return the tractor and trailer along with the cage to the villagers after the 'Operation Rescue of the Royal Bengal Tiger' from the utmost uncomfortable and unbearable environment of such a terrible improvised cage into its luxurious normal habitat of a wildlife park or a forest far away from their village.

After about half an hour or so of my interactions with the villagers and the ACF, Mr. B. C. Konwar, the officer-in-charge of the Police Station, Golaghat, went happily back to his normal policing work without the necessity of wielding his full authority, in view of the resolution of the issues to the greatest satisfaction of the people who came to witness, the villagers, and the police personnel deployed for duty.

Thankfully, I was able to ensure an amicable settlement in the largest interests of the villagers and of course, for the proper safety and security of the Royal Bengal Tiger, in addition to ensuring that none of the assembled crowd took undue advantage to indulge in any sort of mischief.

There were many more difficult law and order situations as well during my tenure of approximately 2 years of eventful stay.

Memorable Experience of Getting Stranded Inside the Kaziranga Wildlife Sanctuary.

It was an interesting and of course, a memorable occurrence in the Kaziranga Wildlife Sanctuary on a particular winter night. In this episode, I would like to narrate how I got stranded late one winter night inside Kaziranga Wildlife Sanctuary (KWLS), later updated as Kaziranga National Park (KNP).

The officers' club of Golaghat organised a grand picnic to visit Kaziranga Wildlife Sanctuary along with their family members on a particular winter afternoon, and that too, on a holiday.

In those days, the KWLS had only 2 lodges, i.e. one tourist lodge and another forest rest house. This was in the year 1978. Of course, later on KWLS was transformed into KNP. Even when I was there, the ITDC had set up a hotel in 1978. The tourist lodge, maintained by the Tourism Department of the Government of Assam, and ITDC hotels were meant for tourists on a payment basis. All these 3 buildings, i.e. Forest Rest House, tourist lodge, and ITDC hotel, were there at that time. I understand now, after several years, many more hotels and resorts have also come up.

The Forest Rest House had only a very few rooms with the drawing and dining hall that was only meant for the visiting senior forest officers of the department. The Forest Range officer was in charge of KWLS and also the Forest Rest House. The Sub-divisional officer and Sub-Divisional Police Officer were always treated as guests of the forest department. Even now, I remember the exquisite culinary skills of the Chowkidar/Cook of the Forest Rest House. His name was Mr. Baruva, and he belonged to the Chittagong area of Bangladesh, and I always called him Chittagong Baruva. The Tourist Lodge and ITDC hotel were fully equipped with rooms, including catering arrangements in those days.

Mr. Baruva of Forest Rest House was such a wonderful gentleman. He looked after us, I mean myself and Mr. Shankar Barua, the Sub-divisional Police Officer, with great care and had made excellent food for both of us whenever we happened to visit KWLS. The Forest Rest House, the tourist lodge, and ITDC hotel were all located at Kohora, on the right-hand side of the National Highway opposite KWLS when one drives from Guwahati to Jorhat.

Baguri is a place at a distance of approximately 6 km on the National Highways from Kohora. It is the border between Sibsagar district and Nagaon district. Baguri is part and parcel of Nagaon district of Assam. Incidentally, more than 80% of KWLS falls in the district of Sibsagar only or within the Golaghat Sub-Division, whereas less than 20% also falls within the district of Nagaon. The total area of KWLS was approximately more than 450 sq. km.

There was a PWD Inspection Bungalow (IB) at Baguri, Baguri is located only a few km from the border of Golaghat Sub-Division. From the Baguri side, one could also enter the KWLS as one could go from Kohara, We had organised our picnic at Baguri IB because there was a very big open space outside the Baguri IB within the big compound.

There were approximately more than 75 ladies and gentlemen, including some children, and most of them were officers of many technical departments. Generally, in Assam, whenever the officers and their families went on a picnic, they carried provisions, vegetables, etc., along with utensils and cooked at the picnic spot. In a way, one could call it a community lunch, and each and every member of the community, i.e. the officers and their spouses, attended to all cooking arrangements without any issue of ego or prestige as to who should do what. It is a kind of collective organisation of the officers and their families which generally promotes a sense of belonging, unity, and friendship among the officers and their families. The only exception was myself, who was a bachelor. So if I may say so in a lighter vein, I was the beneficiary of all goodies for consumption without any hard labour. Of course, I had made it a point to contribute my mite in the form of cash, which my colleagues and their families refused to accept. They informed me that being the head of the administration, they respected me and treated me as their guest of honour, though I was the youngest amongst them at only 27 years old.

The place of the picnic was approximately more than 60 km from Golaghat town. Therefore, all provisions, including rice, vegetables, etc., were brought from Golaghat along with the entire contingent. We all had assembled before 12 noon. Obviously, it took more than 2 hours to organise lunch. Though the IB had a dining hall, only a few people could sit and have food. Since it was a winter day, we had all decided to sit in the open ground with a proper seating arrangement to take food on palm leaf plates.

If I may compare such picnics with our marriages in the south, it is like the food preparation and serving of the food with love and affection on the part of the people themselves who prepared the food without expecting any waiters or other employed staff to serve the food. It was exactly like an extended family get-together of ladies and gentlemen who belonged to different communities and hailed from different parts of the State of Assam, and everybody took part in the organisation of the picnic, preparation of the food, serving of the food, etc., with utmost love and affection without standing on any sort of ego or prestige.

So by the time we finished eating the food that was prepared, it was around 4.30 pm.

So around 4.30 pm, the officers and their families started moving from the Baguri side into the KWLS. Inside the sanctuary, it was a muddy road and, of course, the jeeps could easily move on. Moreover, it was only winter and therefore there were not many obstacles for the vehicles to move inside the sanctuary. I and my driver along with the forest guard started moving into the sanctuary in our car, later along with the Sub-Divisional Police Officer and his family. The Sub-Divisional Police Officer and his wife were travelling in their own jeep, and the driver was driving their vehicle. After all our colleagues' vehicles left the IB towards the sanctuary, the Sub-Divisional Police Officer moved inside the sanctuary followed by myself in an Ambassador Car driven by my driver, Mr. Tahir Ali. There was only one forest guard who had a lathi (stick) in his hand. After some distance inside the sanctuary, we noticed that there was a slushy and muddy patch. Fortunately, all the vehicles except our 2 vehicles had already crossed that patch, and they moved on inside the sanctuary. The whole idea of organising the picnic was after the late lunch we could go inside the sanctuary up to some distance, preferably a few kms. It was only because of the fact that the wild animals normally either came out of their hiding places in the early mornings for their prey or for water in the ponds inside or in the late afternoons when the sun was not too hot. That was the idea why we had all left after 4.30 pm as there was sufficient light to see the wild animals safely at a distance.

When the police officer and I noticed the slushy and muddy patch, the driver of his vehicle, i.e. the jeep, somehow, with great difficulty, could negotiate that patch and thereafter crossed the patch and went into the straight stretch of the road. Of course, there was some difficulty for the driver, but he succeeded in crossing the difficult path. The driver of the vehicle, along with the sub-divisional police officer and his wife, waited for my vehicle to cross that difficult, slushy, muddy patch. Unfortunately, despite the best efforts of my driver, Mr. Tahir Ali, he could not overcome the obstacle, and we got stuck. In this process, it was already around 6 pm, with the sun slowly setting. Mrs. Shankar Barua, the wife of the then Sub-Divisional Police officer, started crying in view of the darkness as she wanted to go along with her husband outside the sanctuary as early as possible. Mr. Shankar Barua, who was a very dear friend of mine and a very young I.P.S. officer, did not want to leave me alone in the sanctuary. However, she did not want to leave her husband and go with the driver outside the sanctuary. She insisted that her driver, along with her husband and herself, should move as quickly as possible from that area so that they would reach the Kohora Forest IB, which was already at a distance of 10 to 12 km from the place of occurrence. It was getting dark, and she was scared and worried about the wild animals which may be a danger to our safety and security at that particular point in time. There was so much haggling and arguments between her and her husband about whether I should be left all alone or they should leave together. I might recall from my memory, the driver of the Sub-divisional Police Officer's vehicle was too smart, and he informed the wife of the sub-divisional police officer, "Sister! Please stay with your husband and take care of the SDO and let me go back with the vehicle and arrange to send some rescue team from the forest IB at Kohora, which was at a distance of more than 10 or 12 km from the place of occurrence." I decided that the SDPO and his wife and the driver should immediately leave the place and arrange to send some rescue vehicle after reaching the forest IB. Once they left, only myself, my driver, and the forest guard with the only weapon, i.e. lathi, were left at the mercy of wild animals and God's will for our safety and security.

After some time, it became pitch-dark and my driver was showing his bravado. He informed me that the wild animals, especially wild elephants, may not come near the vehicle if there was a fire. So what he did was take some petrol and make a fire with the help of some paper lying around. Because of the small and insignificant bonfire created by my driver, the wild animals would not come near the vehicle, according to him. After about a few minutes, the fire also got extinguished. Thereafter, the driver also came inside the vehicle, where I was sitting in the back of the vehicle while the forest guard was sitting in the front seat. At that time, I could only pray to the great God Almighty to ensure our safety and security from the wild animals. Even at that time, my driver had a sense of humour. He told me, "Sir, our ambassador vehicle was like a football for the wild elephant; in case the elephant came nearer to our car, it would play with the car like a football player." So he was also a bit worried after noticing that there was no rescue team within sight.

I was wondering whether the sub-divisional police officer's vehicle and other officers' vehicles were stuck en route as we got stuck in the slushy and muddy patch. If it had happened as I thought, obliviously the rescue team would not come so quickly for our rescue. But fortunately later on, I heard that except for that slushy and muddy patch, there were no other obstacles and the road condition was alright till one reached the national highway and met the forest range officer at the forest IB. Later on, I heard that the Sub-divisional Police officer had sent a wireless message to the Forest Range officer stating the condition of my predicament of being stranded inside the sanctuary due to the very bad slushy and muddy patch en route, and that too, more than 10 or 12 km from forest IB.

Our fellow officers of the sub-division, the Sub-divisional Police Officer and his wife, Forest Range officer and his staff were all worried. They were trying to do their level best in organising a rescue team and sending a well-conditioned vehicle to rescue myself, my driver, and the forest guard from the sanctuary. I had heard about their rescue operation after I had reached Kohora Forest IB.

They had organised a tractor along with a long iron chain, and that tractor was sent from the forest IB to the place of occurrence where my vehicle was stranded. The distance was approximately 12 km or so. The organisation of the tractor and long iron chain and its slow movement inside the sanctuary took a little more time. When we noticed the lights inside, rather than the first lights in the sanctuary in that pitch-dark night, I immediately thought of God's divine grace. Slowly, as the tractor moved, we could hear the sound and were reassured that we were safe after some time. The driver of the tractor came nearer to our vehicle and pulled the vehicle with a long iron chain within a few minutes. Thereafter, my driver thoroughly checked the vehicle, and after some small distance, we crossed the tractor, and the tractor followed us. By the time we crossed the sanctuary late at night on a winter night, which was quite dark, it was after 10 pm. I might say that during the entire ordeal on that night, I, my driver, and the forest guard could hear all kinds of howls, roars, and various sounds emanating from the wild animals. It was like music to us, though I may jovially write so in a lighter vein today.

In a nutshell, if I may say, getting stranded deep inside the sanctuary for a few hours, and that too, in the dark night within the sanctuary, was an unforgettable incident in my life even after more than 4 decades or so as of date. It was nothing but God's will that I could narrate this incident in this book as I was unharmed by the wild animals on that particular night. By the time my car reached the forest IB, it was after 10 pm. At that time, it was a great relief for all the officers who had assembled near the Forest Rest House. I was given a hero's welcome with tremendous applause and cheers from all my colleagues and their families. I was honoured with a very beautiful '*Gamocha*' as soon as I got down from the vehicle. In fact, all of them were waiting with bated breath and straightaway took me to the dining hall in the tourist lodge for a grand dinner. After dinner, after 11.30 pm on that night, all of us left for our headquarters, which is Golaghat.

My time as S.D.O. Golaghat also included events that were more grim. Somewhere in the year 1977 or 1978 (I am not very sure), I received information about a serious law and order situation due to the assaults of by one group or community on another group. Then as advised by me, the S.D.P.O. sent a big team of armed police personnel to that area to conduct the investigation and to proceed further for counter attacks in required. We planned to follow soon after to the spot. The incident took place approximately 25 KM from Golaghat town.

The police party was headed by an assistant commandant of 3rd A. P. Battalion ie. armed police force along with the police personnel as required from Golaghat in addition to police personnel from the local police station.

After the arrival of the Deputy Commissioner, the S.P. and D. I. G. from Jorhat (Sibsagar District Headquarters), myself and the S.D.P.O. also proceeded along with them in our vehicles. The vehicle of the D.C. was an Ambassador with No. 1 as its number plate. Incidentally at that time, D. C.'s vehicle always carried No. '1' as its number plate and the S.P.'s vehicle carried No. '2'.

When we were about to enter the forest area, I suggested to the Deputy Commissioner and Superintendent of Police and D.I.G, that we would enter the area in the D.C.'s Ambassador vehicle which was a white coloured one with its No. 1 name plate. In fact D.C. had suggested that we would get into two Jeeps. It is a fact that my suggestion ultimately was a blessing in disguise by God's Divine Grace. I would mention as to why I meant it like that.

After we went inside the forest area for about half a kilometre or so, the Assistant Commandant of the police battalion came nearer to our vehicle and stopped us. In a hush hush tone, he informed the D.C. that the vehicle in which he and other police personnel went inside, was fired upon by miscreants hiding in the forest. Mr. Buragohain (I vividly remember his name even now) was a very smart and a physically strong gentleman. He informed us that he and his police patrol party was fired at and they had retaliated. Thereafter there was silence. Maybe they were hiding themselves in the interior area of the forest only. He advised us to stop the engine of the car. The D. I. G. and S. P.. immediately jumped outside and took positions lying down as they were armed with guns.

We, i,e., D. C. myself and D. F. O. were sitting inside the car for some time. There was no further firing, My assumption was that after seeing the No. 1 of Deputy Commissioner vehicle, the miscreants might have fled, or they might have been apprehensive about the large police party that arrived with D.C and S. P. of the vehicle.

After waiting for some time, we had left the place after thoroughly ascertaining the fact that the miscreants had fled away. This was a close brush for me with the reality of danger not too far away.

Secretary (from March to November 1979) to Commission of Enquiry, Constituted for Enquiry on the Alleged Misuse of Government Machinery by the Then Government of Assam for the Conduct of Jawahar Nagar AICC Session, in the Year 1976.

Deputy Secretary, Transport, Tourism, and Co-operation Departments from January 1980 to June 1980.

In the month of March 1979, I was transferred from Golaghat on completion of my tenure as Sub-divisional officer, Golaghat Sub-Division and appointed as Secretary, Commission of Enquiry on the conduct of AICC Session at Jawahar Nagar, by the new Government of Assam. In fact, the then Chief Secretary to the Government of Assam had called me on the phone and informed me that the new government wanted to get my services to be placed as Secretary of One Man Commission of Enquiry about the conduct of AICC session by the previous government. The Commission was headed by retired Delhi High Court Judge, namely, Mr. Justice Jaghit Singh. The allegations were that the services of many of the government departmental officials were misused by the previous government for the conduct of AICC session at Guwahati in 1976. I was appointed as his Secretary and had to take care of all administrative arrangements including organising an office building, setting up a courtroom, etc.

I zeroed in on an existing officers' club building at Dispur towards the setting up of the Office room including for the staff members and for the court room. Justice Jaghit Singh used to come only for about 10 days in a month from Delhi. During his absence, I had to issue letters to the officers concerned who were involved in the construction of guest houses i.e. State Guest House No.1 and State Guest House No.2 in addition to laying and widening of roads in and around Jawahar Nagar as well as other infrastructural arrangements for the conduct of AICC session. State Guest House No.1 was constructed on a hilltop near Khanapara, Guwahati to accommodate the then Prime Minister Mrs. Indira Gandhi to enable her to stay near the venue of the AICC session. This place was also considered to provide for the safety and security of the Prime Minister. State Guest House No.2 was constructed for the benefit of other VIPs. The government of the day under Chief Minister Sarat Chandra Sinha considered the hosting of AICC session for the first time in Guwahati an appropriate opportunity to spruce up the areas around the AICC venue by laying new roads and widening existing roads.

The different technical departmental officers appeared before the Enquiry Commission and informed them that they simply carried out the instructions of the government for the laying of infrastructure like roads, buildings, and for providing street lights, drinking water facilities as the whole session venue was in the outskirts of Guwahati City in a semi-urban area.

I would like to mention that the most important witness who appeared before the Enquiry Commission was none other than the former Hon'ble Chief Minister, Shri Sarat Chandra Sinha. In the courtroom, which was otherwise called '*Ejalas*', the Hon'ble Commission of Enquiry headed by Mr. Justice Jaghit Singh requested Shri Sarat Chandra Sinha, who came to give evidence, to sit in the witness box. However, Shri Sarat Chandra Sinha refused to sit and was prepared to stand for a couple of hours and gave evidence about his unambiguous instructions to all the officials starting from the then Chief Secretary to the Govt of Assam, Director-General of Police, and other senior officials to contribute their mite in the developmental activities, viz., for the construction of new roads, and also for the construction of 2 big guest houses. He candidly and categorically stated before the Enquiry Commission Chairman that he took the utmost responsibility and he was only responsible for giving appropriate instructions to the officials concerned. According to him, he had done nothing wrong and he only took advantage of the then conduct of the AICC session and wanted to develop the infrastructural facilities in and around the AICC

Session Venue. Moreover, he had also informed the Enquiry Commission Chairman that a very big exhibition was held at that time to showcase the developmental activities of the various State Government departments in the country, including that of the State Government of Assam, as he had anticipated a large number of visitors to the exhibition and as a large number of delegates had to attend the AICC session, which was held for the first time in Assam where at that time the infrastructural facilities were not so adequate. Furthermore, when the VVIP like the then Hon'ble Prime Minister of India was to spend a couple of days at the AICC Session Venue, in view of the safety and security and also in view of the proximity to the venue of AICC Session at Jawahar Nagar, he had ordered the construction of 2 state guest houses. He had also mentioned that, according to his conscience and according to his duties and responsibilities as expected of him as the then Head of the Government, he had to take care of the successful conduct of the AICC session without any hitch from the point of safety and security of VVIPs and other VIPs, including the members of the public. He had candidly stated that in view of all the precautionary steps and appropriate actions taken by the State Government official machinery, at every level under his direct command and control, if at all the Commission felt that any wrongdoing was committed, he as the then Chief Minister would take the fullest responsibility and requested the Enquiry Commission Chairman not to find fault with any of the officers in the official hierarchy as they had done nothing wrong except scrupulous observance of the instructions of the State Government headed by him.

As I was observing the entire proceedings before the Commission of Enquiry on Jawahar Nagar Session of AICC, I could state without an iota of doubt that the then Chief Minister had not only the conviction to state that what he stated before the Commission was right, but also very strongly defended that the development of infrastructural facilities in the semi-urban areas or the outskirts of Guwahati was absolutely essential. He had candidly stated that it was his foremost duty to help the people at that time notwithstanding the allegations of misuse of the government official machinery during the AICC session.

The Judge himself was pleasantly surprised to observe the sincere conduct of the most important witness who was the then Head of the Government. He preferred to stand in the witness box despite repeated requests of the

Commission. Perhaps that was the first time that the Commission would have noticed that here was the head of the then State Government who took utmost responsibility for whatever was done by the government machinery and requested the Commission to consider his request not to take any action against any of the officers who were only carrying out the instructions of the government headed by him. After the recording of evidence of Shri Sarat Chandra Sinha, the former Chief Minister, the Chairman of the Enquiry Commission had wound up the proceedings. He himself stood up and thanked him with folded hands for the straightforward and honest stand taken by the then Head of the Government.

After a few months and after the recording of all the witnesses, including the head of the then State Government, the Commission office was closed, and before that, the Chairman of the Enquiry Commission, Mr. Justice Jagjit Singh, had submitted his report to the then State Government of Assam. I had also to wind up my office and reported back to the Chief Secretary.

In the meanwhile, in the month of November 1979, as I had to proceed to my hometown in Tamil Nadu for my marriage, I had met the then Additional Chief Secretary looking after personnel and other departments and requested sanction for my earned leave for 15 days. I vividly recall even now that the then Additional Chief Secretary, Mr. B.S. Sarao, called for the file from the concerned officer of the department and wrote in my presence in that file, **"I told Mr. Manoharan that marriage comes once-in-a-lifetime only and his leave for 15 days was considered not enough and therefore, I granted him 75 days' leave and advised him to proceed on leave immediately for his hometown, as Assam can always wait for him."**

I stood up and profusely thanked him and said that I would at the most take a little more than a month's leave only and I would report back in the month of January 1980.

After my marriage, I returned to work in January 1980. I was posted as Deputy Secretary of the Transport, Tourism, and Co-operation departments. After a few days of joining, the then Agricultural Production Commissioner, Dr. A.C. Ray, took me to the then Chief Secretary of Assam, Mr. R.S. Paramasivan, and wanted me to join the office of the Small Farmers Development Agency (SFDA) as its Project Director for the district of Kamrup with headquarters in Guwahati. The Chief Secretary remarked that as I was a very young officer, I could handle both the offices, one in the field and another at the State Secretariat. For about 5 months, I took care of my secretariat assignment as well as my assignment as the Project Director of SFDA in Guwahati. The office of SFDA was later renamed as the District Rural Development Agency (DRDA). I had to go on tours within the district to take care of the activities of SFDA in the larger interests of the farmers.

Things took turn when I was suddenly transferred and posted as Additional Deputy Commissioner (border) in Sarupathar, a block headquarter, in May 1980. This was within the Sub-division of Golaghat. The reason given by the government at that time was that there was tension in the border areas and large-scale violence was expected between the forest villagers, who were mostly encroachers, and the Naga villagers residing in the border areas. The reason given was that I knew the areas very well due to my past assignment as Sub-Divisional Officer of Golaghat Sub-division; I would do very well in that new assignment.

I protested, and it was during the President's rule that this order was issued. Immediately thereafter, I met Mr. Ramamoorty, the then Adviser to the Governor of Assam, and informed him politely that it was a grave injustice for me as I had to go back to stay in a village as Additional Deputy Commissioner in the sub-division where I had previously worked as the head of the administration of the Sub-Division. I categorically informed him that any other officer could have been posted there instead of unnecessarily relocating me as I had just joined after my marriage in January 1980. I informed him that my wife was in the early stage of pregnancy. It would neither be possible for me to leave her alone at Dispur nor to take her to that village called Sarupathar. One had to go through a very bad road to reach that village, and especially, the last stretch of a few kilometres' access to that village was literally very bad with too many bumps. I candidly informed him that I could not afford to take my wife, who was in the early stage of pregnancy, through such an ordeal. I told him that I would obey the government order but on the condition that I may be given 15 days' leave to take my wife to her hometown in Tamil Nadu and thereafter, I would come and join at Sarupathar. I also requested him to reconsider my transfer from Sarupathar as early as possible after I joined there. I strongly felt and informed the adviser that it was total injustice to me for disturbing me within 6 months of my joining at Dispur and also for posting me in a place where I myself was the head of administration of that sub-division for about 20 months. Mr. Ramamoorthy appreciated my bold, free, and frank assertion and with due sympathy, he heard me and assured me that he would do his level best to help me get out of the place called Sarupathar as early as possible.

I had met Mr. Ramamurthy and stated that I had worked as the then Sub-Divisional Officer of the Golaghat Sub-Division for about 2 years and my appointment as Additional Deputy Commissioner was the senior-level assignment, especially to assist the Deputy Commissioner at the District Headquarters. I had felt that appointing me as the Additional Deputy Commissioner of a very small area to look after the border areas and, within the sub-division where I had worked as the then Sub-divisional officer earlier, was absolutely unjustified and certainly unwarranted.

After I had left my wife in her hometown in Tamil Nadu, I returned to Guwahati and proceeded to Sarupathar. I sent a report to the State Government after joining as an Additional Deputy Commissioner (border) at Sarupathar. I had hardly spent a fortnight there. On an evening within a fortnight of my joining at Sarupathar, the then Commissioner of Upper Assam Division, Mr. E.S. Parthasarathy, called me on the telephone and informed me that I was appointed as the Deputy Commissioner of North Cachar Hills district with its headquarters at Haflong. He was extremely kind-hearted and sent me a vehicle to Sarupathar the next morning and requested me to join him for breakfast at his residence before proceeding to Haflong.

Generally, by and large, the Deputy Commissioners were appointed after about 6 years of service only in the State of Assam. However, in my case, as luck would have it, even before I had completed 5 years of service, I had been appointed as the Deputy Commissioner of North Cachar Hills district. It is because of the magnanimity of the then Principal Adviser Mr. H C Sarin to the Governor of Assam as well as Mr. Ramamurthy.

The next morning, I left Sarupathar and proceeded to Jorhat on my way to Haflong to take over as Deputy Commissioner of North Cachar Hills district. I met Mr. and Mrs. E.S. Parthasarathy at their residence and joined them for breakfast. After my sumptuous and very nice breakfast,

I profusely thanked Mr. Parthasarathy and his wife for their wonderful hospitality and took leave of them. I must write here that I had never met Mr. E.S. Parthasarathy before, and it was so kind of him to have invited me for breakfast that morning before I left Jorhat on my way to Haflong, the headquarters of North Cachar Hills District. That was the first and last time I had met them.

In this connection, I would like to state that Mr. E.S. Parthasarathy was one of our very well-respected Senior officers in the Assam Cadre. During the troubled times of the agitations in the State of Assam, Mr. Parathasarathy was the first senior officer to take action against the assembled crowd under his jurisdiction and ordered the police to disperse the crowd when there was violent protest in a District Headquarters. Unfortunately, until that time, no strong action was taken by the administration against the unlawful assembly of people who had indulged in the various modes of agitation.

This had infuriated certain sections of the people who had led the agitation at that time against the infiltration of illegal migrants inside the territory of Assam. It seemed at that time that a conspiracy was hatched to attempt on the life of the very senior civil servant who had taken the action for the first time to disburse the unlawful assembly of people.

Mr. E.S. Parthasarathy was the Commissioner of Upper Assam Division, and his office was at Jorhat. It so happened that some unknown persons, inimical to the strong action taken against the agitation, planted a bomb within the **seat cushion** of the chair in his office. When Mr. Parthasarathy came to his office and sat on the chair, the bomb went off and killed him instantly.

I vividly recall that this particular incident happened sometime in the month of April 1981. At that time, my in-laws had come to stay with us for a few days at Halflong, the District Headquarters of North Cachar Hills District where I was the Deputy Commissioner. My wife and I accompanied her parents from Halflong to see them off in Guwahati.

On our return journey, we stopped in the evening at Nagaon Circuit House to rest for some time. There was an eerie silence and hushed murmurs among the staff members of the Circuit House. When I inquired about what had happened, I was shocked to hear that Mr. E.S. Parathasarthy had been killed in his own office chamber. This news sent shock waves throughout the state. Unfortunately, I was unaware as I was travelling. It was only when I reached Nagaon Circuit House in the evening that I learnt of this unfortunate and deeply saddening news. It was not only a rude shock for me but also for my wife and parents.

Moreover, this was the very first time in the State of Assam during the agitation which had continued for a couple of years since the latter part of 1979, such a violent incident targeting the life of a very senior civil servant was attempted.

It was extremely tragic and very unfortunate that such an honest, straightforward and very pleasant civil servant's life was snatched away by certain unscrupulous and ruthless persons who had indulged in such a dastardly act obviously in collusion/connivance with people who knew the office timings and also who were knowledgeable about his arrival at the office on that particular day during that specific time. Obviously, the bomb was planted on the previous day/night so that on the next day when Mr. Parthasarathy came to the office to take his seat on his chair, instantly he was blown off from his seat. I understood that even the sound of that bomb blast was heard at a distance of a little more than a kilometre. I was personally dejected and upset when I heard this incident as I had met him only once in my life, and that too in his residence when both he and his wife had treated me in the early part of July 1980 with a delightful and sumptuous breakfast as though I was one of their own family members.

Deputy Commissioner of North Cachar Hills District Halflong from July 1980 to December 1981

Experience as the Deputy Commissioner of North Cachar Hills district with its headquarters at Haflong between 3rd July 1980 and the end of December 1981.

On 3rd July 1980, I joined as the Deputy Commissioner of North Cachar Hills district with headquarters at Haflong. It was really a record of sorts as I was posted as the Deputy Commissioner of a District in Assam in less than 5 years of my service. To be very precise, exactly within 4 years and 11 months, during the President's rule in Assam at that time, I took over as the head of the District Administration.

My earlier memory of my stint in Haflong was the Circuit House where I reached the evening before I took charge. This was a very old structure built during the British time, i.e. more than 95 years old at that time, overlooking the Barail hills range. In a way, the Circuit House was a little away from the town, and the location was excellent. The rooms were provided with old-type furniture. I would like to mention a cook cum caretaker called Mr. Ahamed. Even today, I remember his good conduct, and he had very good manners and, more so, a fantastic ability to make outstanding quality of food, especially all sorts of vegetarian and non-vegetarian food items. Also, I had informed the then Deputy Commissioner that I would take over charge the next day morning from him. I spent a year and a half as Deputy Commissioner of North Cachar Hills district with its headquarters at Haflong. It was a very memorable tenure as it was my first district charge. The Commissioner, who was a supervisory officer of that district, was Mr. P.N. Rao. There was a Divisional Commissioner for both the Hills districts in Assam and Cachar District of Barak Valley.

I was also appointed later as Deputy Commissioner of Karbi Anglong District in the years 1984-1985, and my tenure was from October 1984 to June 1985. Incidentally Karbi Anglong was the other hills district of Assam.

At that time, the Divisional Commissioner happened to be Mr. J. Changakakoty, who was the Divisional Commissioner – Mr. P.N. Rao or Mr. Changakakoty, and thereafter Mr. T.K. Kamila was the Commissioner of Hills Division. If I may say briefly about all 3 personalities, I would like to rate Mr. P N Rao as a very strict disciplinarian, and he was very particular about the job undertaken by me as the Deputy Commissioner. In fact, I could not even proceed on leave for a fortnight when my child was born in Tamil Nadu in the month of November 1980. The situation in Assam was fast becoming worse in view of the difficult law and order situation, and therefore, I was denied leave even for a fortnight, which I wanted during my tenure as Deputy Commissioner in December 1980.

As the Deputy Commissioner of North Cachar Hills district, I had a wonderful tenure. Of course, the other 2 Commissioners of the Division, Mr. J. Changakakoty and Mr. T.K. Kamilla, were also very pleasant gentlemen in addition to being strict disciplinarians.

In Assam in the hills districts, there was no separation of the Judiciary, and now also that position remains the same. In other words, the Deputy Commissioner of North Cachar Hills district performed the functions of district and sessions judge. It was there at that time, and it is there as on date as well. As per the Sixth Schedule of the Constitution of India, the Administration of Justice Rules were prevalent, and it is so as on date as well.

As per the Rules of Administration of Justice and as provided under the Sixth Schedule of the Constitution, the Deputy Commissioner discharged the role and functions of the district and sessions judge, though the nomenclature was Deputy Commissioner only.

Of course, there was no need for a separate attire to put on like a district and sessions judge in normal parlance. However, the government Pleaders and the other Defence Counsels appeared in their Advocates' robes. It was a very good and novel experience for me at a very young age to conduct the trial of criminal cases by performing the functions of the district and sessions judge, of course as Deputy Commissioner only in the official court chamber. I might recall one particular instance wherein I had to try a murder case, and the accused was hardly about 25 years old. He was a tribal boy. I was really surprised to see him and what kind of murder charge was imposed on him in view of his innocent look. When I came to know after reading the case record and after listening to him, the Public Prosecutor, and the Defence Counsel, it was evident that out of sheer disgust or anger, the accused hit another person with a bamboo pole, who was also not very old, and who brought his cattle to graze in the land of the accused. As a consequence, due to sheer bad luck on the part of the accused person, the other person died instantaneously because perhaps the hit taken by him might have immobilised him, and it happened due to a severe head injury.

In other words, it was absolutely not premeditated murder but could be inferred as a culpable homicide not amounting to murder. Therefore, I had decided at that time that it was necessary on my part as the presiding officer of the Court to change the charge of the accused as though he had committed a culpable homicide not amounting to murder, and I had decided to punish him under section 304 instead of under section 302 of the Indian Penal Code. Considering the age of the accused, his innocence, his ready acceptance of his guilt, I took pity on him as a compassionate civil servant and imposed only 3 years' rigorous imprisonment. After all, taking into account the future of the life of that young person and his very pleasant manners and his absolute co-operation during the interrogation of the police as well as during the prosecution stage, as Deputy Commissioner in charge of the functions of district and sessions judge, I was convinced that the ends of justice could adequately be met by this so that in the future he would repent his offence and also he would refrain from such unwarranted criminal action on his part. The Deputy Commissioner could impose a maximum of 7 years' rigorous imprisonment for the offences relating to murder charges. However, any quantum of punishment beyond 7 years' rigorous imprisonment would have to be ratified by the Hon'ble High Court of Guwahati.

The Deputy Commissioner discharged the functions of the administration of law and order and other regulatory functions in addition to his regular supervisory role over Civil Supplies and Excise matters, etc.

However, they were not entrusted with Land Revenue Administration as prevalent in the Plains Districts of Assam.

In both the Hills Districts of Assam, namely North Cachar Hills District and Karbi Anglong district, the Land Revenue Administration and the developmental functions for the welfare of the people were entrusted to the Autonomous Hills District Councils of North Cachar Hills and Karbi Anglong Hills Districts. The Autonomous Hills District Council was headed by the Chief Executive Member and was assisted by 6 or more executive members who were responsible for the administration of the District Council. It was a sort of a mini-cabinet at the District Headquarters. The various constituencies or local areas elected their representatives who were called Members of the District Council.

I may attempt to make a corollary of the District Council's administrative apparatus with that of the State Government, viz., with its head as Chief Executive Member (CEM), who is considered as the head of the local self-government at the district. The executive members comprised the Executive Council or the cabinet of that particular mini government who were responsible and accountable to the CEM.

The executive members comprising the Executive Council of the District Council, headed by the CEM, were allotted various portfolios like land revenue and functions of development departments such as PWD, drinking water supply, and road construction, etc.

The Deputy Commissioner was only responsible for maintenance of law and order and other judicial functions in addition to the usual matters of food and civil supplies, excise, and other regulatory functions that were exercised in the case of plains districts. As the youngest Deputy Commissioner of North Cachar Hills district, I also discharged the functions of the district and sessions judge. After a few years, when I was appointed as the Deputy Commissioner of Karbi Anglong District, I exercised the functions of district and Session Judge as well to conduct the sessions cases.

The Deputy Commissioner, in fact, had 2 office chambers i.e., the normal office chamber and the other one was like a court room (*Ejalas*) of district and sessions judge which one would have witnessed in different parts of the country. I was rather very proud to be the youngest de facto district and sessions judge at the age of 29 years at Haflong.

The Deputy Commissioner was entrusted with the duties and responsibilities with full powers under the CrPC (Criminal Procedure Code) to conduct the trial of all cases, including the sessions cases. The Executive Magistrates who had worked under the Deputy Commissioner exercised the functions of the Judicial Magistrates, though they were not designated as the first-class Judicial Magistrates. All their decisions were appealable in the court of the Deputy Commissioner. It was a very interesting phenomenon as the then Deputy Commissioner, while dealing with the session cases, had to depend on interpreters because in both hills districts, the majority of the population were from myriad tribes that have been inhabiting these hills since time immemorial. In the North Cachar Hills District, there were more than 10 tribal communities. Likewise, in the Hills District of Karbi Anglong, there were several hills tribes who were the inhabitants.

So whenever there was a Court Case, I had to depend on the tribal interpreters who were called Dubhasis in the Office of the Deputy Commissioner. The Dubhasis were generally grade IV employees and generally might know a few more tribal languages in addition to their mother tongue. A Dubhasi was expected to stand next to the witness and listen to the statement made by the witness in his mother tongue, which might be of another tribal language. Therefore, a Dubhasi being knowledgeable about a few more dialects or languages of other tribes would translate the statement of the witness in broken Hindi language. So as the Deputy Commissioner in charge of the Court, the Deputy Commissioner's responsibility was to record the statement of the witness in the English language and as per the versions given by the Dubhasis pertaining to the statement of the witness. Amongst themselves, i.e. various tribal communities, they generally communicated in broken Hindi language. It is a dialect known as 'Haflong Hindi'.

On the whole, it was a wonderful experience, and I am indeed extremely grateful to God Almighty for giving me such an enlightened experience as I had discharged the functions of the judiciary and executive of the hills districts, viz., North Cachar and Karbi Anglong districts.

The reader might also be interested to know the kind of relationship between the Deputy Commissioner of the district and the Chief Executive Member of the District Council in terms of their functions. The Deputy Commissioner acted like a friend, philosopher, and guide to the Chief

Executive Member and the elected representatives of the autonomous Hills District Council. As regards the Office of the Deputy Commissioner, there were several Executive Magistrates to assist the Deputy Commissioner in the exercise of executive and judicial functions. Likewise, the Chief Executive Member and the Executive Members were assisted by the Principal Secretary and the Secretaries of the District Councils. The various development departments were supervised by the concerned executive members as well as by the Principal Secretary and his secretaries to ensure the proper discharge of duties by the Heads of Development Departments and their subordinate officers in the district.

The Chief Executive Member and the Executive Committee were only responsible for policy decisions and allocation of financial resources for the functions of the development departments. However, the Principal Secretary in charge of the District Council, who was generally an Administrative Service Officer, was responsible for the proper and prudent expenditure of the financial resources by the Heads of Development Departments in the district. In other words, the financial powers were fully entrusted to the Principal Secretary only.

My official relationship as the head of the District Administration was quite cordial with the Chief Executive Member and the Executive Members, as their friend, philosopher, and guide. Sometimes based on the requests made by them and in order to understand and appreciate their activities in the largest interests of the people, I used to tour the areas wherein several developmental actions were executed by the Heads of Development Departments. I was, however, not expected to interfere in their functioning. During my assignment as the Deputy Commissioner of the North Cachar Hills district, the Chief Executive Member was an elderly person and used to call on me whenever there was any need for me to guide him or to help the District Council for the expeditious implementation of the programmes by the development departments concerned. The functions of the development departments like PWD, Health, Drinking water supply, Roads and Buildings, etc. were called 'transferred subjects' to the District Council i.e. the District Council had the full authority to ensure that the Heads of Development Departments in the Hills District were primarily accountable and responsible only to the District Council's CEM and the concerned executive members.

Moreover, if the State Government wanted to transfer a senior-level officer working in the Development Department, it could not be done arbitrarily without the prior consent or consultations with the District Council's authorities. In case the District Council was not very happy with the performance of a particular Development Department head, the CEM or the Principal Secretary might request the Head of the Development Department of the State Government i.e. the Minister concerned or the Secretary of the Department concerned to seek his transfer from the district.

The District Headquarters, Haflong, was a very pleasant hill station and continues to be the only hill station in the entire State of Assam even today. Interestingly, the entire Office of the Deputy Commissioner was on a hilltop. The residence of the Deputy Commissioner was across the road and was also located on another hilltop. The residence was a fairly large bungalow with very big rooms, a very large, long veranda built during the British-era, with a view of the hill slopes. The kitchen was located separately, and in those days only firewood was used. The security personnel and the staff of the residence were also accommodated within the premises of the Deputy Commissioner's bungalow.

The district had a tradition of village headmen bringing birds of poultry or a few eggs in small cane baskets packed with cotton along with a bottle of rice beer as a gift to the Deputy Commissioner.

I may say in a lighter vein, 'not to drink was a taboo' in the Hills District. The men and women of the hills tribes were used to drinking the love *pani* or local rice liquor/beer, as it was their normal custom.

I was advised by the then Chief Secretary, Government of Assam that it was a great honour for village headmen to come and meet the Deputy Commissioner at his residence with something in their hands like a bird or eggs along with a bottle of rice beer or liquor called '*love pani*' depending on their financial condition. It was not a matter of bribe; it was a tradition, considered a privilege and honour on the part of the village headmen to meet only the District Head of Administration called '*Bhor Saab*'. It means that the Deputy Commissioner was a Bada Sahib in Hindi or a highly respected official as head of the administration. I was informed very clearly and candidly by the then Chief Secretary, Assam, that I should never refuse to accept such courtesy on the part of the village headmen as it would offend their sentiments.

In those days, I used to get up rather late, after 8 am. On many a day, a poor village headman with his humble gifts would be waiting outside the entrance gate. Generally, the village headmen preferred to visit the residence of the Deputy Commissioner with the fond hope and trust of resolution of simple issues like the issue of Gun Licences (i.e. licences for single barrel breach loading/Double barrel breach loading, also called SBBL/DBBL guns) and issues like shortages of food items in their respective areas. For them, the possession of SBBL or DBBL guns was a matter of prestige, and they normally used them only for shooting birds. Their grievances were generally minimal, and their wants were also very minimal. I used to invite them in for a cup of tea or sometimes for a south Indian breakfast of idlis or dosas which in those days, they would have never seen or relished before. My doctor wife was only too willing to host them with love and affection as our honoured guests.

Once, I called my Nazir or Cashier from the Deputy Commissioner's office to come home and after his physical verification of the requirements of the village headman, to buy a new shirt for him and bring it across quickly. Later, I took the village headman to my office and made him wear the shirt for his great satisfaction. I wanted to make the village headmen very happy and comfortable at the residence of the '*Bhor Saab*' whenever they visited my residence in the early part of the day. I always made it a point to redress their grievances, which were always genuine and as quickly as possible.

I considered myself fortunate to look after the village headmen whose conduct was pleasant and to help them in the best possible manner as a very sincere public servant for resolution of the issues brought to my notice by them. Incidentally, I wished to write that such poor people had to walk long distances in the hills to meet me. It was an unforgettable experience and a golden opportunity for me to serve such poor people of the district.

Right from the British days, it has been a tradition of honour for the village headmen to receive shawls from the Deputy Commissioner (DC) during tours to interior areas of hills districts. The major hills tribe of the district was Dimasas, and there were other hills tribes as well. Whenever the DC visited a village, that village headman along with nearby village headmen were informed beforehand, and the Office of the Deputy Commissioner informed the residents of the particular village and nearby villages to meet the Deputy Commissioner during his visit. In the case of the Dimasa village headman, the Bhor Saab was supposed to honour him with an Eri Shawl. In the case of the village headman belonging to Jemi Naga village, the Bhor Saab was supposed to honour him with a red blanket. During my tours in the district, I had made it a point to inform a group of Tribal Villages beforehand, wherein I could present the shawls to the village headmen of the particular area as it facilitated me as their respected Bhor Saab to honour a large number of village headmen as a matter of prestige and honour for them belonging to a particular tribe of those areas. Moreover, it was rather difficult on the part of the village headmen of various tribes to undertake the journeys to the District Headquarters very often to meet their Bhor Saab or Deputy Commissioner. After all, only certain places in the district were connected with motorable roads in those days.

Considering the backwardness and the poor road communications, I considered that it was my duty to frequently tour the various parts of the district which were predominantly inhabited by the tribal population. Moreover, as a matter of a gesture on my part as Deputy Commissioner, I used to carry a lot of chocolates for children and packets of cigarettes for adults and especially for the very poor backward Jemi Naga Villages during my visits.

I would like to narrate a very interesting event in my life when I took my wife and my infant child to a distant Jemi Naga village called Laisong, which was located at a distance of approximately 60 km or so from the District Headquarters with not-so-good road connectivity. Since my office had already informed the village headmen of my visit on that particular day, there were quite a lot of villagers, mostly children and citizens, in addition to more than a dozen village headmen. I was so very happy and considered myself fortunate in honouring those very poor tribal village headmen with red shawls and offered chocolates to the poor children and packets of cigarettes to the village adults. This village was situated at a height of a little more than perhaps, approximately between 4000 and 5000 ft. It was a very important place as it was a tri-junction between the States of Assam, Manipur, and Nagaland, i.e. bordering Manipur and Nagaland. There was a border outpost of Assam Police Battalion as well.

By the time we reached the village, the village headmen had organised a dinner for us accompanied by their typical dance performance. It was a very interesting information for the reader to note in that particular Jemi Naga village, which was fairly a big one, there were 2 dormitories i.e., one was exclusively used for unmarried women and another one was exclusively earmarked for unmarried men. The dormitories were spacious big huts with thatched roofs. There was perfect discipline amongst the villagers. Even though they were rather poor, they were extremely hospitable and made sure that all of us did have food with them.

My doctor wife and I, along with our infant son, had stayed overnight in the police barracks on slept on bamboo beds, with the place having no provision for electricity in the village at that time, and they used only lanterns during the night.

For me and my family, it was an unforgettable experience. This was not only related to the warm and excellent hospitality extended by the local villagers but also by the senior police officer-in-charge of the border police outpost and his colleagues. On the next morning after having a cup of tea, snacks, etc., we took leave of the officer-in-charge of the border outpost and other police personnel after thanking them profusely for their wonderful hospitality. The villagers and village headmen who had assembled in the previous evening were also there in the morning to bid an affectionate farewell. This novel experience of our visit to a distant Jemi Naga village called Laisong, quite far from the District Headquarters in view of very poor road communication, has been very strongly etched in my mind.

Likewise, I had visited another village called Hajadisha, which was more than 80 km from the District Headquarters which was predominantly inhabited by a tribe called Dimasas. I took the Eri shawls for the village headmen and other neighbouring Dimassas village headmen who came to meet me along with the local villagers. Though it was also an interior area of the District Headquarters, there was an Inspection Bungalow that was Spartan with only a couple of rooms. Generally, for the poor villagers, there was no entertainment at all. Therefore, I had instructed the district information and public relations officer to organise a film show, which consisted of only the Films Division's newsreels comprising important events in the country at that time. For the villagers, it was a great entertainment and not like watching a normal Hindi cinema. Nevertheless, it was, of course, a pleasant entertainment, as many of them had not even seen such Films Division news or films.

At this juncture, I would like to narrate that I had an interesting experience of visiting the residence of the village headman nearby. He had requested me to come to his residence for dinner. He himself was a very poor village headman living in a small hut with a thatched roof and having a mud floor only with some utensils and a small kitchen with firewood fuel. I was touched by his kind hospitality and I respected his sentiments and accepted his invitation. I took him in my vehicle and went to his nearby residence, which was nothing but a small hut and not very far from Hajadisa village. I sat along with him on the floor, which was nothing but a mud floor. He offered me a simple dinner, i.e. rice with dal and some chicken pieces with some kind of liquid curry.

The relationship between me and the then Chief Executive Member (CEM) of the district council at Haflong, namely, Shri K.K. Hojai, was always cordial, and there were absolutely no issues in terms of coordination between the Office of the Deputy Commissioner and that of the District Council.

After I took over as DC in the first week of July 1980, Sri K.K. Hojai came to call on me at my residential office. Sri K.K. Hojai was a very pleasant and respectable gentleman and, in fact, by profession, he was a contractor, in addition to being a senior politician. When he came to call on me, I showed him utmost respect and ushered him into my drawing room. I introduced my wife to him and informed him that since he came to my house for the first time in the morning, if he did not mind, I would like to offer him a south Indian breakfast before giving him a cup of coffee. He readily agreed to take breakfast with us. There were no airs about him, though he was the richest man in the district and also holding a powerful assignment as CEM. He liked our south Indian breakfast like *idli* and *dosa* with accompaniments like *chutneys*, etc., including coffee. He came to my residence after a few months and invited me to his daughter's wedding with a Tamil Nadu cadre I.A.S. Officer, who was 2 years junior to me in the service. We had attended the wedding of his daughter at that time at his residence at Haflong.

In this narrative, I will briefly mention 2 instances wherein I accompanied Shri K.K. Hojai on visits to different parts of the district, one hardly at a distance of a few km from Haflong and another one at an interior village called 'Semkhor' at a distance of more than 50 km.

I was pleasantly surprised when he came to take me to Ramakrishna Mission Hostel run for the poor orphan children from the interior villages. Though it was under the care and concern of the organisers of Ramakrishna Mission, Sri K.K. Hojai contributed a lot by providing requisite financial resources. I went around the hostel and I could see around 30 young boys and girls who were given proper shelter, food, and education as well at the primary stage. I was frankly touched by his altruistic act of taking care of the orphaned children of several tribes. I was very much impressed with his tremendous social welfare activities, and he seemed to be an unusual but pleasant samaritan in politics.

Originally, the counter-insurgency jungle warfare training school was functioning at a place called Verangte in the state of Mizoram. The army authorities wanted to shift that **Counter**-Insurgency Jungle Warfare School (CIJWS) from Verangte to a peaceful village around 20-25 km from Halflong. The place was considered ideal by army authorities because it had a hilly terrain, and the nearby villagers were also very helpful and law-abiding citizens.

In order to establish such a big institution of the army, they wanted sufficient land and therefore, there were negotiations between the army authorities who had come from Mizoram to discuss with the District Council Authorities. As explained previously, the Land Revenue Administration was vested with the authority of the district council, and the land ownership pattern was also quite different from that of the other districts of Assam. Since that area was well-known for the naturally growing orange trees, the villagers demanded sufficient compensation for the land as well as the expected loss of income on account of handing over the highly productive land. In the beginning, as Deputy Commissioner, I was not at all involved in the negotiations between the District Council Authorities and the Army Authorities. There were allegations of people demanding more compensation on the issue of a sufficient number of orange trees on the ground; but in reality, there were only small trees/shrubs, etc., and perhaps the villagers and the authorities in the district council demanded huge compensation which was certainly not justified. Therefore, the negotiations struck.

The Ministry of Defence came to know of the impediments being faced in the shifting of the CIJWS from Mizoram to NC Hills district. Therefore, the Ministry of Defence higher-ups took up the issue with the Chief Secretary to the Government of Assam and advised him to instruct the Deputy Commissioner of NC Hills district to involve himself in the negotiations and try to reach an amicable settlement. The real objective behind the move was to relocate the CIJWS in the peaceful environs of the NC Hills district from the point of view of its efficient organisation and also to facilitate their training, accommodation, and future development as and when it would be planned.

As I received clear instructions from the State Government, I got in touch with Mr. K.K. Hojai and requested him to come with his officers for a meeting to be fixed by me on a particular day. I informed him that the Brigadier, who was the Head of the CIJW School at Verangte, had already come with his colleagues and that I had also requested him to attend the meeting. I also informed the Secretary of the District Council to invite the villagers who were not very happy about the establishment of the school and protested regarding the amount of compensation offered. Therefore, as arranged, the CEM, the District Council Authorities, the Brigadier, and his colleagues, and the local villagers assembled in my huge office chamber at 11 am on a particular day.

The meeting took place for nearly 3 hours. I presided over the meeting and made sure at the commencement of the meeting that absolute decency and decorum shall be maintained at any cost during the meeting. As I expected allegations and counter-allegations regarding the quantum of compensation that was sought to be awarded by the army authorities to the District Council and through the District Council in turn to the affected villagers, I wanted to conduct the meeting in an orderly manner with due diligence and dignity.

I listened very carefully to the versions of army officers, the versions of CEM and some EMs, and the officers of the district council in addition to that of the assembled village elders whose lands were sought to be acquired for that purpose. It was no doubt a tortuous negotiation. I made sure that all 3 parties must come to a conclusion regarding not only the extent of land to be provided to the army authorities but also the quantum of compensation to be awarded by the army to the villagers and that too, in the most expeditious manner. I also made it very clear that under no circumstances should there be any delay with regard to land acquisition and sufficient compensation in the largest interest of the villagers. Though there were lots of differences, and there were different views expressed, but ultimately they came to the conclusion that everybody had to respect the decision of the Ministry of Defence and the State Government for the establishment of Counter-Insurgency Jungle Warfare School in the NC Hills district.

The meeting ended with the successful resolution of the issues regarding the extent of acreage of land to be earmarked, compensation to be provided to the affected villagers, and the timeline for taking over and handing over possession of the land on the part of the army authorities concerned, in addition to the timely payment of compensation to the affected villagers. All the decisions were properly recorded, and I insisted that the CEM, the EMs, the Secretary of the District Council, the Army Brigadier and his colleagues, and of course, the representatives of the villagers who had assembled, put their signatures as they had agreed in the meeting and that they would abide by the decisions taken in the meeting.

I vividly remember my visit to a village called 'Semkhor' which was located more than 50 km from Haflong. The interesting aspect is that I came to know about the village's existence, its interior location, and the people, particularly belonging to a sect of Dimasa Cachari tribe living in that village, through Mr. K.K. Hojai. Mr. Hojai had met me one day in my residential office and requested me to accompany him and a few executive members and the leaders of their Dimasa Cachari community the next day. There was a purpose as to why he had invited me to visit that village. Another interesting aspect about this village was it could only be reached by trekking from a place called Maibong, the then block headquarters. Up to Maibong and up to a particular point beyond Maibong, one could take a vehicle, but after that particular point, we had to negotiate and trek through a difficult path in the hills to reach the village called Semkhor.

Though the village was inhabited by the Dimasa Cachari tribals, this particular sect of Dimasa Cachari tribals was speaking a dialect which was not usually understood by the other Dimasa Cachari villagers. For many generations, they had been leading a very secluded life. For instance, even to fetch the essential provisions for their livelihood, like rice, dal, edible oil including kerosene oil, vegetables, etc., they had to trek through the hilly areas by foot every fortnight to visit the Fair Price Shop at Maibong and other shops that used to sell vegetables and other provisions, etc.

In fact, on the way itself, Mr. K.K. Hojai, who accompanied me in my car, briefed me about the peculiarities of the village. He had informed me that according to the villagers, their belief was originally based on their assumption of a story or occurrence, perhaps handed down from their forefathers, that their King had shot an arrow and that a particular arrow fell in that village. Therefore, that was their place to settle down, and under no circumstances would they ever shift from that particular location unless and until a future King of that community would give them a way out.

Mr. K.K. Hojai, being the Community Leader himself, told me candidly that he and his colleagues had tried their level best to convince the villagers of Semkhor and persuade them to shift to a nearby location instead of that particular difficult interior location, which was neither conducive for their livelihood nor for their health facilities as they had to depend on the health facilities at Maibong for which they had to take a long-distance by trekking. I reached the destination after considerable exertion as I was not used to trekking such long distances in a hilly terrain. As requested by the then CEM, I had accompanied him and his colleagues to do my level best to convince the villagers by taking the help of a translator of what I intended to say and convince them about the disadvantages faced by them to continue to live in that inhospitable and inaccessible area, bereft of health facilities or opportunities for good living.

During the negotiations with the villagers, I must mention that they heard me out patiently along with their local leaders. I spoke in a kind of broken Hindi language and the interpreter was somehow able to translate in their own slang/dialect about the disadvantages of their continuous living in that particular interior and remote village away from literally the rest of civilisation. The most interesting thing was that they had been living in a secluded manner for a number of decades; their way of speaking the Dimasa tribal language was certainly different and even Mr. K.K. Hojai and his colleagues could not understand the implications or the contextual references of the responses of those villagers. Despite our best and long interactions with them for more than a few hours on my part as well as the CEM and his colleagues, the Semkhor villagers were certainly not responsive, and they took a stubborn stand that under no circumstances, they would leave their present location and they would continue to live in their village only, despite the many hardships and difficulties faced by them day in and day out.

We were thoroughly exhausted as we had considered that our mission was not at all successful and despite our earnest intentions and our well-meaning interactions with them, we could not convince them about the many advantages that could accrue to them once they shifted from that particular village to a nearby village or elsewhere nearer to Maibong. In view of their obstinate and steadfast repudiation of our saner counsel, I felt very helpless in the wake of such superstitious beliefs and traditions of that sect of the Dimasas of Semkhor Village. The District Council was too willing to help them in the best possible manner with regard to their requirement of land, shelter, and other necessities. I also had offered my services to them in the best possible manner with regard to their food supplies so that they did not have to trek every 10 days or so to fetch their provisions from several kilometres in the difficult hilly terrain. I had to admit that I could not convince them at all but Mr. K.K. Hojai had appreciated my t support to him and his colleagues in such difficult negotiations. If I may say in a philosophical tone that human faith is unshakeable, come what may and in this particular instance, I could understand and appreciate the feelings and sentiments and the age-old faith of the inhabitants of Semkhor village about their strict adherence to the dictates of their King who perhaps had lived more than several decades ago and they had to respect his orders with reference to inhabiting that particular village. It was one of the most unforgettable experiences I ever had and my visit to Semkhor village and interactions with them without understanding a bit of their dialect on my part had always been etched in my memory even after 40 years of the event.

Mr. K.K. Hojai had introduced me to the villagers of Semkhor village as the Deputy Commissioner and the head of District Administration. He mentioned that I hailed from a place called Madras City, which was more than 2500 km away from that village. In addition to introducing me, the CEM had informed that as an administrator and the head of district administration, I had accepted his request and accompanied him to convince the villagers about the advantages of shifting from their age-old habitation, which was a distant village not easily accessible from the block headquarters at Maibong.

Training at the Defence Services Staff College at Wellington, in Nilgiris District of Tamil Nadu from January to November 1982.

In the month of December 1981 while I was serving as Deputy Commissioner of North Cachar Hills district at Halflong, I got a communication from the State Secretariat asking me if I would be willing to join an 11-month training programme at the Defence Services Staff College at Wellington, Nilgiris district, Tamil Nadu. I responded to that communication positively with my willingness to join that course. I thought that I would rather take this opportunity to go to Wellington, Nilgiris district for the purpose of my training and to get exposure to the training of the officers of the rank of Captains / Majors in the Indian Army and equivalent ranks in Air Force and Navy. Additionally the course attracted defence personnel from other countries as well. Therefore, I had to hand over charge of the assignment as Deputy Commissioner in the third/fourth week of December 1981 to proceed to Wellington in Tamil Nadu. I got the intimation later that the training was essentially meant for middle-level officers like Majors and Captains in the army and that of equivalent ranks in the Air Force and Navy.

I was also given to understand that only 4 civilian officers were selected i.e. 2 officers including myself belonging to the I.A.S. and 2 officers belonging to other Class I Services. Approximately more than 350 middle-level officers of Army, Air Force and Navy and from some other countries had come to join the DSSC training programme or course of study. In fact, a Lieutenant Colonel was kind enough to meet me at the reception and took me to the quarters, where I was accommodated, which was a three-bedroomed independent flat on the ground floor. Incidentally, Wellington is a township of the army and it is about 3 km away from Coonoor, which is a beautiful hill station and more than 350 staff quarters meant for officers' trainees were allotted to the officers. By and large, there were individual quarters; mostly the buildings consisted of 2 quarters i.e. upstairs and downstairs. I was allotted No.10 of Castle Quarters. There were different names for various quarters.

In this connection, I would also like to mention that apart from middle-level officers of the armed forces, there were officers of equivalent ranks from abroad, viz., Sri Lanka, USA, U.K. and a few African countries who participated in the training programme of the 38th Staff Course in the year 1982. It was considered to be one of the finest defence institutions in the country meant for training of the middle-level officers of the 3 different wings of the armed forces i.e. Army, Air Force and Navy.

In the case of army officers, they had to appear for the entrance examination before joining the course. If my memory serves me right, officers of the armed forces were entitled to become Lieutenant Colonels only after passing such a course.

During the training period, I was attached to the Army wing of the course. I attended the classes taken by the senior officers of the army for army wing officers. Likewise, for Naval and Air Force officers trainees, their respective senior faculty members took classes for them.

There was no examination system, but there did exist a system of internal assessment of the participation of the trainee officers. The DSSC is affiliated with the University of Madras. Once an officer completed this course for the duration of 11 months, they were entitled to get a Pass Course Certificate. The essential part of the course was also the necessity for the presentation of a dissertation paper of the officers' choice. In my case, I had submitted a dissertation paper on the insurgency in the North East. Once the dissertation paper was accepted and the Pass Course Certificate issued, the University of Madras considered the performance of the officers and they normally were provided a Post Graduate degree called M.Sc in Defence Studies.

I received my postgraduate degree, i.e. M.Sc in Defence Studies, in the year 1983 from the University of Madras. As I had by then left Wellington to Dispur, Guwahati, for joining my assignment as Joint Secretary to the

Government of Assam in the Home and Political Departments at the Secretariat in the month of December 1982, I received the degree by post.

Towards the end of the course, Field Marshal Manekshaw - Sam Hormusji Framji Jamshedji Manekshaw, popularly known as 'Sam Bahadur', was invited as the Chief Guest and he awarded all the officers the Pass Course Certificate. Field Marshal Manekshaw was a resident of Coonoor at that time and continued to live there for many more years.

Coming back to the infrastructural arrangements of the college, I would like to mention that it was a well-equipped institution along with a proper auditorium and lecture halls. There is a military hospital as well for providing medical assistance to the trainees. One of the important highlights was that roughly every fortnight, eminent persons from various walks of life were invited by the college authorities as Guest Lecturers. During my training period, I had come across senior civil servants, religious heads, academics, and other distinguished persons in various fields who had come and presented wonderful lectures. Even today, I vividly cherish the admirable and memorable lecture given by Shri Ranganathananda Swamiji, the then head of Sri Ramakrishna Mission. By and large, the Guest Lecturers were requested to give their talks and before they concluded for about 30 minutes or so, there used to be time for questions and answers. The then Army Chief had visited as a guest lecturer as well.

Thanks to these lectures, one greatly benefitted from the exposure to various subjects like economics, religion, administration, philosophy, etc.

As I explained, I was attached to the Army Wing during my training programme. Another I.A.S. officer was attached to the Naval Wing. One Indian Railway Service Officer was attached to the Air Force Wing. There was a scientist from the Defence Research and Development Organisation who was attached to the Army Wing. I would like to mention that for officers of the Navy and Air Force, as well as the civil services, there was an army attachment for a fortnight at the border areas. I preferred to go to the Jammu and Kashmir border in view of the fact that I had done an army attachment for a fortnight during my initial training period in the I.A.S. at the North Eastern border in Arunachal Pradesh. Another very important programme of this course was the 3 weeks' industrial cum demonstration tour organised for the trainees. In fact, a fully air-conditioned train consisting of more than a dozen coaches with a vestibule for the trainee officers was organised by the staff college in close coordination with the Railways. As a part of this tour, I had the opportunity to visit certain defence institutions like the National Defence Academy at Khadakwasla near Pune, Artillery Headquarters at Deolali. I could witness the tank fire demonstration at Ahmed Nagar, which was a wonderful sight. I had also witnessed an Artillery demonstration during nighttime.

In addition to visiting such defence institutions, we were also taken to certain industrial establishments as part of the tour. I visited Bharat Electronics Limited, Kirloskar Group of Companies, and certain other industrial units during the year 1982.

This is just to illustrate for the reader to understand and appreciate that a holistic approach was adopted by the Defence Services Staff College at Wellington in order to make the officer trainees aware of not only the functioning of important defence institutions at the field-level but also to make the officer trainees aware of the industrial advancements made in the country by various Public and Private Sector undertakings depending upon the tours organised for different groups. For me, it was not only a Godsent opportunity to stay in my home state for a period of almost one-year in Nilgiris district but also to get exposed to the vital functions of some important defence organisations spread across the country. It was a welcome change from my earlier district assignment to my own home state when I became an officer trainee after being the head of the District Administration as Deputy Commissioner for more than a year and 6 months or so in the State of Assam. For me, in addition to attending the course for about a year or so at Wellington, I got acquainted with good friends in some of the other civil services and of course, in the armed forces. I could maintain a few friendships developed during my Wellington days to later periods as well after I had come to Delhi on some central deputation assignments for more than a decade.

Joint Secretary to the Government of Assam in the Home and Political Departments, Government of Assam from 4th December 1982 to September 1983

My reminiscences of extremely challenging, and unforgettable months of an unenviable assignment as Joint Secretary to the Government of Assam in the Home and Political Departments during the years, i.e., from 4th December 1982 - 9th September 1983 and especially, between December 1982 and March 1983.

I reported to the office of the Chief Secretary to the Government of Assam on 4th December 1982 immediately after I had successfully completed the Defence Services Staff College (DSSC) course. I was informed that I was appointed as Joint Secretary to the Government of Assam in the Home and Political Departments. As soon as I called on the then Chief Secretary Mr. Ramesh Chandra, he advised me to meet the Home Commissioner and seek his advice and instructions. Incidentally, the state was under the President's rule at that time. I met the Home Commissioner, Mr. M. Gopalkrishna for the first time on 4th December 1982. He had assumed charge of this office during the most turbulent times and volatile situation in the State of Assam. He was my supervisory officer, and I reported to him as advised by the then Chief Secretary.

In this narrative, I will restrict my reminiscences to the period of approximately 4 months as the second in command in the Home and Political Departments during the President's rule only. I will not be writing on the period of my continued assignment as the Joint Secretary, Home and Political Departments to the Government of Assam thereafter, up to 9th

September 1983, i.e. for a further period of approximately 5 months. That experience under the popular rule was rather qualitatively different and perhaps warrants another interesting narrative. Therefore, I have decided to concentrate in this narrative on my most challenging, difficult, and unforgettable experience during my tenure in Assam.

In my very first meeting with Mr. M. Gopalkrishna of the 1962 I.A.S. batch of Assam-Meghalaya cadre, he told me that he had called for the Annual Confidential Records of some of the young officers and selected me as his Joint Secretary in the Home and Political Departments, based on whatever credentials and criteria he had prescribed, of which I was not aware. He further added that he would serve as the Home Commissioner only for the next few months approximately and thereafter, he would leave Dispur (Guwahati) for Hyderabad. He was business-like in the strictest sense of the term with categorical instructions to me about my duties and responsibilities as his immediate subordinate officer.

He had originally gone on deputation assignment to the Government of Andhra Pradesh from the State Government of Assam. He was literally pulled back only to serve as the then Home Commissioner of the Government of Assam with a clear mandate of his duties and responsibilities for a limited period only. He was affectionate, absolutely straightforward, candid, categorical and very pleasant and transparent in all our interactions during an extremely challenging and tough assignment in that short period. I would also like to mention that he was polite, courteous and business-like and had interacted with me and other senior and junior officers and staff members wearing his infectious smile on his face always with a cool-headed approach and composure. I learnt from him the nuances of the art of governance and literally followed his footsteps in the learning curve of my administrative career in my later years in the Indian Administrative Service. I often used to quote the following dictum all through my administrative career i.e. 'When the going is tough, the tough get going'. This is based on my wonderful experience of working with Mr. M. Gopalakrishna.

My indelible impressions about the outstanding qualities of head and heart of Mr. M. Gopalkrishna in my very first meeting made me feel very comfortable. That positive thought in view of his exemplary conduct certainly led me to my lifelong association with him as one of the elder members of our family to date. It is a fact that he had visited my office and residence in the then City of Madras (later renamed as Chennai) during the years 1985 to 1990 a few times while I had served as the then Joint Chief Controller of Imports and Exports and as Zonal Head of the Imports and Exports Control and Trade Promotion Organisation for the whole of South India, under the Ministry of Commerce, Government of India. I have had official interactions as well with him and more so, with his colleagues so far as the import requirements of capital goods and raw materials, etc. were concerned, when he had served as the then Chairman and Managing Director of Godaveri Fertilisers Limited. If I remember correctly, it was under his able and outstanding leadership, the production asset of the company had been literally built up from scratch to its logical completion stage in due course. I had visited his office at that time and his officials also attended the many periodical meetings that I convened at Madras, in my capacity as the then Chairman of Capital Goods Licensing Committee and the then Chairman of Supplementary Licensing Committee for the import requirements of capital goods, raw materials, components for capital goods machinery, as and when necessary for the many big and small-scale industries to enable the growth and development of the trade and industry of the southern states. He had served as the Chairman and Managing Director of Nagarjuna Fertilisers Limited as well in due course.

Working with Mr. Gopalkrishna was a fabulous experience, even if it was for a limited period of a few months. I learnt to deal with such extraordinary work pressures in such an adversarial and difficult environment. He had informed the then Chief Secretary at that time that he would work even 16 to 18 hours a day; but he would definitely need one hour break for his lunch and also in view of his penchant for listening to Carnatic classical music and melodious songs in the afternoon at State Guest House No. 2, where he was accommodated with full security in addition to the pilot and escort police personnel for providing security to him during transit between the office at the Secretariat at Dispur and Khanapara, where State Guest House No. 2 was located. He had also advised me that I might also take an hour's break from our gruelling routine in the afternoon and had kept the Chief Secretary informed about the necessity for my rest also for an hour during the lunch break. On those days, the regular working hours for us commenced around 9 am every day and concluded around midnight and very often beyond midnight as well across all days of the week.

To provide context, the state was under President's rule at that time, owing to which the whole administration was under the hierarchy of the then Hon'ble Governor of Assam, Mr. Prakash Mehrotra. He was assisted by 2 advisers, namely, Mr. R. V. Subramanian and Mr. N. Natarajan. Mr. R. V. Subramanian was the Senior Adviser and was in charge of many of the important departments, like the Home and Political Departments, General Administration Department, Elections, etc. The official hierarchy of Chief Secretary, Home Commissioner, and Joint Secretary to the Government of Assam in the Home and Political Departments, in addition to the Director-General of Police and the entire police organisation through the Chief Secretary and the Home Commissioner, were primarily accountable and responsible to the Senior Adviser only and no one else at that time.

The Senior Adviser was a very difficult and highly demanding taskmaster, literally holding the reins of the state administrative machinery. He made it unambiguously clear that his word was final and his directions on the complex issues of administration and the entire hierarchy of the police organisation were under his command and control only. For all practical purposes, the Senior Adviser functioned like the de facto Governor at that time. He was vested with that kind of authority as mandated by the Government of India during the President's rule. To mention in a lighter vein, I had never ever seen him smile during our formal interactions with him. He was a serious bureaucrat and meant serious business at all times. Moreover, during those troubled times, at 6 pm sharp on almost each and every day, there was a State Coordination Committee Meeting for an hour and sometimes more than an hour as well under his business-like leadership. The entire administrative machinery right from the Chief Secretary downwards, including my humble self and the Director-General of Police and his colleagues and senior police officers of various wings, had to attend and carry out his directions on the fast-developing law and order situation, as it turned from bad to worse very often in various parts of the state. I was entrusted with the responsibility of recording the minutes of the meetings, especially, on all the decisions that were taken each and every day. I had to send the draft minutes to him through the Chief Secretary regularly for his perusal and approval immediately after the conduct of such meetings.

The situation in the State of Assam was extremely volatile in view of the widespread agitation against the foreigners or illegal immigrants from the neighbouring country throughout the state. There was also an apprehension that the situation would be unmanageable in the foreseeable future, given the serious threat to the maintenance of law and order and safety and security of the people in the entire state. Incidentally, I came to know later on that the Senior Adviser originally belonged to the Assam-Meghalaya Cadre and after his field postings, etc., he had proceeded on deputation to the Government of India and had spent several years on assignments continuously at the Centre before his superannuation.

As the agitation was gathering momentum, a series of violent incidents was reported from many parts of the state. The announcement of general elections for the legislative assembly of the State of Assam, announced in the latter part of December 1982 or the early part of January 1983, was totally resisted by the people of the state. I vividly remember the day when Mr. Bipul Chandra Kalita, the then affable, diligent, well-mannered, and unforgettable Superintendent of Police of the Special Branch, had come to my office chamber at the then Dispur Secretariat and informed me that Prime Minister Mrs. Indira Gandhi, at that time, made an announcement that general elections were ordered and would be held perhaps in less than 2 months' time, i.e. in February 1983. He was literally nervous and told me without the least ambiguity that we would be in for very great trouble certainly in the coming months.

I immediately rushed to the Chief Secretary's Chamber and informed him about the not-so-good news for the state and the people at that relevant time. I came to know that the Home Commissioner was already briefed by the Intelligence Bureau and the higher-ups in the Government of India and Special Branch wing of the state Police. I vividly also remember, even after 40 years as of today, what I said to the Chief Secretary. I quote as follows. "Sir, the state will witness very big trouble. There will be uncontrollable widespread violence and bloodshed. I am extremely concerned about the situation that might follow in view of the undesirable announcement of general elections in the state, when the situation had been steadily deteriorating day by day."

However, I must say that he was totally unruffled and responded in a calm, composed, and unflappable manner to my statement filled with anxiety and strain writ large on my face. He retorted with the following words, "Do you think so?"

I said candidly without batting my eyelids, "Yes, Sir. I am damn sure about it." After all, it was a fact that I had been literally receiving dozens and dozens of wireless messages from the Special Branch of the Police organisation informing of many violent incidents, clashes, and turmoil day in and day out and briefing the impact of such developments to the Home Commissioner and the Chief Secretary regularly. Incidentally, I came to know later, a couple of assistants and a few grade IV staff who had worked with me affectionately called me 'Running Joint Secretary' in view of the fact that I had to rush to the offices of the Chief Secretary and the Home Commissioner holding the important files in my hands every day in those difficult months, at least more than a dozen times every day on average. My statement above is in no sense an exaggeration and is being truthfully recalled.

In the meantime, the entire administrative machinery was geared up to meet the situation. However, the announcement of general elections to the Legislative Assembly in the state triggered and gave a very big impetus on the part of the leaders of the agitation to continue their agitation with much more vigour and virulence. They exhorted all sections of the people of the state to boycott the general elections to the and asked them to resort to total non-co-operation with the government and the administrative setup at each and every level from the higher echelons at the secretariat to the lowermost formations in the districts and sub-divisions throughout the state.

The sway of the leaders of the anti-foreigners movement over the general populace of Assam was so immense that practically, each and every section of the people gave a call to boycott elections and literally announced total non-co-operation with the government departments and organisations entrusted with the conduct of the elections.

In order to ensure proper maintenance of law and order and to immobilise the leaders of the agitation, the prominent leaders were arrested under the National Security Act and other significant provisions of law on several occasions; but it was also a fact that they had obtained bail orders with ease. At one point in time, none of the government officials reported for duty as the non-co-operation movement gained momentum very vigorously.

Literally, only a handful of officers and staff had reported for duty at the State Secretariat, in the districts and sub-divisions, just a few weeks before the conduct of elections. The law and order situation was much worse and it deteriorated rapidly. I could feel this as I was going through a large number of periodical police wireless transmission messages, popularly called 'Sitreps', i.e., Situation Reports received from time to time from morning till midnight on each and every day.

Moreover, it will be appropriate to mention at this juncture that the Superintendent of Police of the Special Branch, Mr. Bipul Chandra Kalita, visited my office regularly with important confidential documents and dossiers relating to the conduct of the prominent leaders of the agitation with attempts to disrupt the normal functions of the government and to foment trouble and unrest amongst various sections of society. He used to come to meet me in my office chamber regularly on several days with the draft orders for the arrest and detention of the most prominent leaders of the agitation, under the National Security Act. This course required the approval of the Home Commissioner, Chief Secretary, and the senior adviser. Hand-to-hand movements of such files were the order of the day between 4 of the functionaries in view of the necessity for ensuring utmost secrecy and one might call us the most important or not so fortunate people in the hierarchy of the administration, i.e. Senior Adviser, Chief Secretary, Home Commissioner, and Joint Secretary, Home and Political Departments of the Government of Assam at that time. I was literally at the receiving end and had to sign all such detention orders forthwith the moment written orders were issued in the files to that effect. It so happened that after such orders were served on the prominent leaders and when they were produced in the courts after their arrest, bail orders were promptly given by the concerned courts. Again in such cases, very quickly and often Mr. Bipul Chandra Kalita used to come to my office with a fresh set of draft detention orders on substantial dosiers and rationale for such detentions after obtaining the requisite approval for my signature. In the secretariat, only a little more than 2 dozen people in addition to 4 of us from the Senior Adviser to the Joint Secretary, i.e. a few of the assistants, stenographers, typists, and grade 1V employees had worked in such a hostile environment. Most often, they used to stay for the night at the Secretariat itself. Of course, very large contingents of security personnel were deployed at the Secretariat round the clock for the safety and security of all the personnel working at the Secretariat, including the Chief Electoral Officer and very few of his trusted officers and limited staff in the Election Department as well. The non-co-operation movement and boycott call to shun the elections foisted on the people as announced by the prominent leaders of the anti-foreigners movement were widely supported by all sections of the people. The senior officers including the Class I and Class II officers and Grades III and IV staff of almost all the government departments hardly reported for duty after the announcement of the conduct of the elections for several weeks or so in view of the non-co-operation movement announced by the leaders of the agitation.

As we had to work 16 to 18 hours approximately during those troubled times, every day a very limited staff risking their lives had worked for us literally round the clock. Except for a few senior officers like us with proper security all the time at the secretariat and during our movements outside the secretariat to our residences, by and large, the junior officers and staff had to spend several nights at the secretariat itself. Of course, in the interests of safety and security of all the junior officers and staff, I took adequate care of their food and security requirements as well as their time at the secretariat to ensure adequate security safeguards for their movements between the secretariat and their houses. They had to literally go to their homes late at night and come very early in the morning.

The entire Dispur Secretariat complex was literally turned into an impregnable fortress. But even though it was such an impregnable fortress under the watchful eyes of the large number of security forces deployed at the front, rear, and on all sides of the secretariat, it was a fact that on one fine day around noon or so, an unruly and criminal-minded person who hid a big knife somehow tried to sneak through the security cordon and rushed to the main building of the secretariat with the clear intention to harm. Fortunately, he was apprehended in time, and the security at the front entrance was further strengthened to ensure that no such untoward incident was ever allowed to recur. As advised by the Home Commissioner, I made sure that the secretariat Canteen Proprietor and his limited staff functioned as required day and night to prepare the food items and various snacks for the limited staff who were on duty each day of the week without even a day off. The requisite financial resources were made available to him in advance for the purchase of commodities, provisions, vegetables, etc. in bulk quantities in view of the non-co-operation movement and frequent calls for bandhs, etc.

The limited number of grade III and grade IV officials, in addition to the security personnel working with us in the departments, were taken very good care of. Especially, their food requirements, including arrangements of tea, snacks, etc., were adequately taken care of so that each and every one working at the secretariat did not have to go hungry at any time on any day. This was thanks to the very clear instructions of the Home Commissioner that I must take full care of them and cater to their requirements.

I would like to recall one office assistant by the name of Mr. R. C. Malakaar who worked hard with due diligence and commitment, assisting me with absolute sincerity and dedication. Later on, I came to know that perhaps due to the good annual confidential reports given to him by me, the Home Commissioner, and many of his superior officers, he was selected as the Regional Passport Officer in Guwahati in the early 1990s.

As a slight digression, if I may say so, in the month of October 1994 when I proceeded on a one-year foreign training programme in the United Kingdom, it was the same gentleman who was so very delighted to issue a Diplomatic Passport (as I was in the super-time scale of the I.A.S. by then) to me and my family with joy and happiness writ large on his face when all of us had met him at his office in Guwahati.

Closer to the election days, as most of the junior officers and staff, perhaps except a very few officials detailed and deployed for the conduct of elections, refused to work and did not report for duty, the Government of India in the Home Ministry and the Election Commission of India had to deploy very large contingents of the Central Government Class II and Class III officials, numbering several hundreds, in addition to one hundred odd I.A.S. probationers as well for the conduct of the elections in Assam. They were sent by air to Guwahati and other airports in the state for discharge of their duties as presiding officers and polling officers at the innumerable polling centres spread over all the 126 legislative assembly constituencies.

It certainly and literally became a herculean task for the Chief Electoral Officer and the Home Commissioner, in addition to all the Deputy

Commissioners and Sub-Divisional Officers who were the District Election Officers and Returning Officers, to look after their logistic requirements like transport, stay, and food arrangements. Many of the Class I and Class II officers of the State Government, in addition to a very large number of Class III office assistants and grade IV staff, etc., obeyed the call for non-co-operation and did not respond to their duties as perhaps their conscience did not permit them to discharge their duties and responsibilities as expected of them. Moreover, they did not wish to risk their lives and wanted to play safe in such a surcharged emotional environment and with widespread violent incidents in many parts of the state. I might like to quote one incident which was widely reported at that time in the newspapers. When some of the I.A.S. probationers were going around the Panbazar areas of Guwahati, some young students including a few girls accosted them and wished to verify who they were and what they were doing. Without realising the gravity of the ground-level situation, a few probationers proudly responded by reporting that they were I.A.S. probationers and deputed to work for the conduct of the elections in Guwahati at that time.

This immediately provoked the assembled boys and girls, and they assaulted the I.A.S. probationers indiscriminately, causing severe injuries to some of them. Of course, fortunately, the security personnel deployed at the police picket stationed nearby immediately rushed to their rescue. Immediate instructions were given all over the state to all the Deputy Commissioners, Sub-Divisional Officers, and the entire police organisation to ensure that no such untoward incident ever happened and that all the very large contingent of officials and staff who came from outside were provided more than adequate security. Each and every official was advised that they should never venture out and should stay put only at their prior arranged places of accommodation until the conclusion of the conduct of the elections.

As all the shops were closed on most days, it became a big issue to provide food for the scores of Central Government officials and staff who were sent to the state for the purpose of conducting elections. To tide over such difficult and unforeseen situations in the initial stage, some very senior I.A.S. officers were deployed for duties to receive them at Guwahati airport and provide them with food packets for their onward journeys to various destinations. For such requirements, several planeloads containing dozens of large cartons of bread, cake, biscuits, and other packed snacks were sent from Delhi to Guwahati airport to take care of the immediate food requirements of several hundreds of officials and staff deputed by the Government of India from many departments in New Delhi.

The Resident Commissioner of the Government of Assam at Assam House, New Delhi was roped in along with the Home Ministry officials and Indian Airlines officials who had coordinated the dispatch arrangements from Delhi for transportation of several planeloads of such huge and heavy consignments of food items which were sent to Guwahati airport and for onward transmission to other cities and towns through the coordinators deployed at Guwahati airport and in the districts and sub-divisions of the State of Assam. I constantly monitored the situation and I was aware of such dispatches to the offices of Deputy Commissioners and Sub-Divisional Officers regarding the requirements of the officers and staff deputed by the Central Government to perform the duties of presiding and polling officers for all the earmarked polling stations in the state.

The officials and staff, numbering around 2 dozen people, who were working in the Home and Political Departments at the Secretariat, had requested to be provided with consignments of bread, biscuits, and varied namkeen packets received from Delhi. This request was made in view of their continuous slogging of several hours day in and day out, including late-night work, with utmost sincerity and dedication despite risking their lives. I immediately complied with their requests. I had requested our senior I.A.S. officers, who were deployed for the distribution of snack items, bread, biscuits, etc., at the airport in Guwahati, to ensure that several dozens of such cartons were sent in vehicles with security to the Secretariat Complex as well. This was in addition to the dispatch arrangements made by them to the districts and sub-divisions. It was my responsibility to ensure the welfare of not only the limited number of assistants and staff of the Home and Political Departments and some assistants and staff at the Election Department but also to look after the large contingents of security personnel deployed at the Home and Political Departments, in addition to the Election Department at the secretariat. Their constant and continuous discharge of duties and responsibilities in such an adversarial environment and amidst so much turmoil and violence in the state was extremely critical.

As and when the elections were nearing and conducted with unprecedented security arrangements, it was virtually like a civil war zone, despite the presence of police and paramilitary personnel. Violent incidents on a large-scale did occur, and several hundreds of people lost their lives. There were conflicts and clashes between tribals and non-tribals, inter-community conflicts and clashes, and the inevitable communal conflicts and clashes between various groups. It was really a very pathetic and certainly an unenviable environment in the entire state, to say the least. The total number of people officially declared dead was perhaps a little more than 2 thousand, but unofficial reports indicated a much higher number of casualties in view of such mad and terrible violent incidents.

After the conclusion of such unforgettable and undesirable violent incidents, elections that were conducted amidst so much of unprecedented violence, popular rule was established, and the President's rule was revoked.

Mr. Hiteshwar Saikia took over as the Chief Minister of the State. The Senior Adviser and the other Advisers subsequently left the state. Mr. M. Gopalakrishna, the Home Commissioner and my mentor, candidly informed me at my very first interaction that he would leave the state on his reversion back to the State of Andhra Pradesh after a couple of months and that too after completion of the election most likely in the month of March 1983. I continued in the same assignment for another 5 months or so before my transfer and posting, ironically, as Secretary to the Commission of Enquiry on Assam Disturbances. I was especially selected as the Secretary to the Commission of Enquiry on Assam Disturbances, as desired by the then Chief Minister, to assist Mr. T. P. Tewari, the one man Commission of Enquiry headed by the former Chief Secretary and former Vice-Chairman of the Uttar Pradesh State Planning Commission.

Just for the information of the reader of this lengthy narrative, I would like to mention that in those bygone years, the officers and staff at the secretariat had to depend on PBX/PABX telephone exchange systems at the secretariat and elsewhere for passing on the instructions to their colleagues and subordinates. It was a time-consuming process and did create so many hurdles and obstacles in the communications of instructions on the landlines or fixed telephone systems from the senior officers of the State Secretariat to the field officers of the districts and sub-divisions. The only dependable and reliable fast communications were through the police wireless network.

The senior officers had to depend on the stenographers for issuing instructions and orders by dictation. The assistants and typists had to depend on manual typewriters and cyclostyling machines for typing and making copies respectively. The advent of computers came in the later part of the 1980s along with the photocopier machines, popularly called Xerox machines. The subscriber trunk dialling facilities, popularly called STD facilities, with various code numbers for districts' headquarters and Sub-divisional headquarters' towns, in addition to other cities and towns, were implemented in the later part of the 1980s. The advent of fax or facsimile machines for the fastest communication of orders or instructions through such machines attached to the landline phones or fixed telephones from one office to another office in times of emergency in another city or town was also witnessed later, perhaps after several years in the late 1980s.

Therefore, one could easily understand and appreciate the importance of physical human labour and the significance of the utility of machines like manual typewriters and cyclostyling machines, etc., during the early part of the 1980s when the limited number of devoted, sincere, and hardworking officials and staff had to perform their onerous duties and responsibilities in such an unavoidable and stressful working environment with many difficulties, including long working hours, restlessness, fatigue, etc., in times of adversity at various levels in the hierarchy of the governance of the state.

Ever since the elections were announced and concluded later around the end of February 1983 with the end of the process of counting of votes, etc., the whole exercise was full of so much strain, stress, and tension amongst the few trusted officers and staff who had worked at the secretariat and at the districts and sub-divisions relentlessly for a couple of months much against the wishes of the general people of the State of Assam.

Unfortunately, it is undoubtedly an undeniable fact that it did leave a bitter taste and indelible impressions in the minds of not only the people of the state but also amongst the officers, assistants, stenographers, and grade IV staff who did contribute their humble mite to attend to the call of their duties in such a stressful and tension-ridden environment in the state capital and in the districts and sub-divisions, though they were a very small and insignificant fraction of the entire state administrative machinery.

I shudder to think even today after more than 4 decades about the nightmarish occurrences of large-scale violent incidents of killings, arsons, and lootings that were the order of the day and especially before the conduct of general elections and immediately thereafter as well in the midst of unprecedented violent incidents and terrible bloodshed that the State of Assam witnessed in its history. I do not like to pass any value judgement at this stage of my life about the entire process of elections that was conducted in such an adversarial environment with so much of unprecedented violence, communal clashes, inter-community and intracommunity conflicts and clashes and the explicit lawlessness at its worst form. Nowhere in the country, such elections in thoroughly undesirable and unwarranted law and order situations were ever perhaps conducted in the past and hopefully, if God willing and God forbid, such farcical elections in the name of the restoration of democracy would and should never ever be held. The scars inflicted and rivalry experienced amidst so much violence, loss of lives, loss of homes by the varied groups belonging to very many sections of the people would continue to remain in their hearts forever, especially those who survived even after such bloody clashes and conflicts in view of such unprecedented violence, which was seen and experienced by the people.

One would only hope and trust that such violent acts and inhuman behaviour with perhaps animal instincts, abominable and reprehensible conduct of several sections of the people witnessed in that year would never ever recur again in the State of Assam, or anywhere else. I only pray to God the Almighty that such a curse and unprecedented violence would never ever befall on the land and the people of the State of Assam who were always peace-loving citizens. When I had entered the state as an I.A.S. Probationer in 1976 and in my first field posting as Sub-Divisional Officer of Golaghat Sub-division in the years 1977 to 1979, it was a beautiful, charming, delightful and of course, peaceful paradise on earth, as I had widely travelled as a very young I.A.S. officer in the sub-division under my jurisdiction, as the head of the Sub-divisional administration.

Secretary, Commission of Enquiry on Assam Disturbances from September 1983 to July 1984

In the later part of August 1983, the Chief Minister, in the presence of the Chief Secretary, advised me to proceed to Lucknow and meet Mr. T. P. Tewari, Vice-Chairman of Uttar Pradesh Planning Commission and Ex-Chief Secretary of the government of Uttar Pradesh, and seek his opinion as to whether he would accept an assignment as a one-man Commission of Enquiry on Assam Disturbances and to let us know the terms and conditions of his appointment.

Accordingly, I went to Lucknow and met him to ascertain his convenience and his terms of appointment. He readily agreed to be the Chairman of the Enquiry Commission on Assam Disturbances. He informed me that he would like to take up this assignment and requested allowing him to take with him 2 retired state civil service officers to assist him during the conduct of his enquiry on Assam Disturbances. He also informed me that he would like to stay for 2 weeks at a stretch and in between, he would like to return to Lucknow. He had requested proper accommodation for himself and his 2 retired state service colleagues, in addition to the provision of the requisite remuneration.

I came back and informed the Chief Secretary and Chief Minister of the terms and conditions of Mr. T. P. Tewari for his appointment as Chairman, Commission of Enquiry on Assam Disturbances, and they accepted the terms and conditions as suggested by Mr. T. P. Tewari. Thereafter, formal appointment orders for his assignment as Chairman, Commission of Enquiry on Assam Disturbances and the appointment of his 2 retired colleagues as Officers on Special Duty to the Chairman of the Commission of Enquiry on Assam Disturbances were issued. I took care of the issues of accommodation and transport for all 3 of them. They were accommodated in the State Guest House No. 2 at Khanapara, Guwahati. I made arrangements for the provision of transport for their place of stay and for their transport to the office at Dispur, Guwahati on a regular basis. In fact, I had organised the office accommodation for all 3 of them in addition to myself in an adjacent vacant building nearer to the State Secretariat. It was originally built for the Guwahati Tea Auction Centre. It was a new building and yet to be put to use for the purpose for which it was built at that time.

I was appointed as the Secretary to the Chairman, Commission of Enquiry on Assam Disturbances during the period from September 1983 to July 1984.

Mr. T.P. Tewari advised me to issue notices to the concerned Deputy Commissioners, Superintendents of Police, and senior officers like the concerned senior civil and police officers who happened to be their supervisory officers during the relevant periods. They were called to depose before the Commission of Enquiry on different dates and times as intimated to them beforehand and narrate truthfully as to what exactly had happened with regard to the law and order situation during the relevant periods. His OSDs were present in addition to the stenographer engaged by me for helping them. My duties and responsibilities were limited to the issue of the notices beforehand to ensure their presence for giving evidence based on their personal knowledge and experience of various occurrences in their respective jurisdictions. Of course, I was very much present along with the Chairman during the relevant period when such evidence was given by our erstwhile Deputy Commissioners, Superintendents of Police, D.I.G.s, and other concerned officials who were issued notices to depose.

In addition to the recording of evidence relating to several incidents of law and order situations during the unsettled period and especially during the statewide disturbances, the Chairman of the Commission decided to visit many districts and wished to interact with the general public of certain areas and the concerned senior officers to ascertain the issues of law and order and whether appropriate actions were taken for the prevention of violent incidents and what exactly the outcome of their efforts was. The general public who had come to meet him expressed their views and requested him to take appropriate action against certain officials who were responsible for the cause of such violent incidents. In their opinion, such widespread disturbances had resulted in several loss of lives and loss or damages to public property in a reckless manner. By and large, the people gave their views in a very fair and frank manner during their discussions with the Chairman of the Commission of Enquiry on Assam Disturbances, and I only occasionally intervened to translate the views communicated by them in the local Assamese language to English for his information.

Though occasionally every month after his recording of evidence at his office in Guwahati, he used to leave for Lucknow for a week or 10 days, his 2 OSDs were present at Guwahati only and performed their assignments as allotted to them by the Chairman during his absence. In fact, they were very nice gentlemen, and I did my level best to make them feel comfortable and help them in providing the requisite assistance of stenographers and necessary co-operation based on their requests. Based on the request made by the Chairman, I organised a short-duration tour to Imphal in the State of Manipur. I went with him and visited the Govindajee temple at Imphal and also a place distant from Imphal called Moirang, on the India-Myanmar border. It is the place where Netaji Subash Chandra Bose hoisted the Indian National Flag for the first time - much before the Independence of our country. A Museum was established at that place in honour of Netaji Subash Chandra Bose. It contains several photographs of Netaji Subash Chandra Bose and the former members of the Indian National Army who fought against British Rule. I was delighted to have had the opportunity to visit Moirang and to have paid my respects to Netaji Subash Chandra Bose. The pole bearing the Indian National Flag is kept intact at the Museum.

After a few months of recording evidence of many more officials, the Chairman of the Commission of Enquiry on Assam Disturbances, with the help of 2 OSDs and other officials and staff who worked with him, prepared a report which he wished to submit directly to the then Chief Minister of Assam. Of course, it was crystal clear that he did not seek my assistance in the preparation of his enquiry report. It is a fact that I only provided the requisite logistical support and did not assist in the preparation of his enquiry report. As requested by the Chairman, in due course, I organised the appointment time at the beginning of July 1984 for Chairman Mr. T. P. Tewari with the then Chief Minister of Assam. I was not present during his meeting with the Chief Minister. As requested by Mr. T. P. Tewari, I waited outside the office chamber of the Chief Minister. During his meeting with the Chief Minister, Mr. T. P. Tewari personally handed over his enquiry report. I was certainly not aware of the contents of that enquiry report. Only his 2 OSDs were aware of the contents of that report.

Afterwards, I had to organise the return trip of the Chairman and his 2 OSDs back to Lucknow. Moreover, I had to organise the closure of that temporary office. I had performed my limited role as expected of me as the Secretary to the Commission of Enquiry on Assam Disturbances as per the mandate of the government and as per the direction of the Chairman of the Enquiry Commission.

Principal Secretary, Karbi Anglong District Council from August to September 1984 and Deputy Commissioner of Karbi Hanglong District at Diphu from October 1984 to June 1985

My next assignment was the Deputy Commissioner of Karbi Anglong District.

There is only one big iron gate which separates the office of the district council and the Office of the Deputy Commissioner. Soon the next day, I went and took over as the Deputy Commissioner of Karbi Anglong District with headquarters at Diphu. For the reader, I would like to say that the office of the district council is on a hill and likewise, the Office of the Deputy Commissioner is also on a hill. The residence of the Deputy Commissioner is on another hill nearer to the Office of the Deputy Commissioner.

As I had served as the Deputy Commissioner of North Cachar Hills district, it was rather easy for me to serve as the Deputy Commissioner of Karbi Anglong District. However, area-wise, the jurisdiction of Karbi Anglong district was far bigger, and a lot more officers were posted to assist me. Here again, the judiciary was not separated from the executive. The Deputy Commissioner had an office chamber for his administrative work and another big courtroom which was otherwise called '*Ejalahs*'. It was a big courtroom with a raised platform for the Deputy Commissioner to preside and conduct the court proceedings with the usual witness box, accused box, and other paraphernalia like that of North Cachar Hills District. Unlike in the NC Hills district, I had to handle a greater number of cases as the de facto district and sessions judge. As per the provisions of

Administration of Justice Rules and as provided under the Sixth Schedule of the Indian Constitution, the Deputy Commissioner was entrusted with the judicial functions. Moreover, other Class I officers were posted to work as Judicial Magistrates, whose judgements could be appealed in the court of the Deputy Commissioner.

Of course, in addition to my normal routine work regarding administration and judicial matters, I had to frequently tour the district as well. Karbi Anglong district was the biggest district in the State of Assam, and though it was called the Hills District, approximately one third of the area was in the hills and the rest of the area was in the plains. To enable the reader to comprehend the size of the district, I would like to mention that it was approximately 3 times the size of the entire state of Goa in terms of area!

Of late, I understand that Karbi Anglong district has been divided into 2 districts, Karbi Anglong and Hamren. However, during my time, Hamren was part of Karbi Anglong district and it was another big hill station at a distance of approximately 150 km from the District Headquarters, Diphu.

I had many interesting episodes in my administrative and judicial functions which may be of interest to the reader. However, I had only stayed for approximately 10 months, which included a little over 2 months as the Principal Secretary of the District Council.

To begin with, I had noticed that the existing accommodation of the Deputy Commissioner was not adequate for the purpose of holding conferences and conducting meetings due to the absence of sufficient space in the hall where the meetings were held in the Office of the Deputy Commissioner or the Circuit House. Therefore, I organised the construction of a structure within the office premises of the Deputy Commissioner as there was ample vacant space. I initiated the work with my straightforward and tough approach, directing the Executive Engineer, PWD to complete the building within a period of 7 months. Eventually, a very nice and spacious Conference hall was constructed as per my instructions within approximately 7 months, thanks to my constant supervision.

The Circuit House at Diphu had only a few rooms in those times. So, I had decided that there should be an additional Circuit House building and advised the Executive Engineer, PWD to draw up a plan for the construction of a few more rooms in a separate building within the premises. Before I got transferred, I made sure that the construction work of the five-room additional Circuit House was started.

In Hamren, there was no Circuit House worth the name except one PWD Inspection Bungalow. Therefore, I made sure that a beautiful Circuit House was planned, constructed, and implemented within a period of 7 months. The then Hill Areas Development Minister was requested to unveil the new 5-roomed Circuit House at Hamren. I always believed in my confidence and trust, i.e. 'Where there is a will, there is always a way'. The reader may have his own suspicion as to how it could have been possible to construct a 5-roomed Circuit House in a backward Hills District and that too, at a distance of more than 150 km from the District Headquarters. The technical officers of PWD were aware of my timelines and in no uncertain terms my conditions imposed on them that there shall be any sort of delay in the construction activities. Moreover, in addition to my tours, the Minister himself, being a native of the district, also frequently inspected the pace of construction. I informed them that as the Minister of Hill Areas Development had hailed from the district, only he would unveil the Circuit House before my term came to an end and there should not be any compromise on the quality of construction.

At Diphu, i.e. the headquarters of the Karbi Anglong district, I organised football matches during the celebration of Republic Day and exhibitions as well. After all, the areas were very backward and except for one cinema hall in the District headquarters, the people of the district had no other form of entertainment available. Coming to the cinema hall issue, I would like to record that after my thorough inspection, I ordered the closure of the cinema hall and directed the cinema hall manager who was present at the time of inspection to carry out all modifications, repairs, etc. from the point of safety and security of the people. In this connection, I also advised the proprietor of the cinema hall, who happened to be a well-known politician, that unless the repairs/modifications were carried out as per the provisions of the Cinematograph Act/Rules, I would not budge from my decision whatever pressure might be brought to bear upon me to reopen the cinema hall. During the period when the cinema hall was under closure, the local Minister was staying at the Circuit House for a couple of days, and I was informed by the *Chowkidhar* (caretaker) that he wanted to have a word with me on some administrative issue. When I went there, I found the cinema hall manager coming out of his room. I just looked at him and told him sarcastically that perhaps he might think that the Minister would interfere and request me to open the cinema hall. I went and met the Minister. I told him that I just saw the Manager of the Cinema Hall coming from your room and asked the Minister whether the manager requested the Minister to put in a word to me to open the cinema hall. The Minister smiled and told me that he made the same request. Thereafter, I took some time to explain to the Minister about the provisions and rules, etc., of the Cinematograph Act and based on the provision of the act, only the Deputy Commissioner issued the licences for the operations of the cinema hall. I informed him that unless the rules are scrupulously followed by the cinema hall Proprietor/ Manager purely from the point of safety and security of the people who come to witness the cinema, the cinema hall licence would be cancelled and temporarily suspended. In this particular case, I suspended the operations of the cinema hall and directed the Proprietor/Manager to address all the deficiencies and report to me. Thereafter, one more inspection will be done by me or my officers for the reopening of the cinema hall subject to the fulfilment of instructions given by the Deputy Commissioner.

The Minister patiently listened to me, and to his credit, I might say that after my detailed explanation about the safety and security of the people, which was uppermost in my mind rather than the entertainment aspect, the Minister advised me to close down the cinema hall for another month. He also candidly informed me that unless the proprietor/Manager carried out scrupulously the instructions issued by the Deputy Commissioner regarding the fulfilment of the rules and regulations for running the cinema hall, under no circumstances should the cinema hall resume its operations.

Another interesting episode I may like to touch upon with regard to my interactions with the Minister of Hill Areas Development in the same Circuit House after a couple of months.

In the Hills District, drinking is not a taboo at all. However, I had a display on the notice board in the Circuit House at Diphu stating that drinking was prohibited. That meant whoever came to stay at the Circuit House, irrespective of the categories like politicians, members of the legislative assembly, or Ministers, was forewarned that drinking of liquor was strictly prohibited. The caretaker of the Circuit House was given very clear instructions by me that under no circumstances should there be any consumption of liquor on whatever pretext by anyone who opted to stay at the Circuit House, whether he may be an officer, MLA, or a Minister.

On one fine morning around 11 am on a working day, the caretaker of the Circuit House called me on the phone and requested me to come to the Circuit House immediately, as the then hills Areas Development Minister was completely inebriated and wanted to meet me for a discussion. When I went inside his room, the very first question I asked him was why he had violated my instruction displayed at the Circuit House by drinking in his room. He immediately apologised and tried to justify his act by becoming emotional. He was aware of my no-nonsense attitude. He became emotional and told me that he was not at all happy with the affairs of the district council and I should take over the entire administration of the District Council. He had already invited the Development Commissioner of hills Areas Development Department to come to the Circuit House at Diphu with the concerned file from Dispur, Guwahati, and was awaiting his arrival. So, in the meanwhile, I tried to convince him that it was not alright for him to do so in such a state when he was not behaving normally, as I was very much aware of his excellent qualities of head and heart. In the meanwhile, the Development Commissioner of hills Areas had come from Guwahati as per the instructions of the Minister. After seeing the inebriated condition of the Minister, the Development Commissioner was rather upset, and took me out, and we had a detailed conversation in the drawing room of the Circuit House. He explained to me that it was not that easy to dissolve the district council and hand over the reins of administration to the Deputy Commissioner of the district. After all, it was a major decision to be taken by the state Cabinet and had to get the approval of the then Governor of Assam. After I had a detailed discussion with the Development Commissioner, I told him that I would handle the situation, and he might simply be present with me.

When we both entered into the room of the Minister, the Minister was in a hurry and he wanted the file to be given to him so that he would issue the order for dissolution of the district council and its takeover by the Deputy Commissioner of the district. I tried to convince the Minister and informed him rather in a lighter vein that I would be the happiest person to take over not only the district council's affairs but also more than 2 dozen vehicles at the disposal of the CEM, EMs, and officers concerned. In fact, this provoked him to tell me that I should immediately organise to take over all the vehicles of the district council and bring the same under my control. I even jovially told him that I would be very happy to use a new vehicle every day and park a them all in the office compound of the Deputy Commissioner, Circuit House, and Deputy Commissioner's residence premises. I informed the Minister that there was a procedure to be followed even though he was a Cabinet Minister for the Hill Areas Development, and that even though it was his prerogative to take a decision to dissolve the district council's administration, it was certainly incumbent on his part to take the approval of the state Cabinet and also that of the Hon'ble Governor of Assam on the file. I told him that I did respect his authority but under no circumstances would I be a willing partner for his inappropriate decision to be taken in a hurry by such a wrongful method. I told him that I was speaking not only as a Deputy Commissioner of that district but also as a civil servant who had taken an oath to abide by the Constitutional provisions in letter and spirit. Of course, the Minister was aware that the Autonomous Hills District Councils were the creation of Constitutional provisions only and as per the Sixth Schedule of the Constitution of India. It took quite some time for me and the Development Commissioner to convince the Minister for Hill Areas Development that we would not give him an opportunity to give the approval in the file without the requisite cabinet approval and the approval of the Hon'ble Governor of Assam. I also categorically told him that despite our saner counsel if the Minister still decided to give his direction on the file to me, the Deputy Commissioner of the district, such illegal orders were not binding on me and I would certainly not carry out his instructions. In a nutshell, the Development Commissioner and I had convinced him to proceed to Guwahati the next day and place the matter before the state Cabinet for approval for the dissolution of the district council and also the approval of the state Governor of Assam.

Ultimately, after more than an hour of our continuous counsel to the Minister, he reluctantly agreed to our suggestion and left the Circuit House. It is a fact that he hailed from that district and he proceeded to his own house thereafter. The Development Commissioner of Hill Areas profusely thanked me for my intervention as he was rather in an unenviable position and looked very tense when he came all the way from Guwahati to the Circuit House at Diphu. I made him relax and informed him that he need not take tension hereafter. Therefore, when the matter ended on a peaceful note and after his lunch, the Development Commissioner proceeded to Guwahati and carried the file with him. This episode, of course, did not leave any bitter taste in the mind of the Minister, and he was always kind-hearted, jovial, and interacted with me on quite a few occasions thereafter.

As the Deputy Commissioner of the district happened to be responsible for the proper administration of the district Jail, I had to occasionally visit the district Jail in order to not only verify the conduct of the Jailor and his staff but also to listen to the grievances of the inmates of the jail. As pointed out earlier, the Deputy Commissioner of the Hills District is the de facto district and sessions judge. Thus, it was incumbent on my part to visit the district Jail at least once in 3 or 4 months or so.

Whenever I visited the district Jail not only in this Hills District but also in my previous Hills District, I not only interacted with the staff of the jail administration but also tasted the food items to ascertain the quality of food given to the inmates. So, on one occasion when I visited the district Jail at Diphu, I interacted with the jail Staff and inmates. I also went to the kitchen and tried the quality of the food items given to the inmates. During my interactions with the staff of the district Jail, I suddenly noticed a child crying inside the jail. I was flabbergasted and directed the Superintendent of the Jail to bring the child before me along with the person carrying that child. Lo and behold, to my utter surprise, I was told that the accused person was undergoing trial in my own court for the offence of murder of his wife. It is a fact that in a fit of anger and disgust, he killed his wife due to allegations of her misconduct and illicit relationship with another person. After her death, when the trial proceeded based on the charge sheet given by the police, the accused, who happened to be the father of the girl child who was hardly 2 to 3 years old, did not have anyone to look after the child. Therefore, he had to come with the child to face the trial. I did not come to know about his predicament during the trial. It so happened by fortunate coincidence that I could meet the girl child along with the accused at that time of my visit to the district Jail on that day. Perhaps if she had not cried, I would not have noticed her presence. I was so angry, disgusted and agitated,

I rebuked the Superintendent of the Jail and the Staff as to how they did not bring to my notice earlier the presence of the girl child inside the prison. It was absolutely unwarranted on their part to have allowed the girl child to be not only with her father but also amongst the other convicted and under trial prisoners. I ordered the Superintendent of the Jail to take immediate custody of the girl child and bring her to my office thereafter. I told the child's father before I left the jail that it was absolutely not only an illegal custody of the child inside the jail but also inhuman on his part to bring the girl child without the knowledge of the de facto district and Session Judge, which was me. I admonished the police officers later and directed them that henceforth under no circumstances a child, that too, a young girl child on some pretext or the other should be allowed by them to proceed with the accused to the jail. The moment I reached the office, I had called the district Social Welfare Officer and a Lady Officer of Integrated Child Development Scheme (ICDS) to meet me. Also, I had contacted the custodian of an organisation of SOS functioning in a border village in the neighbouring district of Nagaon. In fact, the organisation of SOS in that border village had only come into existence more than a year before in view of the untold violence and disturbances in the State of Assam and in view of the conflicts between various communities during that unfortunate and dismal situation of law and order. Many children had become orphans. Therefore, this organisation, rather a voluntary organisation of dedicated people, was taking care of such orphaned children for their accommodation, food, and education as well. I had informed the office bearers of this voluntary organisation about the necessity on my part to ensure the safety and security of the girl child whom I had met inside the jail along with her accused father. Thereafter, I had also informed them that I had given clear-cut direction to the district Social Welfare Officer and a lady officer of ICDS at Diphu that they would proceed from my office with that unfortunate girl child and hand over that child for her safe custody in the premises of that SOS organisation. I also informed them that within the next fortnight or so, I would personally visit the neighbouring district and verify that they were taking good care of the particular helpless child. It was certainly due to God's divine grace that I could contribute my humble mite for the safety and security of the young girl child who was hardly 2 to 3 years old by taking her outside the district Jail so that she could live happily and peacefully in her future life. On that particular day, I still remembered that the under-trial prisoner who was the father of that girl child wanted to bend down and touch my feet to thank me. I prevented him from doing so. I consoled him and informed him that I would make sure that his trial would be speeded up and he would have an opportunity to meet his own child on a later date after his conviction and period of time to be spent in the district Jail in due course. If I might recall, this particular incident had left an indelible impression in my mind that it was due to God's divine grace and nothing but God's divine grace that I could be of some little help for that poor child and for her future. I always believed right from day one when I joined the I.A.S. that 'Service to humanity is Service to God the Almighty'. On that particular day, I was of the opinion that God the Almighty had ordained me to ensure not only the safe custody of the girl child in good hands but also for the growth and development of the child in a well-meaning ambience.

In a way, I should consider that my visit to the very old, congested jail accommodation within the headquarters of the district was a blessing in disguise to me, as I thought the need of the district was a new jail premises and that too, at least a few kilometres from the District Headquarters, Diphu. I requested the district council to immediately allot a few acres of land for the purpose of construction of a new jail, and I also took up the issue with the State Government Authority concerned for immediate sanction of funds to the PWD for construction of the new jail, after relocation of the present existing old jail which was absolutely not at all warranted in the midst of the town.

I took up this issue very strongly and made sure that the State Government Authorities did sanction funds quickly and allot sufficient land by the district council for the construction of the New jail building with relevant facilities. The reader might be doubtful as to whether in my very short period of stay i.e. approximately months as the Deputy Commissioner after my stint as Principal Secretary of the District Council for a little more than 2 months if I could really take steps for the construction of a new jail. It was a fact that I got the requisite land allotted and funds sanctioned, for the PWD to begin the work. I personally laid the foundation stone for construction of the new jail before I had handed over the charge of my assignment as the Deputy Commissioner of the district.

During my district assignments, I always made it a point to tour different places and interact with the villagers in interior locations for at least 10 days a month in order to understand and appreciate their problems and grievances. I tried my level best to address them. The role of the Deputy Commissioner was the most important and vital aspect of a civil servant. This was a golden opportunity available only to Civil Servants in the Indian Administrative Service and in no other service. I am very proud that I did contribute my humble mite in attending to various problems and issues facing the people in the interior parts of the districts I had served in the State of Assam.

One such example was when I got the opportunity to contribute to the peaceful resolution of the grievances of the workers of a Cement Factory at a place called Bokajan around 80 km from Diphu. The Cement Factory was owned by the Cement Corporation of India, a Public Sector Undertaking under the Ministry of Heavy Industry. There was a time when there were serious differences between the management and the workers, and I had to halt a day and night to resolve the issues raised by the workers, as they had struck work for an indefinite period putting the cement production in jeopardy. Ultimately with the help of the senior officers of the Labour Department, I did try my level best to get a settlement signed by both sides with considerable effort as they had their genuine grievances as well and also their immediate objective was to continue production of cement and to resolve their issues raised with regard to pollution control and prevention of health hazards. Of course, it took a lot of time and negotiations between the management and workers. Finally, at midnight, the negotiations concluded, and the issue resolved to the satisfaction of all concerned. After successfully signing the agreement, I joined them for dinner after midnight. In order to avoid unnecessary and unpleasant law and order situations, I had advised the Superintendent of Police to deploy adequate police force as well as a matter of abundant precaution. Fortunately, no untoward incident happened, and I left the Bokajan Circuit House the next day after making sure that everything went off peacefully and the cement production was resumed.

During my time, there were only 10 districts in Assam. The Karbi Anglong district was the biggest district in terms of geographical area. Hamren was the sub-divisional headquarters of the district. Of course, the distance between the District Headquarters, Diphu, from Hamren is approximately 150 km. I took the initiative to construct a nice Circuit House with 5 rooms at Hamren. During my very short stay of approximately 8 months or so as Deputy Commissioner of Karbi Anglong District, a beautiful Circuit House was constructed at Hamren. It was inaugurated by the then Minister of Hill Areas Development. Since Hamren was far away from the District Headquarters, I had taken an initiative to organise a district-level exhibition of various departments at Hamren town in order to make the people understand and appreciate the various developmental programmes that were being undertaken by the departments concerned not only in the District Headquarters of Diphu but also in the entire sub-division of Hamren. Hamren sub-division has been converted into West Karbi Anglong district. Hamren, which was the original sub-division headquarters and a slightly hilly region, is presently the headquarters of West Karbi Anglong district. Many years after I had left Karbi Anglong district as Deputy Commissioner, I had gone once or twice as the then Commissioner of Hills and Barak Valley division. At that time also, Karbi Anglong district was the only one district with Hamren as the sub-division headquarters town. When I started my first field-level posting as the Sub-divisional officer of Golaghat Sub-Division, there were only 10 districts in Assam. Today, perhaps there are 35 districts in the state. Many of the sub-divisions have become districts, and the original sub-division headquarters town has become the District Headquarters town. For instance, Golaghat has become the District Headquarters of Golaghat district. The very purpose and objective of me as the head of the District Administration in organising a district-level exhibition of various development departments was to make the people understand and appreciate the works that were being done for the benefits of the people such as drinking water supply, rural electrification, and pipe water supply scheme, etc. It was a novel experience and was very well appreciated by the political representatives as well. The then Minister of hills Areas Development enthusiastically participated not only in the organisation of the exhibition but also in giving sufficient suggestions for further improvement of the functioning of various development departments in addition to beautification of the Circuit House with greenery around. As Karbi Anglong district was one of the most backward districts of Assam, it was the bounden duty of the district administration and district council to organise such programmes in coordination with different development departments and to make them responsible and also responsive to the needs of people who had inhabited interior areas with less accessibility to meet the official hierarchy in the District Headquarters town.

On the whole, I would consider my assignment as the then Deputy Commissioner of North Cachar Hills district and also as the then Deputy Commissioner of Karbi Anglong District was a godsend opportunity to serve the people of different tribes in both the districts. I used to say in a lighter vein that I was the Deputy Commissioner, district Magistrate, and district and sessions judge all rolled into one, as I had performed different roles while sitting in the courtroom as the responsible Court Officer but while sitting in the district Deputy Commissioner's office chamber as the head of the District Administration. The demarcation of the duties was very clear. In other words, I used to sit in my regular office chamber every day for one session and in the courtroom for another session enquiring into the issues of criminal complaints against the accused brought by the Police and presented by the Public Prosecutor. There was clear demarcation of duties and hence there was no confusion at all. At the cost of repetition, I would like to candidly say that in both District Headquarters Towns while discharging my judicial functions, I had to necessarily depend upon the interpreters or Dubhasis as they were the government employees in view of the fact they were proficient in 2 or 3 more languages than their own tribal language to help the Deputy Commissioner record the evidences of the witnesses during the trial proceedings. If I may say so for an outsider, it was rather interesting to note that the accused might belong to a particular tribal community and the Dubhashis might belong to another community. However, the Dubhashis had to interpret and translate whatever the accused or witness as the case may be called upon to narrate as to what had happened during the time of occurrence. So, the Dubhashis had to interpret and help the court in somewhat broken Hindi language which I had to literally translate into English for the purpose of recording the evidences of the witnesses or the statements of the accused. It was not only amusing but also very interesting to observe such court proceedings in both the courts presided over by me in the 2 hills districts of the State of Assam.

In the last week of June 1985, as I received a formal appointment order as the then Joint Chief Controller of Imports and Exports at Madras under the Ministry of Commerce, Government of India, I had to bid farewell to all my officers and staff at the District Headquarters town, i.e. Diphu. I was so touched by the farewell organised by my officers and staff in the brand new Conference hall, which was hurriedly erected due to my continuous and constant supervision over the period of a little more than 7 months during my tenure.

It was by God's divine grace and my sheer good luck that I had got my first Central Government deputation assignment after 10 years of my service and that too, in my home town i.e. the City of Madras. On a very important and crucial assignment under the Ministry of Commerce, Government of India at the age of 34 years only, I was appointed as the head of the Imports Trade Control and Exports Trade Promotion Organisation then called the Joint Chief Controller of Imports and Exports for the entire southern region of the country.

In fact, I came to know about that assignment from one of my own colleagues only at the Office of the Deputy Commissioner, Karbi Anglong district at Diphu, that the orders had already reached the state Govt headquarters with the direction that I should report for duty at Madras after handing over the charge of the assignment of Deputy Commissioner in the last week of June 1985. I always believed in destiny, and I had tremendous faith in God the Almighty for my position and status in my life in different assignments during my entire official career of 35 years or so.

I had stayed at Diphu in Karbi Anglong district in 2 different assignments for a period of 10 months only, i.e. as the Principal Secretary of the District Council for a little more than 2 months and as the Deputy Commissioner of the district for a little more than 7 months only. I would fondly cherish my good deeds as a young civil servant in the 2 hills districts as the head of the District Administration. God was kind enough to give me an opportunity to serve in my own hometown in the state of Tamil Nadu for a period of 5 years even though I belonged to a different cadre, i.e. the Assam-Meghalaya cadre. I would not have dreamt of serving in my own home state for a period of 5 years and that too, on a very sensitive and crucial assignment as the head of the organisation in charge of Imports Control and Exports Trade Promotion for the 4 southern states and heading not only the office in Madras but also in 6 different places under my charge, i.e. Bengaluru, Hyderabad, Vishakhapatnam, Cochin, Tuticorin, and Puducherry.

JCCI&E, Madras, Tamil Nadu, on Government of India Deputation – Ministry of Commerce from 5th July 1985 to 2nd July 1990

While I was serving as the Deputy Commissioner of Karbi Anglong District, I received a letter from my very dear batchmate and friend Mr. N. K. Raghupathi who was posted as the Regional Director, Staff Selection Commission under the Government of India in Madras in the year 1985. Mr. Raghupathi informed me of a vacancy for the post of Joint Chief Controller of Imports and Exports under the Ministry of Commerce, Government of India in Madras. He advised me to try my luck in getting that assignment. Until then, I had not known about that vacancy and the significance of the assignment.

Due to the timely information and guidance from Mr. N. K. Raghupathi, I could contact and get help and assistance from some of my well-wishers in the higher echelons of bureaucracy in Guwahati and Delhi.

By God's divine grace, I was fortunate to join as Joint Chief Controller of Imports and Exports in Madras on 5th July 1985. I served in that role for 5 years from 5th July 1985 to 2nd July 1990. I am indeed extremely grateful to my very dear friends and sincere well-wishers for securing a 5-year tenure appointment under the Government of India in the Ministry of Commerce in my home state, i.e., Tamil Nadu.

The Role and Functions of the Joint Chief Controller of Imports and Exports (JCCI&E), Government of India in Madras as the South Zone Head of the Imports Control and Exports Trade Promotion Organisation.

The role and functions of Joint Chief Controller of Imports and Exports (JCCI&E) were not only to administer the office and ensure its regulatory functions in the best possible manner but also to participate in several meetings connected with import and export policy provisions, procedures, and related to trade and industry. I regularly attended meetings convened by the Chambers of Industry, Trade and Commerce not only in the City of **Madras** but also in other cities like Bangalore, Coimbatore, etc. I also attended various functions organised by the Commodity Boards, Export Promotion Councils, and meetings of the Exporters associations and used to listen to their grievances about the delay in the disposal of their applications received in the office of JCCI&E, Madras.

Participation in these meetings was necessary in order to make them aware in a transparent manner of the highly complex import policy provisions that were in place in those days so that there was not only an understanding and appreciation of the policy provisions on their part but also for providing an opportunity to submit their issues to me for resolution. In a way, I made it a point to emphasise that there should be no misunderstanding on the part of the various exporters, members of the trade and industry, and chambers of commerce and office bearers of the export promotion councils about the functioning of the Licensing Authority. I was absolutely friendly and responsive in listening to the grievances and to request them to bring to my notice on any later date if there were any issues to be resolved, especially with regard to the policy provisions. I also sought their suggestions which would enhance the image of the Import Control and Export Promotion organisation. As I myself was quite new to the issues of imports and exports and to understand the regulatory functions of the organisation, initially for a couple of months, I took the help of one of my experienced junior colleagues who was capable of making me understand and appreciate the difficult policy provisions, etc., as I had come from field postings from the State of Assam.

Within a few months, I could gather some knowledge and experience of handling different and difficult issues of imports and exports not only in the office files but also during my interactions with the members of the public in various meetings of the export and Promotion Councils, Commodity Boards, Chambers of Commerce and Trade. This was a wonderful opportunity for me not only to gain knowledge during my interactions but also to take up several such issues with my headquarters office during the meetings of the port licensing officers located at various destinations under the administrative control of the Chief Controller of Imports and Exports, New Delhi.

During one such meeting, I brought to the notice of the Chief Controller of Imports and Exports in New Delhi that there were several life-saving drugs, life-saving equipment, surgical instruments, etc., all of which came under the licensing category. This amounted to a lot of inconvenience and unnecessary and avoidable harassment for the members of the public due to too many regulatory functions for such vital needs of society. To ensure that my voice was fully heard in the meeting, I specifically raised an issue regarding a drug called *cyclosporine*, which is an essential drug for patients suffering from kidney ailments, particularly for those who underwent kidney transplant operations. I came to know about this when many patients from the North Eastern states, who used to come to Madras for kidney transplant operations, approached me to obtain the import licence for the drug.

One day a gentleman came into my office and, showing his hands, mentioned that he was a kidney patient and needed *cyclosporine*. He could not afford to buy it in the open market as it was a licensed item. I immediately called the public relations officer to find out whether he encountered such patients regularly who needed such an essential drug. He responded in the affirmative. I promptly gave very clear directions to him that if any such patient came to see him, he should bring him to my office chamber. He was to ensure that the required import licence for the procurement of Cyclosporin either by him or by a particular hospital authority was issued on the spot. After all, it was a matter of life and death for a particular citizen who had come all the way from a distant part of the country to receive treatment for such a kidney ailment.

This was the condition prevailing in the years 1985 to 1987 or so i.e. more than 4 decades ago. During his next visit to Madras, the Chief Controller of Imports & Exports (CCI&E) in the years 1986-87 wanted to go to the Apollo Hospitals. I made arrangements for both of us to meet Dr. Pratap Reddy, the Chairman-cum-Founder of Apollo Hospitals. He was the first and foremost gentleman to introduce private healthcare facilities in this country. Dr. Pratap Reddy was kind enough to take the CCI&E and myself around the entire hospital and show us the various modern amenities, latest gadgets, etc., in different wards. It was also nice of him to take us to an operation theatre where he showed us the open-heart surgery that was being performed by a team of doctors. We happened to see the operation through the glass partition. He explained to us how the bypass surgery was performed. It was rather an education for both of us to understand the nuances of such complicated surgery. Before leaving the hospital, the CCI&E requested Dr. Reddy to send to the office of JCCI&E the complete list of life-saving drugs, life-saving equipment, surgical equipment, etc., that were to be brought under the Open General Licence within the next couple of weeks. He informed Dr. Pratap Reddy that since I already accompanied him, it was my duty and responsibility to make sure that once a list was received from the Apollo Hospital, it should be sent to the office of CCI&E New Delhi for his further appropriate action.

The Open General Licence facilitated the import of a life-saving drug, life-saving equipment, etc., without going through the tortuous process of obtaining a licence from the Licensing Authority. The import policy provisions listed the items requiring an import licence. After a couple of weeks, I received a list of more than 350 life-saving drugs and another list of more than 350 or so life-saving equipment, surgical instruments etc., from the Apollo Hospital.

Within the next few months when the new Import and Export Policy and Handbook of Procedures for Imports and Exports were announced, the lists received from Apollo Hospitals containing life-saving drugs as well as life-saving instruments and surgical equipment, etc. were brought under the Open General Licence through a formal notification. There were no deletions or omissions in the list. This was of immense benefit for the entire population of the country. This was a revolutionary step during those years when the licence regime was at its peak and the regulatory functions of the Organisation very strict. In view of the proactive policy or decisions taken by the then CCI&E and of course with the help of the Chairman of Apollo Hospital, hundreds of life-saving drugs, life-saving instruments, and life-saving surgical equipment, etc could be imported by any person/any firm/any organisation without the need to go to the licensing office at all for the import of such items.

As a matter of corollary, when one of my sincere well-wishers, who was a senior and retired officer in the Government of India, brought his younger brother, a Cardiothoracic Surgeon serving in the United Kingdom, for a visit to my house for a cup of coffee, I took the opportunity at that time to show him the new import policy provisions containing the complete list of life-saving drugs, instruments/equipment, etc., that were brought under the OGL for the first time in the country. I requested him to spend some time and go through the complete list and let me know whether he was of the opinion to add any other life-saving drugs or life-saving instrument or equipment, etc., which could enable me to immediately send the details of such information to the CCI&E for further inclusion if needed. He informed me candidly that there was absolutely no need as the list was completely alright and exhaustive. I later informed the then CCI&E about my interaction with the Cardiothoracic Surgeon from Wales, England, and his appreciation of the list of life-saving drugs and life-saving instruments and equipment, etc. In my opinion, one singular proactive decision of the government in the import policy provisions during the strict regulatory regime was one welcome step which was appreciated by the people in general and the entire medical fraternity in particular.

Likewise, wherever it was possible, the CCI&E wanted to make further improvements in the licensing policy by reducing unnecessary and unwarranted regulations in the form of processing applications for the issue of import licences and export incentives provided to importers and exporters respectively in general as per the policy provisions.

I would like to touch upon another significant introduction of a laudatory decision that was taken in the meeting of all the port licensing officers presided over by the CCI&E in the years 1986-87. He wished to introduce, with the help of the National Informatics Centre and the Department of Electronics and Communications, Government of India, computerisation in the issue of various kinds of import licences as well as export incentives to curtail the unwarranted delays in the matter of disposal of such applications valued at crores and crores of rupees. He emphasised that this would benefit importers and exporters.

A national training programme was organised in the office of the Joint Chief Controller of Imports and Exports at Madras. This was a first in the country in the organisation of Chief Controller of Imports and Exports under the Ministry of Commerce, Government of India.

The very fact that the introduction of training for officers and staff in the matter of computerisation of import licences and export incentives, and that too in Madras, was a conscious and conspicuous decision taken by the CCI&E. I may sound a little immodest if I might mention that in an open meeting of all the port licensing officers spread over the entire country, the CCI&E openly announced, "If Manoharan could succeed in this computerisation programme, it would be introduced and implemented in the entire organisation of Imports Control and Exports Promotion in the country." This was the level of confidence he had exhibited about my capabilities in the presence of my colleagues in an open Conference. He also stated that JCCI&E Madras should take the pioneering role in the matter of computerisation of Import licences and export incentives for training of officers and staff and to acquaint them with the latest techniques for the issue of import licences and export incentives, thereby cutting delays at every level of hierarchy during the scrutiny of such applications.

Of course, it took more than 6 months and nearly a year to motivate and make the officers and staff understand the implications of the computerisation programme and also the advantages that it might accrue not only to the members of the public who used to come for several types of issue of import licences and export incentives but also in enabling the officers and staff to avoid fatigue which would otherwise be more pronounced while manually processing all such applications without the knowledge of computer applications for various scrutiny purposes.

No doubt that it was a herculean task to organise the training programmes and introduce the methodology to be adopted for scrutiny of the applications and for the issue of various kinds of import licences and export incentives as there were varied types of requirements of documentation that were necessary for scrutiny. It was a difficult task not only for the people who came to train all our officers and staff but also for the officers and staff to get familiarised with regard to the innovations that might be warranted for scrutiny of the applications through the computer system. While the strength of the Madras office was approximately 250, the numbers of applications every day for Import licences and export incentives were many times over. Today we may express satisfaction about the digitisation programme and computerisation of so many functions of the government in the realms of administration in the largest interests of the people of our country in general and for the benefits of the society in particular for cutting down delays and for ensuring transparency for the fullest satisfaction of the people who visit the government offices. Times have changed over the last more than 3 decades.

It was not so during the years 1985 to 1988 when the computers were first introduced for the functions of certain departments of the Government of India, especially in a licensing organisation in which there were so many regulations in addition to the submission of many supporting documents. It was a very difficult task for the trainers as well as for the trainees to introduce innovations and adaptations that would suit the issue of import licences and export incentives in a transparent manner. It was also necessary to avoid unwarranted mistakes that might creep in due to any probable deficiencies in feeding the requisite documents to support the issue of import licences and export incentives in a methodical manner, thereby avoiding any sort of mistakes or mischief on the part of the people dealing with such sensitive documents.

I would like to mention that in respect of the scrutiny of the applications for the issue of import licences as well as export incentives, there were certain time stipulations depending upon the nature of the applications. Once computerisation was introduced, we also brought many graded, systemic, and methodological steps in its usage. In respect of simple issues such as applications for Importer and Exporter Code numbers and the issue of Import Licences and Export of Incentives based on the requisite documents, the applications were to be submitted in the morning hours, i.e. from 9 am to 11 am. A computerised acknowledgement receipt was also to be given then and there on the ground floor where the office of PRO was located. The computers were located on the ground floor, which was meant for the issue of importers and exporters code numbers, export incentives through cheques, etc. Things were simplified to such an extent that if an exporter gave an application for the receipt of an export incentive in the form of a cheque based on his export of commodities and other items, his cheque was ready for collection by the evening.

By way of illustration, if we were to consider export incentive for a particular type of product say, export of Leather Garments. The exporter was expected to submit his application, the bank certificate of exports, the shipping bill indicative of the quantum of exports of that particular leather garment along with the copy of the registration cum membership certificate obtained by him from the Council for Leather Exports, etc. Such documents were received at the ground floor from 9 am to 11 am by the staff concerned after making the requisite entry in the computer and an acknowledgement slip was given to him. The papers thereafter were scrutinised in line with the policy guidelines. The exporter was supposed to come to the JCCIE office the same evening between 5 - 6 pm and collect the cheque in the presence of PRO. On an average each day not less than several dozens of such applications for issue of export incentives in the form of cheques were submitted by the exporters for different types of eligible products and appropriate follow-up actions were taken by the officers and staff of the office of JCCI&E, Madras in accordance with the existing rules and regulations.

There were different types of percentages of incentives for exports of different types of products. The above scheme was called the simplified payment scheme.

Even here, depending upon the quantum of export incentives to be given to a particular exporter, the licensing authorities were given the delegated responsibility for signing of the cheques. For instance, for up to a sum of Rs. 5 lakhs, a Deputy Chief Controller of Imports and Exports was competent to sign the cheque before it was delivered through the counter in the office of PRO; but if the exporter was eligible to get a payment of more than Rs. 5 lakhs for that particular application, the cheque had to be signed by the JCCI &E. Generally, under the simplified payment scheme, not too many documents were accepted because the time was short between morning and evening and moreover, there was an absolute need for thorough scrutiny to avoid submission of fraudulent documents on the part of the undesirable characters masquerading as exporters. Obviously, each and every applicant could not be subject to suspicion and one had to go through the documents very carefully. For instance, for the issue of export incentive beyond an amount of Rs. 5 lakhs for issue of cheques either through the simplified payment scheme or otherwise, the buck stopped at the table of the JCCI&E.

The reader might be wondering whether, in this sort of simplified payment scheme, an applicant exporter submitted documents for the export of a particular commodity for a period of one month or for a period of 3 months together, how exactly the scrutiny would be done and how much time would be taken by the office for scrutiny as well as the issue of export incentives. Obviously, such applications with voluminous documents could not be and would not be scrutinised in one day as it required quite some time, which was absolutely necessary for ensuring the correct incentives went to the correct exporter based on the correct documentation on his part. There were time stipulations as well for the issue of big export incentives in the form of bulky documentations based on the quantum of exports of products as per the eligibility criteria.

The very objective of a simplified payment scheme for the issue of export incentives through cheques was to help the exporters in ensuring the continuance of their activities for exports of goods and for the usage of that particular money which would otherwise be delayed if they submitted too many documents at once. In other words, an exporter was most welcome to submit an application every day for the same export product with the requisite documents, and every day they could collect the cheques in the evening. It was a facilitation only to help their business. It was up to them to avail of the scheme or submit their bulky documents for the export of their product for one or 2 months together and thereafter receive the cheques by post from the office. If I remember correctly, in respect of such bulky documentation for a large quantum of exports for export incentives that needed detailed scrutiny at every level in the hierarchy for the issue of export incentives, the cheques would be dispatched by registered post only to their office address.

In such cases, obviously, the issue of export incentives or popularly called Cash Compensatory Support by the government could, by and large, exceed several lakhs or several crores of rupees. It was incumbent on my part as the head of the office to take complete responsibility for the thorough scrutiny of the applications before signing the cheques. So, obviously, in order to ensure that I never committed any mistake and never fell into a trap for submission of any fraudulent documents on the part of unscrupulous elements, occasionally, I did the scrutiny of the documents carefully, especially bank certificates of exports, some shipping bills, etc., whenever and wherever I had some suspicion out of my own intuition only. I kept the files separately without making decisions in a hurry. Moreover, I could not afford to delay each and every file just because of my intuition or suspicion. On the possibility of an ineligible exporter getting export incentives based on such undue advantage taken by him with the presumption that it would escape detailed scrutiny on the part of the officers and staff of the office, the officers and staff dealing with all the applications for the issue of export incentives had to be extremely cautious and careful.

Whenever I felt some kind of suspicion in any case on the nature of documents submitted by the exporters, I referred the matter to the CBI authority quietly. As my assignment as the head of the licensing office was extremely sensitive, I had to keep in close touch with the CBI authorities depending on the circumstances. Whenever I had a suspicion on cases which came to my notice with regard to the signing of high-value cheques, I called the concerned Deputy Superintendent of Police of CBI to my office and brought to his notice the submission of such fraudulent documents purely based on my suspicion and intuition. I requested him to quietly investigate the matter in absolute confidence as I did not divulge to my officers concerned as to why I had kept the files aside without sending them down to the office after signing the cheques. Obviously, there would have been a kind of inquisitiveness on the part of the subordinate staff as to why the files were not sent down, as by and large I used to be very quick in the disposal of files. Of course, every day as I had to attend to too many visitors to ascertain their issues or grievances and also attend sometimes public meetings involving exporters and importers etc. I used to carry the files home and bring back the files the next day. I had given strict instructions to all the officers and staff that none should visit my house on any pretext. That particular stipulation was equally made known and applicable to all the applicant exporters or importers throughout my five-year tenure.

I knew that the organisation of JCCI&E was extremely complicated, complex, and difficult, and more sensitive in view of the fact that crores and crores of rupees worth of licences and cash incentives were issued day in and day out to the eligible importers and exporters. In such an organisation, obviously one had to be very careful in view of the possible vested interests within the organisation and also the possibility of undesirable elements or applicants with fraudulent documents, through vested interests submitting applications. I introduced a notice board on the ground floor where the PRO used to function with the words 'Beware of touts' for the benefit of the visitors. Occasionally, I used to go to the ground floor on a surprise visit. I used to enquire from the assembled visitors/people as to what their issue was and why they were waiting there. Of course, I never disclosed my identity. Some people did wonder about my identity and why I was asking questions on the purpose of the visit. One day during my visits, one gentleman asked me about my identity. I told him smilingly that I was the head of the office and came to enquire whether he faced any sort of harassment from the PRO or from the office or whether any unwarranted delay was experienced by him in the process of his application either for the issue of an import licence or for the issue of export incentive. Some of the visitors were taken aback as they weren't used to this kind of unusual interaction by the head of the licensing office himself. My purpose of such surprise visits had 2 objectives, one was to know whether the PRO was polite and courteous in attending to the visitors and solving their problems and the other was to know whether there were any genuine grievances on the part of the visitors in getting their problems resolved. Wherever and whenever I came to know there was some delay, I advised the PRO to check with the visitors and ascertain whether there were serious delays on the part of the office in attending to their problems. It was a fact that I had selected a very good officer as the PRO to take care of the visitors during my tenure.

I had appointed 2 PROs at different points of time, and both of them were perfect gentlemen, helpful and sincere in their interactions with the members of the public. As I held a high-profile office, very often people from the so-called higher strata of society used to visit for different types of licences and export incentives, including customs clearance permits for the import of foreign cars.

The office of JCCI&E was not empowered to issue CCPs for the import of cars from abroad. The decision was made at the office of CCI&E New Delhi and then the matter was referred back to the licensing office in Madras. The licensing office in Madras would hand over the CCP as per the decision of the CCI&E to the particular applicant after scrutinising the application and their credentials. I had given clear instructions to the PRO that regardless of the status of the visitors, whether they arrived on a bicycle, a cycle rickshaw, an ordinary car, or an imported Mercedes Benz, everyone visiting the office of JCCI&E in Madras should be treated politely with due courtesy and respect.

I was administering the office in an absolutely strict and transparent manner only with clear and precise instructions, and I did not tolerate indiscipline on the part of officers and staff. Though I was strict with the officers and staff, I used to look after their welfare and also used to meet them regularly in the staff meetings. There was a statutory arrangement that the officers and staff in a group i.e. their association members should have an opportunity to meet the head of the office for resolution of their grievances. As I had 7 offices spread over South India including Madras, meetings were arranged periodically in different cities like Bangalore, Hyderabad, Vishakhapatnam, Cochin, Tuticorin, and Pondicherry. That was also in a way an incentive for the officers and staff to visit different offices in the cities at the time of our meetings. During my tenure, I tried to set up an office of DCCI&E at Coimbatore, which perhaps later came into existence in due course.

I introduced a time stipulation for visitors to meet me in times of necessity. I made clear arrangements that importers and exporters would have absolute freedom to access the 4 different DCCI&Es (Deputy Chief Controllers of Imports and Exports) depending on issues after getting their convenient time and date from the PRO in the afternoon between 2 pm to 5 pm. I kept myself available between 11 am to 2 pm on all working days for visitors to meet me. I gave clear instructions to the PRO that these timings should be scrupulously adhered to and that gentlemen who met me in the morning should not go and meet the DCCI&E in the afternoon. The purpose and objective were that in case they were not very happy with the response of the DCCI&E for the resolution of their issues, they might as well come to meet me after some time. I made comfortable arrangements for visitors to sit in the visitors' room on the first floor. I made sure that each and every visitor to my office should be given due courtesy, and I would listen to them with rapt attention. I kept the slip pad on my table and noted down their issues, informing them that in due course, I would call for the files and ascertain why there was unnecessary delay wherever such delays were brought to my notice. I tried my level best to cut down the delays at every level in the process of scrutiny of applications in the office.

As I very often had to attend meetings of exporters and meetings organised by the Chambers of Trade and Industry and different offices of export promotion councils, etc., in the morning hours, the PRO was fully aware of my engagements and used to fix the timings of my meetings with the visitors on a day accordingly.

On one particular day when I came to the office after attending such meetings at 2.30 pm, the PRO talked to me on the telephone from his chamber on the ground floor that a lady with her ten-year-old son had been waiting for the last few hours to meet me. He told her that I was not available at that time on that day, they might come the next morning; but they insisted they wanted to meet me. I requested the PRO to bring that lady and her son to my office chamber to ascertain from them what exactly their grievances were. She informed me that her husband was the branch manager of the Indian Overseas Bank posted in Seoul, South Korea. She and her son would be joining him soon. She informed me that her son was interested in having *idlis* for breakfast every day. She came to know that rice and urad dhal were not permissible to be carried by her when she would be visiting Seoul. The moment I heard her grievance, I assured her that whatever the quantity of rice or dhal or any other condiments or provisions that were necessary for her and her son would be allowed to be taken by them. I requested her to first go and have lunch and then come back to meet the PRO.

Before she went out, I told the PRO in her presence to ascertain their requirements of rice or dhal or any other food items that might be necessary and help her in writing her request in the form of an application. I informed the lady that the PRO would take down the details and she should immediately go out for lunch along with her son and come back after an hour or so. I also told her that by the time she returned, her permit would be ready and she would be welcome to meet me again along with the PRO after 4 pm. I had given clear instructions to the PRO to inform the concerned CI&E (Controller of Imports and Exports) to prepare the export permit for enabling her to take the required items. I particularly gave this instruction in view of the fact that she was a housewife and perhaps would have come to the import licensing office for the first time and was totally unaware of the procedural requirements. At this stage, I must convey my very sincere appreciation to the then PRO who scrupulously followed my instructions in letter and spirit.

As it was certainly a genuine request and I was in a position to help her not only as the head of the office but also as a responsible civil servant, expected to serve in the largest interests of the people. I instructed the PRO that exactly by 5 pm I must get the file with the export permit duly signed by the concerned Controller and the PRO would once again accompany the lady and her son to my office chamber, and I would hand over the export permit to her after giving my approval in the file. This was very well appreciated by the lady visitor. She collected the export permit in the evening from me with absolute gratitude and happiness. Of course, it was very responsible of the PRO to immediately inform me the moment I came to the office about her plight.

This particular incident was informed to a Member of Parliament by the Branch Manager of IOB himself when the MP came across the concerned Branch Manager of IOB at Seoul. After several months, my PRO contacted me on the telephone and informed me that a Member of Parliament had come to meet me and he would accompany him to my office. That was the first time I came across The Member of Parliament. As soon as he came, I requested him to take a seat and wanted to know if he would like to take coffee or tea; he smilingly told me that he did not require a cup of coffee or tea. Moreover, he informed me that the only purpose of his visit was to know who exactly Mr. Manoharan was, i.e. the then JCCI&E at Madras. I was flabbergasted to get a response like this. I was a little amused to hear him say that. During his meeting with the then Branch Manager of IOB at Seoul, South Korea, he came to know that I had helped his wife and son when they had come to meet me some months ago. When he heard that incident from the gentleman and his family, he was pleasantly surprised to know of the incident and then explained to me that the then Branch Manager of IOB at Seoul and his family were indeed grateful to me and conveyed their happiness and gratitude about my helpful attitude to his family during his visit to Seoul.

I was really touched by his kind gesture when he told me that he had just come to see me as a person only and wished me all the very best in my civil service career and conveyed his sincere appreciation for adopting a helpful attitude to the members of the public who had come to meet me for their genuine needs. I conveyed my sincere thanks to him and saw him off after about 15 to 20 minutes of his interaction with me. I must say that he did not accept a cup of tea, coffee, or water and, as stated by him, his purpose of the visit was to meet me, as he has not heard about my name in the past, and as I did not serve under the government of Tamil Nadu.

During my five-year tenure as head of the office of JCCI&E, Madras, I had come across industrialists, many exporters and importers, and a few MPs if they had any issues or if they had submitted any applications for import licences, etc. I vividly recall on a particular day the PRO informed me that a Hon'ble MP had come to meet me. I immediately requested him to accompany him to my office. After he entered my room, I showed him due courtesy and, as usual, I offered a cup of coffee, tea, or water, and he politely declined. He later informed me that he himself was an Industrialist and he had his own manufacturing unit. He had submitted an application for an import licence for the import of capital goods to the extent of Rs. 25 lakhs at that time. I noted down the particulars of his application and his submission date, etc. Thereafter, I explained to him what exactly was the procedure followed in such cases of applications for import licence based on the import policy provisions and Handbook of procedures published by the office of CCI&E, Ministry of Commerce, Government of India. I took some time to explain to him that there were 8 committees headed by me regarding the disposal of the different types of applications of import licences. In the case of applications for the issue of import licences for the purpose of capital goods worth Rs. 25 lakhs or so, there was a separate committee called the Capital Goods Licensing Committee headed by me with the members drawn from the different departments of the State Government and also Government of India organisations depending on the nature of the import of capital goods. Moreover, there was a time stipulation given in the Import Policy/Handbook of procedures for the issue of import licences by the licensing Office.

For instance, in respect of capital goods worth Rs. 25 lakhs as it came under the small-scale category, the Industry Department officers would make inspections of such units, based on the genuine needs of those units.

For all such imports of capital goods pertaining to different industries, the concerned departmental officers of the State Government and Government of India, after thorough inspection, make recommendations to the licensing office. Every month, the Capital Goods Licensing Committee would meet, and such applications would be taken up for discussion in the deliberations of the Capital Goods Licensing Committee. In such committee meetings, in addition to the members of the committee, the concerned applicants were also welcome to attend the meetings and explain their strand and justification for the import of such equipment or machinery.

The Hon'ble MP patiently heard the procedures explained by me and wanted to know whether he needed to remind me after a week or fortnight. I politely told him that there was absolutely no need for him or his manufacturing unit's representatives to remind me on the telephone or by post, as I had already noted down the details. I told him that most likely, based on his date of application, this would be coming up in the next Licensing Committee meeting and the matter would be taken for discussion along with the rest of the applications received during that time.

In addition, I told the MP that once the committee decided to issue the import licence in respect of his unit or any other manufacturing units based on their credentials and inspection reports of the concerned departmental officers and based on the decisions taken after the deliberations in the Licensing Committee headed by me, the import licences would be sent by registered post to the particular applicant based on the address given by him in his original application. I assured him that automatically the licence would reach his unit or office in due course of time. This is a standard procedure applicable to all such applicants for import of capital goods based on the financial delegation of powers given to me as the head of the office. I also informed him for his benefit that I would only see the files at the time of issue of licences for my approval but the licenses would be signed by the concerned Controller of Imports and Exports depending upon the nature of the item of imports. He went back satisfied. This meeting between me and the MP happened perhaps in the years 1987-88.

I handed over my assignment as the head of the office after my 5-year tenure as JCCI&E, Madras on 2nd July 1990 as my successor had not joined at that time. I took 4 months' leave after my deputation period and thereafter, I reverted back to my parent cadre, i.e. Assam-Meghalaya.

I held several assignments thereafter in Assam and proceeded on a Government of India deputation in January 1997 as the then Joint Secretary, Government of India in the Ministry of Steel. From 1997 until the date of superannuation in 2010, for 14 years, I served in New Delhi in Government of India assignments as well as those of the State Government.

During the years from 13th December 2001 to 6th September 2006, I served as the then Principal Resident Commissioner, Government of Assam at the office of Resident Commissioner at Assam Bhavan, New Delhi. During this period of my assignment as the Principal Resident Commissioner, I served as the Chief Representative of the Government of Assam at New Delhi in order to attend various meetings convened by the Government of India. I had accompanied the then Hon'ble Chief Minister of Assam to attend his meetings with various cabinet Ministers of different Ministries of the Government of India. Very often during my tenure, I had to accompany the Chief Minister of Assam for participation in the CMs' Conferences presided over by the then Hon'ble Prime Minister of India. The meetings normally used to take place from 10 am to 5 pm or 11 am to 6 pm depending on the scheduling of the meeting.

In one of the conferences attended by several Chief Ministers and presided over by the Prime Minister, and Cabinet Ministers of the Government of India, after listening to the speech for one or 2 hours, I quietly exited to take a glass of water or juice in the adjoining big hall which was used for coffee break and lunch break at the appropriate timings. When I was looking to see if any glass of juice was available, I did not notice any glass of juice except water/coffee/tea offered by the staff. At that particular time, somebody called me in a louder voice, 'Hello Mr. Manoharan! What were you looking for?' I immediately looked in the direction where the voice had come from and noticed that the then Union Minister of Forests and Environment was present along with another gentleman. I politely told him that I was looking for a glass of juice as I felt thirsty. It was very nice of him to have called one of the staff members who served coffee/tea etc to go and fetch a glass of juice for me. He talked to me for a while and wanted to know if I knew the gentleman standing next to him. I politely told him that I did not know him. He was a senior I.A.S. officer called Mr. Gokhale and he was an Additional Secretary to the Government of India. The Minister asked Mr. Gokhale if he knew me, and he also did not know me at all. After hearing that, the Minister told him that I was Mr. Manoharan from the Assam-Meghalaya cadre and he would never forget me as I was an unusual civil servant. When he said that, the Additional Secretary to the Government of India was rather bewildered. The Union Minister tried to explain why he said it like that. He informed Mr. Gokhale about what had happened when he had met me while I served as the JCCI&E in Madras more than 15 years ago. He vividly narrated in detail the conversation between me and the Minister when he came to meet me as the MP, more than 15 years ago. Thereafter, he said that Mr. Manoharan was an unusual civil servant and categorically told him that more than 15 years ago when he had met me regarding the issue of an import licence, I had told him that there was no need for him to remind me of the issue of the import licence for which he had originally applied. He also informed Mr. Gokhale that, as promised by me, the licence reached his office automatically and he never reminded me even once.

The then Additional Secretary to the Government of India, who was hearing this conversation from the Minister concerned, was happy to know about my helpful attitude and my forthright way of dealing with an applicant, irrespective of the fact that he happened to be the Hon'ble MP when he mentioned the pending application in that office. I was really surprised to know that it was a conversation between me and the then Hon'ble Member of Parliament, maybe for about 20 minutes in my office, and that too, more than 15 years ago. He remembered every word of my conversation and narrated it in detail to another senior civil servant, which is why he mentioned that he never forgot me in his life.

I recalled this incident only to indicate that despite being a politician and that too, a Member of Parliament for very many years, he might have met a very large number of the members of the public, officials and non-officials in very many places in the country. I was myself surprised when he remembered me and that too when he had met me only once during my tenure in Madras. Generally, people may have wrong notions about politicians as well as civil servants. Perhaps, both categories of persons may be maligned due to certain wrong perceptions or presumptions based on interactions with them. In other words, if I may say so, there were very many members of the public and politicians who were gracious to remember whatever little help they might have got from very many officials of the government even on simple issues, and they would always cherish such pleasant meetings. It was so very gracious of him to have complimented me to another senior civil servant.

During the years that were between July 1985 to July 1990, while I served in my assignment as JCCI&E under the Ministry of Commerce, Government of India, I used to receive a very large number of applications for transfer to my office, mostly from LDCs/Typists, i.e., grade III staff from Government of India offices in New Delhi. In those years, the salary structure was not very high, even for Class I officers. Many girls and boys who went from the state of Tamil Nadu as LDCs/Typists would have hardly earned a salary of Rupees 6 or 7 hundred approximately. They found it extremely difficult to live within that meagre salary if they did not have relatives or any other support system for them who had gone away from their faraway native places in Tamil Nadu to New Delhi. Generally, the Staff Selection Commission of India at various regions recruited grade III staff members like LDCs/Typists after conducting requisite examinations as per the procedure existing at that time. They used to send the selected list of candidates to various Central Government offices spread over the country. The Government of India offices in Madras or any of the other big cities were expected to appoint such candidates recommended by the Staff Selection Commission only to fill up the vacancies if any that might arise in that particular office. But in case a Department of the Government of India, for instance, in Madras did not receive any such list of candidates for filling up the vacancies in their office, it might be left to them to consider the requests of the LDCs/Typists who were serving in various Central Government offices in New Delhi for their transfer to a Central Government office. For example, for the boys and girls of Tamil Nadu who were finding it rather difficult to survive within the limited means of salary in the capital city of the country, they were always anxiously waiting to come to Tamil Nadu to join any particular Central Government office depending upon the vacancy and their good luck.

When I served between 1985-90 as the head of the office of Joint Chief Controller of Imports and Exports, I used to receive a very large number of requests from employees working in New Delhi. Very often, their parents used to come and make requests to me to consider the applications of their children. I introduced a procedure in my office to deal with all such cases of requests. At this juncture, I would like to make it very clear that if there were no objections by the Staff Selection Commission (SSC) and if there were no recommended categories of candidates sent by them to our office for filling up the vacancies, it was left to me to consider such pending applications with a request for transfer to my office at that time.

I requested the administration section to maintain a register compiling all such pending applications date-wise received seeking to come back to Madras to serve in a Central Government office. I made it a principle and explicitly clear to my office as well as the applicants or their parents who came to meet me that all their applications were organised in a chronological order. I informed the applicants or their parents whenever they came to meet me or made requests by post that I would certainly help the people on the principle of first-come, first-served basis, i.e., based on the order of receipt of such requests chronologically maintained in my office during that period.

Over a period of time, as and when the vacancies were available and as and when the SSC did not object or did not send its list of recommended candidates for appointments in my office at Group III level, I issued orders for their transfers strictly on the basis of thorough scrutiny on the basis of dates of application of requests and allowed them to join with the usual joining time. In this straightforward manner, I would like to record that more than 5 dozen young government servants were transferred to the Chennai office over a period of 5 years. I candidly informed them that though I had a helpful attitude for consideration of their applications for accommodating them in our office depending upon the availability of vacancies as and when possible, I made it a point to inform them that this particular office where I was working was a different cup of tea unlike their offices at New Delhi. I made it clear to them whenever they came to join this particular office where they would be working thereafter was an extremely sensitive, complex, and difficult one. Perhaps, they were not aware of the functions of the licensing office during the regulatory regime, especially when the import licences and export incentives worth of crores of rupees were dealt day in and day out.

I categorically informed them, at the cost of repetition, that under no circumstances would I tolerate it if I happened to know that they were trying to take undue advantage of the situation in view of the possible motivation for dealing with applications in a manner which was not desirable, contrary to the import and export policy and procedures. It was my bounden duty to explain to them the consequences of inaction or unwarranted action with a malicious approach in dealing with such sensitive matters of the licensing regime with vested interests.

From the very beginning of joining this organisation, I made it a point that I was extremely strict with a no-nonsense approach in dealing with recalcitrance on the part of the few members of the officers and staff in the office who used to delay applications on some pretext or the other or who deliberately created obstacles in the form of unnecessary references back and forth to the applicants who happened to be in the private sector organisations or public sector organisations or individual applications from exporters for their export incentives based on their own exports.

As I was rather strict and insisted on office discipline in addition to ensuring a very good work culture in the organisation, some of these staff nicknamed me as 'Maharaja' in a sarcastic manner. I came to know later that in one of their staff association meetings at the beginning of my joining in the year 1985, the gentleman, i.e., me after coming from Assam Jungles, tried to teach us discipline and tried to conduct the office in an autocratic manner. They even commented, as I came to know later, 'Let's see for how long he would continue to be the head of the office.' Of course, there were quite a few anonymous complaints against me which were all motivated and biased ones. In the New Delhi headquarters, the senior officers did not give any credence to such complaints. Within a few months of my joining, the then head of the organisation, i.e. CCI&E, visited my office and interacted with me. Of course, he was very happy to know the manner in which I was conducting the office with proper enforcement of discipline, which was rather warranted in such a sensitive and difficult organisation dealing with a large number of applications of import licences and export incentives, to the tune of crores of rupees. When the CCI&E himself was very happy after visiting my office and after meeting the officers and staff, he assured me that I could go ahead and advised me to improve further the conditions of the office furniture, furnishings, etc., in addition to bringing out a very good image of the functioning of our office.

As some of the employees sarcastically called me 'Maharaja' of the office, I deliberately called one of my office staff to purchase a call bell with the insignia of Air India Maharaja Symbol on the top of the call bell. I fixed it outside the door of my office chamber. I made sure that whenever I pressed the call bell, there was a nice musical tune as well. Thereafter, when some of the office staff came to meet me for a discussion on some issues pertaining to their association, I informed them that they had given me a peculiar epithet as the Maharaja of this office regarding my style of functioning as the head of the office. I, therefore, informed them that I accepted the epithet with humility and made sure that whenever they entered my office chamber, there was a Maharaja sitting inside by keeping a call bell with the Maharaja Insignia on top of it outside my office.

I had to deal with some difficult members of the staff associations whenever they raised rather impossible demands as an alibi to put pressure on me for consideration of their unreasonable requests sometimes. Of course, I used to listen to them very patiently and whatever I felt was right according to my conscience and as per the rules and regulations of the government in dealing with import and export policy provisions and as expected of me as the head of the organisation, I took the correct stand in listening to their grievances for the redressal of their genuine requests only.

Of course, I considered one of their demands that instead of meeting the staff association every time at the headquarters in Madras, one could visit the licensing offices in Bangalore, Hyderabad, Cochin, Visakhapatnam, and Pondicherry so that the staff association members could visit these places for attending the meetings convened by me but also gave an opportunity to them to see some places of interest in these cities. I did help them in visiting many places and organised transport through the help of the private sector organisations and public sector organisations to educate them on the manufacturing processes involved in many of their industries in these different cities.

It was an eye-opener for them that they were dealing with important applications whenever such units approached our office for the import of capital goods and/or for the import of raw materials, components, etc. The office staff was dealing with only the applications and had no idea about the manufacturing processes or the difficulties involved in the import of goods, which would otherwise help them in the process of manufacture in a reasonable timeframe. I used to visit such units along with them to acquaint myself, in addition to helping my colleagues give such opportunities for them to expand their knowledge about the matters dealt with in the office files.

Perhaps the reader may be aware that more than 3 decades ago we had only 3 types of passenger vehicles in our country i.e. Ambassador Car, Premier Padmini Fiat, and Standard Herald. This is very much unlike the modern days wherein after more than 3 decades, now all types of cars are plying throughout this country, including rural areas and villages. Gone are those days of the monopoly of car manufacturers.

At this stage, I would like to recall my visit to the Standard Herald Car factory on an invitation of the Senior management of the company. This was located in the outskirts of the City of Madras. They were keen that I see the luxury car they were attempting to manufacture for the first time in the country. Being inquisitive, I sought their permission and took my wife also to the factory. We were warmly received by the senior management and shown around the factory. The new luxury car, christened standard 2000, seemed comfortable and comparable to any of the luxury cars currently in use. We were taken around the factory premises in a cream-coloured car. I was impressed that our country was capable of manufacturing such a luxury car, a Standard Herald innovation, even at that time. Unfortunately, due to difficulties in manufacturing such luxury cars which were rather expensive in those days, their well-begun attempt became futile and perhaps they could not market it in due course. As it was totally a new introduction, obviously due to the increased cost of imported components or whatever raw materials that were needed for the manufacture of the new luxury standard 2000 cars, they could not succeed in the end for marketing that particular beautiful car. Older readers might remember the Tamil movie, *Apoorva Sagotharargal* (dubbed as *Appu Raja* in Hindi). A famous song in that movie, *Raja kaiyyavechha* (dubbed in Hindi as *Raja naam mera*), was shot inside the Standard Herald factory on the standard 2000 manufacturing line.

I used to participate in various meetings organised by the export promotion councils, Chambers of Commerce, and Trade the Exporters

Association Meetings in order to understand and interact with them not only for understanding and appreciating their problems and grievances in an open forum but also as an opportunity for them to voice their grievances without fear or favour. I considered it as one of my duties to interact with trade and industry as after all they could not afford to come and meet me every now and then in my office. They also welcomed my straightforward approach with absolute clarity of mind to interact with them in a transparent manner. That also gave them an opportunity to understand and appreciate the latest amended import policy provisions. They were free to ask any questions or any doubts, and these were accordingly clarified. At this juncture, I would like to mention that one of my very well-experienced junior colleagues prepared an extensive guide indicating the various policy provisions and procedures, etc., that would help me in such interactions.

Over a period of time, I was also invited to attend lectures on import policy provisions and procedures on various matters in institutions like RBI Staff Training College, Indian Bank Staff Training College, and IOB Staff Training College, etc. I also addressed the office bearers of the local branch of the Institute of Materials Management regarding the issues raised pertaining to the import policy provisions. In other words, whenever I went and attended several such lectures in the City of Madras in different institutions, I made it a point that I would never accept any honorarium, whatever may be the amount that was prescribed by them. Since I was rather particular about not accepting any honorarium for such lectures, they presented me mementoes which I gladly accepted. It was a welcome relief for me whenever I attended the bank officers' meetings in their training institutions and attempted to clarify their doubts, etc. I had even started using blackboards with chalk which were provided by the institutions to help them understand with the examples given by me on such blackboards. Such meetings used to take place for 2 to 3 hours at a stretch. It was not only a monologue from me on such occasions but interactions with the participants as well in order to make them attentive and to understand and appreciate the nuances of the import policy provisions. The banks had a significant role regarding the issue of bank certificates of exports whenever the exporters wanted to get such a certificate of exports in view of their constant business relations.

Last but not the least, if I may say so, my biggest contribution as the then JCCI&E and that too, as a Zonal head of the organisation was that I could introduce computerisation of the issue of import licences and export incentives, Import and Exporter Code Numbers, and issue various clarifications to the applicants as and when they had approached the office. I would like to state that I was rather privileged to work in such a difficult environment when there was tremendous opposition to the introduction of computerisation in a licensing office as that would cut down the delays, and the functioning was also made effective and transparent. Probably, the reader will understand and appreciate that this took place more than 3 decades ago when there was only talk of the introduction of computers in government offices, unlike the present-day modern environment of the digitisation process and extensive usage of computers in government offices throughout the country. In the years between 1988-1990, after so much persuasion and training, when the whole computerisation process was put through disregarding the objections from the subordinate officers and staff as the head of the organisation, I must say that I was successful not only in introducing the computerisation process but also in motivating the officers and staff by inculcating a spirit of dedication with commitment to the success of the programme.

As I had mentioned in one of the foregoing paragraphs, the head of the organisation in New Delhi, i.e., the then CCI&E, had mentioned in an open meeting of all the licensing offices in New Delhi that he would attempt to introduce computerisation of the issue of import licences and export incentives beginning at the office of JCCI&E in Madras. It was rather a challenge given to me by him, and he candidly informed all my colleagues that he had the confidence and faith that I would succeed in this new innovative process. He also mentioned that if Mr. Manoharan would succeed, thereafter the issue of computerisation would be introduced in all the licensing offices. He would send the officers and staff from other zonal offices located at Bombay, Calcutta, and New Delhi, in addition to other licensing offices functioning in the country, not only for training purposes but also to see for themselves how the process was made successful under my leadership at that particular point in time.

As the computerisation was a successful experiment in the zonal office of the JCCI&E from the years 1988 onwards up to 1990 before the first week of July 1990, which was the end of my tenure, I once went to Delhi and met the then CCI&E and Commerce Secretary as well. In fact, the CCI&E only advised me to meet the Commerce Secretary and make my suggestion regarding the formal inauguration of the computerisation process. At that time when I met the Commerce Secretary after seeking a formal appointment, I expressed my disappointment to him that for more than 2 years, I had successfully introduced the computerisation process, yet there was no recognition at all by the Government of India at the higher echelons. He, of course, appreciated my bold stand and immediately responded that either he would come to inaugurate formally or he would request the Minister of state holding independent charge in the Ministry of Commerce for the formal inauguration. The very purpose of my meeting the then CCI&E and the then Commerce Secretary in the month of May 1990 was because of the fact that I would complete my tenure in the first week of July 1990. If I remember correctly, in the month of June 1990, the then Union Minister of state for Commerce visited our office. Before his visit, I had already organised the distribution of certificates, medals, etc., as a matter of encouragement for the best employees who were instrumental in ensuring the successful introduction of computerisation at our office for the first time in the organisation of CCI&E, New Delhi. I deliberately wanted to ensure that all the officers and staff should have the recognition for their hard work in a very transparent manner.

Frankly speaking, I did not want to get any certificate or medal for myself; it was only a matter of encouragement to my colleagues and staff as I was only the team leader. So, at least a few weeks before the end of my tenure in the last week of June 1990, I was delighted to organise a beautiful function to provide incentives like medals and certificates to our officers and staff for their excellent performance. They were very happy that I could organise such a function when the Union Minister of state for Commerce himself came and presented the awards and certificates to them.

After a couple of weeks after this function towards the end of June 1990, I was given a grand farewell. On that day, I deliberately mentioned to all the assembled officers and staff that despite their serious doubts, reservations, and misgivings about my continuance as the head of the office for more than a few months after July 1985, I told them in a lighter vein that I did complete the full tenure of 5 years with their fullest co-operation. I did complete my farewell address by saying that when the going was tough, the tough got going.

During the course of my Indian Administrative Service career spread over a period of approximately 35 years, I had travelled overseas extensively representing the country in my various assignments under the Government of India. For instance, I had visited New York in the month of March 1990 on an exports promotion tour and had participated in an International Garments Exposition Show for 4 days as part of a three-Member Trade Delegation. This was when I held additional charge as Executive Director of the Council for Leather Exports under the Ministry of Commerce. In that capacity, I also visited Lucca, Italy for a week in the latter part of May 1990 to attend an important meeting of the Leather Importers and visited several leather units for interactions with the buyers of the leather products in different places in Italy.

One of the greatest pleasures of my stint in Madras as the JCCI&E was the opportunity to meet and forge unforgettable friendships. A batchmate and a very dear friend, Mr. N. Bala Baskar, from the Haryana cadre of the I.A.S. was already the Secretary, Handloom Exports Promotion Council at Madras under the Ministry of Textiles, Government of India. On my arrival in Madras, he hosted a grand official welcome reception and introduced me to all the officials and important personalities in the industry and trade associated with Imports and Exports at Madras.

I also came across another senior I.A.S. officer, Mr. A. Sahasranaman of the Jammu & Kashmir cadre, who was the Executive Director of the Council for Leather Exports, Ministry of Commerce, Government of India. He became one of my very dear friends and sincere well-wishers. After completing his 5-year tenure in the post and when he left for his cadre in Jammu and Kashmir in the early part of 1990, I took over his assignment as an additional charge in addition to my regular assignment as JCCI&E at Madras.

During my 5-year tenure as JCCI&E, I also came across Mr. N. Gokul Ram, an I.A.S. officer of the Karnataka Cadre, who was the Secretary, Handloom Exports Promotion Council and later General Manager of Handlooms and Handicrafts Exports Corporation in Madras. He literally followed Mr. N. Bala Baskar in both those assignments as his successor.

This was a sort of pan-national friendship among I.A.S. officers serving in Madras at the same time. Mr. N. Balabaskar belonged to the Haryana cadre, Mr. A. Sahasranaman was from the Jammu & Kashmir cadre, Mr. N. K. Raghupathi was from the West Bengal cadre, and Mr. N. Gokul Ram from the Karnataka Cadre. Finally, I belonged to the Assam-Meghalaya cadre. I was fortunate in forging these wonderful, indelible friendships during my very first Central Government Deputation at Madras. All of them remain my very dear friends and sincere well-wishers. Unfortunately, Mr. N. Gokul Ram is no more, having lost his life due to the cruel fate of destiny just less than a month before his superannuation.

Commissioner and Secretary to the Govt of Assam in the Health and Family Welfare Dept from November 1990 to November 1991

After my successful completion of a 5-year tenure on Central Government deputation posting at Madras, I had to revert to the Assam Cadre in the year 1990. I had taken 4 months' leave as my mother was unwell those days. In October 1990, when my most affectionate and beloved mother passed away, I left Madras after a few weeks for the State of Assam. In the meanwhile, of course, my wife continued to serve at the ESI Dispensary at Saidapet, Madras under the government of Tamil Nadu Medical Service as a Civil Assistant Surgeon. I had requested the retention of my official quarters at Besant Nagar for a couple of months as I needed some time for the transhipment of my personal effects to Guwahati.

I had informed the Chief Secretary of Assam that I would report on such and such date in the middle of November 1990. I was pleasantly surprised when I landed at Guwahati Airport that there were 2 vehicles belonging to the Health and Family Welfare Department which were arranged for me, and an officer of the Health and Family Welfare Department met me and informed me that I was promoted to the super-time scale of I.A.S. and appointed as Commissioner and Secretary to the Government of Assam in the Health and Family Welfare Department. I was taken by surprise with such an immediate posting after my reversion as generally when officers revert back to the cadre after a tenure of Central Government posting, they might have to wait for a few more days, even months, to get an appointment order.

As soon as I left the airport, I reached the Circuit House in Guwahati and left my personal baggage because a room had already been reserved by the officers concerned in the Health and Family Welfare Department. I immediately went to the Secretariat at Dispur and reported to the Chief Secretary of Assam, Mr. P. C. Mishra. He warmly welcomed me and informed me in a very jovial manner that generally when senior officers revert back to the parent cadre, they are expected to wait in the corridors of the secretariat for their posting orders. However, he said the following: "Mr. Manoharan, in your case, there was a total exception, perhaps the appointment order might have been handed over to you in mid-air during your flight." Of course, he was a thorough gentleman and made me very comfortable. At that time, the popular rule (i.e. rule by the elected government) was very much in place. So, after I received the formal appointment order through the Deputy Secretary to the Government of Assam in the Health & Family Welfare Department in the office of the Chief Secretary, Assam, I signed my joining report and left his office chamber. I enquired from my colleagues where exactly the Health Minister's office was, as I considered it my duty to call on him as the new Commissioner and Secretary of the Health and Family Welfare Department. The gentleman himself was a medical doctor and he was happy that I had come back to Assam after my reversion to serve in the Health & Family Welfare Department, as he had heard about my work and reputation.

In the evening, I called all the senior officers of the department to get introduced and to know the issues and subjects that were dealt with in a big Department of the State Government of Assam. During that time, the state had only 3 government Medical colleges and 3 Homeopathy colleges, and of course, the medical institutions as such were limited in those days. Out of the 3 medical colleges located at Guwahati, Silchar, and Dibrugarh, Dibrugarh Medical College was the oldest medical college in Assam. In those years, perhaps, around the time of independence, the doctors who studied at Madras Medical College used to go and serve in those medical colleges, which I came to know later during my visits to all these medical colleges. Of course, compared to the period in the 1990s when I served as Health Secretary to the Government of Assam, I understand that nowadays there are very many private medical institutions in addition to a few more government medical institutions as well.

After a few days of my joining in the Department of Health and Family Welfare, I had to proceed to New Delhi to attend a conference of Health

Secretaries of various State Governments. I stayed in Assam Bhavan, New Delhi, which was the State Government Guest House. On the day I left for New Delhi from Guwahati, the Hon'ble Chief Minister of Assam was also on the same flight. There was a huge crowd to cheer him at the airport before our departure. I had to stay for a few days to meet the senior officers of the Ministry of Health and Family Welfare of the Government of India and to address various pending issues of the Health and Family Welfare Department of the State Government of Assam with the Central Ministry. When I was about to leave New Delhi for Guwahati on that morning for my return journey, I received a telephonic call from one of my well-wishers that the State Government of Assam was dismissed and brought under President's rule. There is a purpose as to why I was mentioning this particular information, which I will narrate below.

On my return from New Delhi to Guwahati, the Hon'ble Chief Minister of Assam, who has now become the Ex-Chief Minister overnight, also travelled on the same flight. When I reached Guwahati Airport and collected my baggage, I came out of the airport and witnessed a kind of eerie silence. To my utter surprise, there was no crowd, not even a few people, to receive the Ex-Chief Minister of Assam. A few days ago, when he had travelled to New Delhi, he was serving as the head of the state Government of Assam. But when the same gentleman returned after a few days, I could see the so-called cold reception he got from his own people. This indicates that power and pelf suddenly vanish the moment the person no longer holds a position or exercises authority.

Perhaps people thought during the President's rule he was nobody and there was no point in meeting him at the airport to receive him as it might not be beneficial to them in their own perception. Generally, it was known to everybody that nothing was permanent in this world and neither one's life, nor one's acquisition as every item could vanish the moment the particular time comes or it becomes part of the destiny in which one might be placed. This particular incident made me realise that once a person becomes an ordinary individual bereft of his erstwhile authority, influence or position, nobody would ever even attempt to exchange a simple smile or exchange of words as a matter of normal courtesy. It was a strange world, especially in politics. So, one comes to think of it in politics; sometimes people would reach dizzy heights in view of their favourable stars and again after some time or some months, if destiny decided otherwise, the same gentleman in politics would become a persona non-grata to his own relatives, his own party men and his own friends.

As soon as I went out of the airport, I could see a strong deployment of police force everywhere in the city, right from the airport to the secretariat. There was an uneasy calm, and one could sense the people's anger, tension, and restlessness en route. Many shops were also closed. When I reached the secretariat, all the Ministers' chambers were vacated, and later on, I heard the Chief Minister's chamber became the Governor's chamber. Whenever he came to the secretariat, he would occupy that chamber.

During President's rule, as Ministers were no longer serving in the State Government, the concerned Secretaries to the government would be responsible for the discharge of the duties and functions as the head of that department under the supervision and control of the Chief Secretary and the advisers to the Governor of Assam. I occupied the Health Minister's chamber as it was slightly more spacious and reported to the Chief Secretary, Assam. I came to know that the advisers were also likely to join in a day or 2. I called my officers and staff and categorically told them that all pending files should be sent regularly in time without the least delay. I also informed them that the proper briefing material concerning the functions of the Health and Family Welfare Department should be made ready for my benefit as well as for the benefit of the adviser who would be entrusted with this particular department in addition to many other departments. For instance, in a State Government during popular rule, there were more than 30 Ministers taking care of various departments. Obviously, during the President's rule, by and large, only at the most 3 Advisers to the Governor would be appointed with each adviser entrusted with a good number of departments. The concerned Secretaries to the State Government should send the files to the particular adviser who looks after his particular departments for his advice or suggestions or orders. As and when it was necessary, it was left to him to send the relevant files depending upon the importance of the subject to the Governor of Assam who functioned during the President's rule not only as the head of the state but also as the Head of the Government.

There were 3 Advisers who joined in a couple of days' time. I had to report to Mr. I.P. Gupta who was the adviser looking after Health &

Family Welfare Department in addition to many other departments. He was a pleasant and affectionate gentleman. In another couple of days, I had decided to call on the Hon'ble Governor of Assam. In my life, I would never ever forget Mr. Devidas Thakur who was the Hon'ble Governor of Assam at that time, in view of his outstanding qualities of head and heart. He hailed from the state of Jammu and Kashmir and in the past, he was the then Hon'ble Deputy Chief Minister of the State of Jammu & Kashmir. My meetings with him were always very cordial, pleasant and absolutely straightforward.

In the meanwhile, we were told that a senior Adviser would be reaching in the afternoon to join. I was told that he would be meeting all the Secretaries to the Government of Assam at the Secretariat Conference Room. His name was Mr. K.N. Prasad. He belonged to the then Imperial Police Service and he had served as Director of the Intelligence Bureau during Mrs. Indira Gandhi's tenure when she was the Hon'ble Prime Minister of India. He appeared to be a very tough gentleman when he presided over the meeting of all the Secretaries to the State Government numbering more than 45 or so. The meeting started as soon as he came from the airport at 3.30 pm. He started discussing with each and every Secretary to the government with a request to thoroughly brief him about his Department about the pending issues and important decisions that had to be taken which might have been delayed. He started his interactions with the Secretaries to the government one after another, in a business-like manner and he took at least 15 to 20 minutes with each and every Secretary to the Government of Assam. By the time he completed about 15 departments during his interactions it was around 6 pm. Generally, the State Government officers were not used to sit in the Secretariat complex beyond 5.30 pm as per the office timings or at the most up to 6 pm. Most of them looked thoroughly perplexed and rather worried as to when such interactions with all the remaining 25 or more Secretaries to the government would be over with that pace of discussions. They were rather apprehensive that the kind of detailed interactions by the senior adviser would continue on and on and perhaps, until late in the hours of the night. When I looked around, the officers were rather extremely worried and perhaps, cursing their fate on that particular day regarding the return journey back home late in the night.

When it came to my response to his interactions, it was already around 7 pm and perhaps there were other secretaries numbering around 15 to 18 looking anxiously at me. Since the atmosphere was rather tense and the senior adviser also appeared to be very tough with a no-nonsense type of approach, I took advantage of the situation when I responded to him as below when he enquired about the functioning of the Health & Family Welfare Department. I candidly told him "Sir! I was holding as Secretary in charge of one of the unhealthiest Departments of the State Government of Assam, called the Health & Family Welfare Department." The moment he heard my response, he burst into boisterous laughter and told me as below: "Mr. Manoharan, we could discuss separately more about your department's functioning in my office chamber later." I immediately took advantage of the opportunity, noting his pleasant mood, and told him "Sir, if you did not mind, could we break up our discussions with me as well as with other secretaries and continue the discussion with the rest of the 15 or 18 Secys to government on a later date as it was already 7.30 pm." Perhaps he understood and appreciated my boldness and readily agreed, saying "Yes Manoharan! Friends! We will right now wind up the discussion and meet later in the coming weeks" and he thanked all our officers and left the Secretariat Conference Room. The moment he left, all assembled secretaries had a huge sigh of relief and thanked me profusely and happily left the secretariat.

After a day or 2, the senior adviser Mr. K N Prasad called me to his office chamber and had a detailed discussion about the functioning of the various wings of the Health and Family Welfare Department like medical education, administration of hospitals in the district in addition to other medical institutions, like homeopathy colleges and pharmacy colleges. I gave him a thorough briefing and also told him that I would like to take him to an important institution called Dr. Bhupaneswar Baruah Cancer Institute. He was a philanthropist and he only founded that institute several decades ago, and later it became part and parcel of the State Government. During my interactions with Mr. K. N. Prasad, he appeared to me as a very strict, straightforward, no-nonsense gentleman with a very large heart. He wanted to do something worthwhile during his stay in the state. Strictly speaking, the Health and Family Welfare Department was not assigned to him. He was in charge of police administration and all enforcement agencies, law and order and personnel department, etc. Somehow, he developed curiosity and interest in the functioning of the Health and Family Welfare Department. Of course, later I had a very pleasant meeting with Mr. I.P. Gupta who was the adviser to whom I reported for getting his orders on several files. Whenever I interacted with him, he was very thorough, knowledgeable and would like to go into the depth of the issues dealt with in the files. Incidentally, he belonged to the Indian Frontier Administrative Service (IFAS). Those officers later on were treated on par with the senior I.A.S. and IFS officers only. Originally, they were expected to serve the North East Frontier Administrative Regions i.e. the border areas of the North East states of Arunachal Pradesh and certain border areas of Nagaland, Tripura and Mizoram etc. During the British time, there were different rules for administering those far-flung areas, and they were posted only in those regions throughout their service. The idea was to try to administer those areas with the fullest co-operation and support from the local tribal people. In other words, there were many tribes speaking with different dialects, and they were not so very amenable to be governed with the kind of authority that would be evidenced in other parts of the country. Moreover, their designations were also rather different at the field-level, and some of them were called Political officers or Assistant Political officers serving in those regions.

Since they had longer tenures in those regions, they were expected to learn different local dialects for interactions with those local tribals and to make them understand and aware of the developmental functions of the State Government departments in their own largest interests. Moreover, in those times before independence during the British Regime, they did not want to force them to adopt a kind of regimentation by the authorities of the State Government departments. Their willing co-operation was only sought whenever the government attempted to introduce some welfare measures for their own benefits. Unfortunately, the literacy levels in those regions were pretty low. Most of such tribal people living in the far-flung areas were all animists. They were not expected to be ruled by a kind of authoritative regime. In other words, IFAS officers were expected to serve the people with more understanding and awareness of the inadequate development and to motivate them with patience and for interactions between themselves as well.

As I reverted to the State cadre in November 1990 and after taking over the assignment as Commissioner and Secretary of the Health & Family Welfare Department in the State of Assam, President's rule was imposed within a period of 10 days or so. My tenure as the Commissioner and Secretary of the Health & Family Welfare Department lasted for a little more than a year. Thus, half of my tenure was during President's rule with the other half under popular rule. The President's rule was only for a brief period, i.e. November 1990 to April/May 1991. There was a qualitative difference in my functioning as the Secretary to the Government of Assam, considering that whatever decisions were taken by me were largely approved by the Adviser to the Governor of Assam and, where necessary, by the Governor of Assam, who functioned as the Head of the Government in addition to his status as the head of the state. In other words, I had a very free hand and could try to clean the system in the department to reduce delays in the issuance of appointments, transfers, etc. of medical professionals.

However, in the latter case, i.e., when after the restoration of popular rule in the government, I had to report to the Cabinet Minister of Health & Family Welfare department after April/May 1991 and convince him about several issues that were pending. I had to educate him as to what was required and what was certainly essential for not only the administration of medical institutions but also for the general medical care of the people of the state. During the succeeding paragraphs, I will, of course, narrate my experience as the Secretary to the Government of Assam during my tenure, which would give an idea to the reader of how and why the qualitative difference was evident in my functioning during the 2 types of rules of the state.

To begin with when I joined in November 1990-91, I was astonished to know that there were more than 500 vacancies for medical doctors available in the state. Had they been effectively utilised in time after their appointment by following the requisite procedure, the state and the people would have greatly benefitted. Generally, the medical and health officers were considered as Class I officers in the state and they were selected by the state Public Service Commission after the requisite procedure. But at the same time, there were provisions under the relevant rules of recruitment that in times of need and emergency, the State Government could appoint medical officers for medical institutions like Primary Health Centres, Community Health Centres, sub-divisional Hospitals, and District Hospitals. I informed the Adviser to the Governor of Assam that I would take the initiative to follow the procedure for the recruitment of medical doctors to fill up the vacancies by the state Public Service Commission as early as possible. In the meantime, in order to cut down delays and to ensure that the people of the state in the far-flung areas get medical care and medicines and their personnel are available in the rural areas, I would take appropriate action for filling up the vacancies by the State Government. My suggestions were readily agreed to, and I immediately called for applications from the qualified medical officers of the state after ascertaining the total number of vacancies in different districts in the Primary Health Centres, Community Health Centres, sub-divisional Hospitals, and District Hospitals.

I activated the Health & Family Welfare Department and formed an interview committee headed by me as the Chairman, and the Director of Health Services, a Joint Secretary and Superintendent of the Office, as Members of the Committee. All such applications were scrutinised simultaneously, and interviews were also organised in my office. The advertisement was given as required by the government rules and regulations with a time limit of hardly 10 days as we could not afford to keep the vacancies pending for months on end. When the applicants i.e. Male and Female doctors attended the interviews along with the certificates etc., their credentials were verified by the staff who assisted me. Then and there the decisions were taken to appoint them as medical and health officers of the state. I had the complete list of vacancies in the various medical institutions on my table. As most of the candidates preferred to work in their own home districts, which was rather natural, I tried my level best to help them in the best possible manner as per their requirements and informed them of their places of postings during the interviews.

The appointment orders were also readied within a week or so for dispatch. Unfortunately, most of the well-educated and qualified doctors were not willing to serve at a distance of more than 50 or 100 km away from their hometowns. But I had to cajole them and advise them that it was a golden opportunity for them as they had been unemployed for a few years. I also assured them that whatever appointments were issued would be ratified by the state Public Service Commission at an early date. I informed them that I would do my level best to help them in the best possible manner. Within a month of conducting interviews to fill all such vacancies, most of the appointments were issued to the deserving doctors. The interviews were held intermittently every day, and the appointment orders were also issued as quickly as possible, as my sole objective was to ensure the filling of the vacancies and to make sure the medical doctors were posted in the rural areas and in the hospitals so that the people of the state could get the maximum benefits of medical care.

Of course, I made sure that the interviews were business-like and did not take much of their valuable time. While I was talking to the candidates, the concerned officials were verifying their credentials. I only asked 2 questions: Number 1, whether they would be willing to work in a rural area within their own district or outside the home districts. Though most of them preferred to work in their home district, I had to convince them that it would not be possible in the absence of many vacancies in their own district, and as far as possible, I tried to give them appointments in their neighbouring district. My senior colleagues, the Commissioner and Secretary of the Industries Department and the Commissioner and Secretary of the Transport Department, came to my room and asked me what was the need for a big pageant of so many good-looking young doctors flocking into my room day in, day out. They were rather perplexed. So, they entered my room and observed the conduct of the interviews. It was very nice of them to have disturbed me, taking advantage of their seniority as they were rather curious to know what was happening in a friendly manner.

After the schedule of interviews and as per the expected time given by me to the office staff, within a period of 10 days, several hundred appointment letters of medical and health officers were issued directing them to join immediately. I also took the initiative to make sure all such appointments were regularised in due course by the Assam state Public Service Commission. I wanted to pen a factual narrative to reflect on the point that we ensured that not only the unemployed doctors got appointments but also the people in the rural areas got the medical help and assistance in time by filling up such vacancies in a transparent manner. Most importantly, my actions were duly ratified by the Adviser to the Governor of Assam.

There were, of course, vacancies in the medical educational institutions like medical colleges, homeopathy colleges, Ayurvedic colleges, etc. in the State of Assam. I took initiatives to fill up the existing vacancies based on the relevant rules and regulations of the State Government of Assam. However, I was a bit cautious in taking the initiative for not only filling up of the vacancies but also for filling up of vacancies for promotions that were due in the medical institutions. At that time, I wanted to apprise the Adviser to the Governor of Assam of the issue of promotions and filling up of the resultant vacancies in various Grades of the official hierarchy like Professor and head of the Department, Associate Professor, Assistant Professors, and Lecturers and junior doctors etc. I knew at that time that the medical fraternity working in the medical institutions were from the influential sections of society of Assam. A word had already spread around that I would take up the initiative for filling up of promotions at various levels in the hierarchy as well as filling up of resultant vacancies in the lower levels.

Somehow in a group or gathering, they all went and met the Governor of Assam to ensure justice in the matter of filling up vacancies and promotions, etc., in the State of Assam. On a particular day, I was informed by the Secretary to the Governor of Assam that both the Governor and the advisers would be present at the meeting of the various members of associations of the medical colleges in the state. There was a big gathering of senior doctors from various medical colleges who had assembled in the lawns of Raj Bhavan at Guwahati. The meeting was presided over by the Governor of Assam, and both the former advisers and I were present. I silently observed the proceedings, and some of them mentioned that there were several pending promotions, which would result in possible vacancies increasing at the lower levels, affecting the teaching faculties and the administration of the medical college hospitals. Many of them spoke in the meeting about the necessity for the issuance of orders by the Health & Family Welfare Department at an early date. After some time, maybe an hour or so, every senior faculty member voiced his or her grievances or suggestions. It was nice of the Governor to request me to respond to their complaints, suggestions, and grievances.

I informed the assembled gathering in the presence of the Governor and advisers that I had already initiated the issuance of posting orders on promotions which were rather due and also filling up of the possible resultant vacancies. I apprised the Governor that I would do my level best to ensure filling up of the promotions and also for filling up of the resultant vacancies in all the medical institutions depending upon the necessity for transfer of a faculty member from one medical college hospital to another medical college hospital. I also informed the Governor of Assam that as there were 3 medical colleges located at Guwahati, Silchar and Dibrugarh and therefore depending upon the vacancies to be filled up due to the promotion of medical faculty members, they have to be shifted from one medical college hospital to another medical college hospital.

I took a little time to inform the Governor that obviously, the doctors at the senior levels based on the eligible criteria as and when promoted, depending upon the vacancies either available in their own existing medical institutions or in a distant medical institution had to be transferred. I wanted to apprise the Governor that once the transfer orders were issued, the senior doctors would have to join in their new places of posting without any grudge. Moreover, I told the Governor and the advisers that once such orders would be issued within the next fortnight after thorough scrutiny on my part, no one should raise any objections and try to bring influence for cancellations of such orders and for requests to comply with their own preferences for joining in a particular medical institution where they were not the preferred candidate. I made a very pertinent and rather provocative statement as below:

"Sir, the senior faculty members who had assembled and were sitting in front of all of us were from the utmost influential sections of the Society in the State of Assam, and I knew that the moment the transfer orders were issued for their promotions purely based on merit and vacancies available in a transparent manner and under no circumstances, I would brook any interferences at any level in the hierarchy of State Administration at that time, including the Governor of Assam. I begged my pardon and informed the Governor of Assam that I would not like to be interfered with either by the Governor or by the advisers once such postings and transfer orders were issued in a proper and transparent manner. After all, as the Secretary to the Government of Assam, I knew my duties and responsibilities, and I would make sure that all such appointments, promotions, and transfer orders would be issued after detailed scrutiny in an objective, dispassionate, and transparent manner, and I would make sure that no slippages would occur." After I made this statement, there was pin-drop silence. Neither the Governor nor the advisers said anything. I was particularly very straightforward and made my comments so that everyone sitting in the audience understood what my position on the matter was, as I knew that

I would be subject to criticism in due course. After listening to me, the Governor of Assam advised me to issue the orders as early as possible, as that was considered necessary in an absolutely transparent manner. The meeting ended with a vote of thanks to the chair.

After the meeting, I went and sat in the office chamber of the Secretary to the Governor, who was a dear friend of mine and a few years junior to me. Since it was lunchtime, I wanted to inform my wife that the meeting was just over and, as informed by the Secretary to the Governor, that I had to wait before I left Raj Bhavan. He mentioned to me that the Governor would like to meet me before I left the Raj Bhavan. After a few minutes, the ADC to the Governor requested me to come inside the Governor's house. He guided me straight to the dining hall where the Governor of Assam, his wife, and one adviser were present. I was rather perplexed, and I thought I would get some reprimand from him in view of my very bold statement just a little while ago in the meeting. The Governor and the Advisor advised me to join them for lunch. During lunch, neither the Governor nor the advisor mentioned anything about the proceedings of that day's meeting. It was a very lively discussion, and the Governor and his wife were extremely hospitable to the advisor and me. When I came out, I went and sat in the Secretary's office. I talked to my wife about what had happened there and also in the meeting and requested her to have her lunch as I had already finished mine. As my lunch was over, I would go to the secretariat.

I would like to narrate another interesting meeting with the Governor at his office. He told me that recently he visited Silchar Medical College/Hospital. He told me very bluntly that the moment he stepped inside, the place was stinking and he told the Principal of the Medical College that he would send Mr. Manoharan, the Secretary to the government, to visit your hospital and to meet all your medical fraternity, office staff and all your associations' representatives and to listen to you for the redressal of their grievances or suggestions for further improvement in the hospital administration. He came out of the hospital immediately. He narrated the incident to me as it happened. He advised me to visit all the 3 medical colleges i.e. Guwahati Medical College, Silchar Medical College and Dibrugarh Medical College within a period of the next fortnight and I should give a detailed report about their representations or redressal of grievances or suggestions or for any other issues of relevance that were to be attended to, on top priority, for each and every medical college. In other words, he wanted me to give him 3 different reports for the respective medical colleges and my suggestions for any improvements or for infrastructural requirements in addition to my suggestions for redressal of their genuine grievances. He advised me that I should meet all sections of employees individually and listen to them and give him a factual report on what exactly their problems and issues of such medical college hospitals were and what further improvements could be made in all such 3 medical institutions. Of course, it was a laborious task for which he gave me a time limit of a maximum of 3 weeks only, if not within a fortnight.

As advised by him, after a fortnight and after my detailed interactions and inspection of various faculties of the 3 medical colleges, and my meetings with the representatives of the medical fraternity and employees, I prepared very detailed reports and took the reports with me to the Governor's office. He took a day or 2 for the examination of my reports and thereafter called me once again to his office. This time he advised me to take the Principal of one medical college institution and the Director of Medical Education along with me to visit the following institutions i.e. All India Institute of Medical Service (AIIMS) at New Delhi, Sanjay Gandhi Post Graduate Institute of Medical Science and Research at Lucknow within the next fortnight and after detailed discussions and visits of various departments in both those medical institutions, I had to submit a report to him. In other words, what exactly he wanted was a comparative analysis of the infrastructural facilities and modern medical aids and surgical equipment available in those 2 advanced medical institutions and what we could provide in our own 3 medical colleges in the State of Assam.

I undertook this task as well, and a team of 3 members, including me, the Principal of Guwahati Medical College and the Director of Medical Education, visited AIIMS in New Delhi and thereafter Lucknow. I made all the arrangements beforehand for meetings with the Directors and Heads of Institutions of those 2 important prestigious medical institutions. After interactions with the Directors and Heads of Faculty Members in both the institutions, I returned to Guwahati along with my team members and prepared the reports, submitting them to the Governor of Assam as per his desire and instructions.

I made some suggestions to the Governor of Assam after my visits to Delhi and Lucknow about further improvements that were necessary in view of the lack of infrastructural facilities in 3 Medical Colleges of Assam and also for the introduction of new medical equipment and surgical instruments, etc., that were absolutely necessary based on the inadequate availability of such facilities in the 3 Medical Colleges of the state. Moreover, for providing additional infrastructure facilities and also for the purchase of new medical equipment and surgical instruments, etc., substantial financial assistance was needed. Hence, I submitted a comprehensive report in consultation not only with the Director of Medical Education but also with all 3 Principals of the Medical Colleges at Guwahati, Silchar, and Dibrugarh.

To quote an example, after thorough examination of my report, the Governor, through his advisor, sanctioned certain projects in all the 3 Medical Colleges. If I remember correctly now, after more than 3 decades, 2 big hostel buildings for men and women, a patient's and attendant's rest house, in addition to the necessary medical instruments and surgical equipment needed and projected by the Principal of Guwahati Medical College Hospital, and likewise the infrastructural requirements, etc., that were suggested by the other 2 Principals of the 2 Medical Colleges and hospitals at Silchar and Dibrugarh, were sanctioned by the government.

I remember very vividly based on the directions of the Governor of Assam and the advisor concerned, the Public Works Department of the State Government undertook immediately the initiative for the Foundation Stone Laying Ceremony of 6 projects at Guwahati Medical College Hospital within a month or so and thereafter, the formal function was organised. It was a rather historical occasion for the Guwahati Medical College Hospital. Simultaneously, the Governor of Assam laid the foundation stone for the 6 projects i.e. 2 hostels for boys and girls separately, Patients 'Attendants' rest house and 3 more projects which I am unable to recollect now, in the presence of all the members of the Medical Fraternity Faculties, medical students and members of the Public on that particular day. Incidentally, if I may say so, I had the fortune of serving in the President's rule for approximately 6 months or so and in between I also undertook certain tours to district hospitals along with the Governor of Assam. Of course, the Governor of Assam Mr. D Thakur was already serving as head of the state before 14th November 1990 when I joined. Since the President's rule was imposed within a week after my joining, I had the privilege and pleasure of working under a very dedicated, straightforward gentleman called Mr. I P Gupta, an advisor who was looking after the Health Family & Welfare department in addition to some other departments and of course, under the leadership of the Governor of Assam himself.

In the meantime, I had heard from the then Chief Secretary of Assam that the Governor of Assam wanted to present Gold Medals to the Civil Servants and the Police officers who had performed with excellence during his tenure of hardly 10 months. Suddenly, there was news that within the next few days, he was leaving the state and a new Governor was supposed to take over on a particular day in the month.

It was a closely guarded secret that none in the administrative hierarchy, right from the Chief Secretary downwards, knew who exactly had been selected for the award of Gold Medals from among the Civil Servants and Police Officers of the state. I was informed that before the meeting, excepting the Governor, no one knew who would be the recipient of the medals.

On one fine morning, there was a beautiful function organised in the premises of the Assam secretariat. All the assembled guests included the Chief Secretary, all 3 Advisors, all the Secretaries to the government, all the senior Heads of Departments, and other members of the officers and staff of various departments. It was a suspense as to who exactly would receive the medals. I was told later that the Governor had requested the Chief Secretary to keep the certificates for the issue of medals ready without filling up the names. He told the Chief Secretary that during the function, only he would announce the names, and simultaneously the officer deputed for keeping the medals and certificates on hand would fill up the names as and when the names were announced by the Governor in the function. Another interesting feature was that the Governor requested the Chief Justice of the Guwahati High Court, who was present on the Dias, to present the medals to the best-performing officers.

After the function started, I was pleasantly surprised that the Governor began announcing the names one after another in the I.A.S. category first. So the moment he announced the particular name, that name was recorded on the certificate. Thereafter, along with the Gold Medal, the certificate for such outstanding service on the part of the civil servant was handed over to the recipient. Here again, the Governor only made the announcements and requested the Chief Justice of Guwahati High Court to present the medals to the officers concerned. In total, 6 I.A.S. officers and 4 I.P.S. officers were selected and provided with Gold Medals and Certificates by the Chief Justice of Guwahati High Court as and when the Governor of Assam announced the names.

As a civil servant, I was surprised to know that the Governor maintained the seniority of the officers concerned and accordingly announced one after the other without any mistake. Out of the 6 I.A.S. Officers, when my name was announced, I was pleasantly surprised as I had hardly worked for approximately 4 to 5 months during the stay of the Governor. Another wonderful feature of the Governor's address was that he extolled the exact qualities of head and heart and the performance of the officers concerned in a beautiful narration while the Chief Justice was handing over the medals to the officers concerned. Of course, there were heartburns among other officers and especially in my case as I had just reverted back to the State cadre and hardly worked for a few months in the Department of Health & Family Welfare compared to the other senior officers who had worked for longer durations. From that particular experience, one could easily know the large-heartedness and sincerity on the part of the Governor of Assam even in selecting the officers of civil service as well as the police service based on his direct knowledge and interactions with the officers concerned only in an impartial and transparent manner.

For me, working as the Commissioner and Secretary, Health Family & Welfare Department during the President's rule under the guidance of the advisor, Mr. I. P. Gupta, and as per the directions of the Governor of Assam, is an unforgettable and very pleasant experience even today.

One fine morning during the President's rule, the ADC to the Governor called me on the phone and informed me that the Governor was being shifted, and a new Governor would take over after a day or 2. Therefore, the Governor wanted to host a dinner for all the senior officers of the government i.e. Advisors, the Chief Secretary, Commissioners, and Secretaries to the Government of Assam, and other Heads of Departments at Raj Bhavan. I was rather taken aback to know about the sudden exit of the Governor, and perhaps there was no time for the State Administration to organise a formal farewell for him.

In other words, it looked as though he himself had given the farewell to the officers and wanted to say goodbye with personal interactions with each and every one during the dinner hosted by him. Drinks and snacks were served before dinner. The Governor was moving around and interacted with each and every individual senior officer who was his guest that evening. When he came to me and my wife, he insisted that I should keep him company at least to have a small drink, which I politely declined. I informed him that due to a commitment made by me to my wife after our marriage for several years, I did not touch the liquor at all. He provoked me and requested me at least for that particular day; I could forget the commitment and join him, which I again flatly refused politely. My wife was a witness during our conversation, and she smiled as I was rather candid, despite his sincere request. This is to indicate the love and affection of the head of the State not only to me as a junior officer, who had just become the Commissioner and Secretary to the Government of Assam after only 15 years of service.

In brief, he was extremely free, frank, and outspoken with each and every officer. He welcomed the officers to be candid and straightforward not only in their responses to his interactions but also during the implementation of the schemes of the State Government in the largest interests of the public. The interesting finale for me was when I took leave of the Governor. He came outside, stood near the car, and opened the door for my wife. At that time, he told my wife the following words, which I quote below: "Madam! I am very proud and delighted to have worked with your husband and interacted with him on many occasions. He is an outstanding officer, and I wish him good luck and all the very best for his future career." Afterwards, he closed the door and took leave from both of us with his folded hands.

On the day of the Governor's departure for New Delhi, I thought as a matter of courtesy I should visit Guwahati Airport and bid farewell to him personally. When I reached the airport, I could hardly see a few senior officers and certainly not any of the political leaders or members of the public. I was really taken aback that a person who did so much for the state during his tenure as head of the state for their own welfare and development was given such a slipshod farewell. As a citizen and as a senior civil servant, I felt very bad. I came across only one Member of Parliament, Mr. Atavur Rehman, at the airport. He belonged to the Imperial Police Service and served the state and later joined politics after his superannuation. He was an elderly and well-meaning person. Incidentally, I happened to know him and expressed my anguish to him about the absence of people in politics in adequate number when the head of the state was leaving the state after serving the state with so much love and affection for the development of their own people. When I mentioned this to him, he gave a very brief response and told me, which I quote below and remember even today after more than 3 decades: "Manoharan Sahib, I will only tell you an Urdu saying after listening to your anguish, '*isiko kahthey hain – jane wale ko laatmaaro; aane wale ko salam karo*'. Mr. Manoharan, tomorrow you will see the difference when the new Governor will come to take over as head of the state of Assam."

When I and other senior officers visited the airport at Guwahati on the next day to welcome the new Governor, there was a very large crowd. Political leaders and representatives were jostling with each other to welcome him with *Gamochas* and bouquets. "What a fine and distinct presence, as exactly predicted by the Hon'ble Member of Parliament on the previous day." I would like to state that the statement made by The Member of Parliament was very true. This is what is called human psychology, i.e. it is better to welcome a new person, whoever he may be, a Governor or a Minister or a bureaucrat when he comes to take over because he might be of some help, assistance, or guidance to the person who would meet him during his course of stay. The human mind also works in a peculiar way; the person who had already served and left would be of no use or help or assistance by unnecessarily coming to the airport to bid farewell to him.

After the new Governor of Assam, Mr. Loknath Misra, took over, I went and called on him as a matter of courtesy and briefed him about the Department. He was polite and courteous and listened to me about the issues in the Department and also my suggestions for further improvement. In another couple of months, the President's rule was revoked, and popular rule was established. A new government took over, and I had to report to the Health Minister after the introduction of popular rule. The new Health Minister hailed from the North Cachar Hills District of Assam, where I had served as a Deputy Commissioner and head of the District Administration in the years 1980-81. However, at that time, I had not interacted with him. As a matter of courtesy, after he took over as Health Minister, I went and called on him.

Of course, the reader would like to appreciate and understand the difference of working in the realms of the President's rule and popular rule. It does not mean that during the popular rule the officers need not be candid and should be more circumspect while dealing with the political leaders as one's superior person. After all, the buck stops with him when a file is sent to him. The files are generally submitted by the Secretary to the government to the Minister concerned. Wherever necessary, the Minister might have to send the files to the Chief Minister unlike in the President's rule. In the President's rule, one had a free hand and the Secretary to the government reports to the adviser and by and large, there were no occasions for frictions, especially for decision-making on important issues. But it may not be so in times of popular rule whenever it comes to taking crucial decisions while a Secretary to government in a particular Department and especially in my case when I was Secretary to the Health and Family Welfare Department, it was my bounden duty and responsibility to explain to the Minister the issues involved and what exactly was the correct decision to be taken in certain circumstances.

In this regard, I would like to frankly state that the then Health Minister was not very knowledgeable, and his understanding was limited due to the fact that he was not well-educated. Very often, I used to go and meet him and tried to make him understand the importance of making correct decisions whenever certain files were sent to him in the best interest of the public. I also reiterated my stand that as a people's representative and as the Minister of that particular Department, the advice of the Health Secretary in a straightforward and impartial manner should be understood and appreciated by the Minister. I would not brook undue interference in the matter of making the correct decision, whatever compulsions might be expressed by the Minister concerned.

I would quote certain examples as below:

In fact, in respect of the medical college admissions conducted by the state Public Service Commission as per the rules and regulations, obviously, the selected candidates fulfilled the criteria laid down as per the rules and regulations of the government. Some of the unsuccessful boys and girls met the Health Minister and informed him that they had done very well and therefore they should get admission. Whosoever approached him with this kind of request and submitted their representations said that they had done very well in the examinations and somehow they were not selected. On such representations, he started writing the following words 'admit him' with his signature and sent back such representations to myself via the rejected candidates!!!

I was really surprised when boys and girls approached me with the orders of the Minister on their representations asking for admissions. I advised them to wait outside and went to the Minister's chamber. I told him that he had no authority to admit the candidates to the medical colleges just like that. I explained to him that there was a very clear-cut procedure, and the candidates were selected only after the thorough examination of their answer papers. Those who fulfilled the criteria were selected. Those who did not fulfil the criteria or obtain the requisite marks in the examinations had their requests or applications rejected. After listening to me, he asked me what the way out was to solve their requests or representations.

I informed him that the only way was to call for the answer sheets of such candidates and have a select Committee of Examiners to go through the answer sheets of such candidates. I told the Minister that the procedure suggested by me would be implemented in a very fair, impartial and transparent manner. During the scrutiny of their answer sheets, if it was ascertained that there was any mistake in the calculation of the marks obtained in the examinations, such cases could be reopened provided there were genuine mistakes. I informed him candidly that as per the rules there were no other options and the Minister did not have any discretion whatsoever to admit a candidate based on his representation only.

After I came back to my office chamber, I called the candidates who made such representations and informed them that at the most I could help them in the re-evaluation of the answer sheets as they were very sure about their excellent performance in their examinations. It would be done through a Selection Committee of Experts under my direct supervision. Incidentally, there was a gentleman who had worked with me long ago as my subordinate officer and had joined politics, and he had perhaps become an MLA. He told me that his daughter was brilliant and she got a fever; however, she did very well in the examination. I told him that the procedure that I explained to all other candidates was also equally applicable to his daughter as well. I told him and also the other candidates about the procedure that I suggested to the Health Minister for re-evaluation of the answer sheets of the examinations written by them, and the same was also accepted by the Minister. Therefore, there could not be any exception to anyone. In case during the re-evaluation by the Committee of Experts, if any mistake was identified, it would be set right. I also gave them an opportunity that the re-evaluation would be done in their presence and in my presence.

When the whole exercise of the re-evaluation was completed in all such cases, in respect of one particular candidate who belonged to the weaker section of the society, her application or representation was only found to be eligible for admission to the Medical College. The reason was that there was a mistake in the calculation of marks obtained by her, and the Committee of Experts understood that and recommended that because of this unintentional mistake of miscalculation of the total marks obtained by her, her candidature should be accepted, and she should be given admission in the first year of the MBBS Course in a Medical College, after observing proper formalities. I put up the file to the Minister for his approval for her admission in view of the procedure that was implemented in an absolutely transparent manner. Thereafter, no more representations came to the office, and I told the Minister that the only candidate would be eligible for admission in view of the mistake in the calculation of her answer sheets marks, and none else would be eligible. I also advised him to stop receiving any more representations and sending those representations and asking me to admit, which was illegal, and I would simply not accept such instructions.

I told him also very clearly that as the Commissioner and Secretary to the government of the Health and Family Welfare Department, I knew what I was doing with regard to not only the issue of medical college admissions but also in the proper adrministration of the Health & Family Welfare Department. At the cost of repetition, I categorically told him that it was my duty and responsibility to guide the Minister as per the rules and regulations not only in the matter of admission of candidates to the medical colleges but also in the matter of transfers and postings of officers and staff in various medical institutions in a fair, impartial, and transparent manner. He understood the style of my functioning as he knew about my posting earlier more than a decade ago as the then Deputy Commissioner in his own district. Sometimes I used to meet him with files and sometimes, I used to send subordinate officers to explain the details in the files clearly to him in the local language.

During my tenure as the Commissioner and Secretary of the Health and Family Welfare Department in the popular rule, another interesting incident took place. Another I.A.S. officer, 2 years junior to me, was also posted as Secretary to the Government of Assam in the Health and Family Welfare Department. The moment he received the order, he came to my room and requested me for work allocation. I told him that since he was a senior officer, he himself could decide his duties and responsibilities, and I would simply approve. He told me, "Sir, whatever you decide about the work allocation, I will abide by." In the meantime, there was an interview conducted by the Assam Public Service Commission office for filling up the vacancy of the Director of Health Services. As per the Service Commission rules and regulations, the Director of Health Services, being the head of the department for the whole state, underwent an interview conducted by the Chairman and Members of the Public Service Commission. I was invited to be present in case I had to give my opinion about the candidates who would appear before the selection committee. There was no issue of giving marks for anything like that by the Chairman and Members of the Commission, including myself, as a kind of observer during the selection process.

After the interview had begun, several candidates appeared before the Chairman and Members of the Service Commission and responded to their questions. If I might recall, the majority of the members decided to select the senior-most Joint Director of Health Services as Director of Health Services. Afterwards, it was sent in a sealed cover to the Commissioner & Secretary to the Government of Assam in the Health & Family Welfare Department, as it was an important assignment in the hierarchy of the Health and Family Welfare Department. Being an important head of the field-level formation of the Health services, the file had to be put up through the Chief Secretary to the Chief Minister. Of course, the file was sent by me only with the recommendation of the Chairman, Public Service Commission and Members of the Commission about one particular candidate who was selected purely on merit. The interesting thing was that the file was approved and sent by the Chief Minister the same afternoon. I advised the Deputy Secretary concerned to issue the formal orders. He informed me that the orders were issued and the selected candidate, i.e. the new Director of Health Services, collected the order from the office, went back to his office, and took over his new assignment in the Directorate of Health Services immediately.

Late in the night, the Chief Minister called me to know whether the orders were issued, and I informed him that as it was already approved by him, orders were issued. He again informed me that it would be better to cancel that particular order, and he would send the next day an instruction in the form of a note. On the next day, the Chief Minister's advice in the form of a written note came, informing that the selected candidate's order may be cancelled, and another candidate who had also attended the interview might be issued the order of appointment. This particular gentleman felt that he would be able to influence the Chief Secretary and Chief Minister because of his connections and that it would be very easy to get the appointment order for him by cancellation of the previous order, which had been issued for the other selected candidate on merit. He knew very well that he was not recommended by the Service Commission for posting as Director of Health Services, as his performance during the interview was far from satisfactory.

As was expected by me, there was a note or instruction from the Chief Minister's Office to the Department of Health & Family Welfare on the next day. The Deputy Secretary concerned put up the file with the Chief Minister's instruction to the Chief Secretary. On that file, the Chief Secretary simply signed without giving his remarks. I was really very much upset, and therefore I made the following observation:

"The Chief Minister was aware that the orders were issued in the previous evening only for the selected candidate as recommended by the Assam Public Service Commission as Director of Health Services. At this stage, it would be unwise to reconsider that particular order or cancel the order as it might involve a legal wrangle. I apprehended that in case the selected candidate who already joined as Director of Health Service would certainly approach the Hon'ble High Court of Guwahati if his order was cancelled and the new candidate was allowed to join in his place. Of course,

I informed candidly that the Chief Minister may kindly consider consulting the Legal Remembrancer (LR) or the Law Secretary regarding my suggestion. I made this remark and sent back the file to the Chief Minister's Office."

During that particular period, I had already applied for a few days of leave with headquarters to visit Darjeeling for some personal commitment, and the same was approved by the Chief Secretary to the Government of Assam before this issue was raised. Since I had to go on leave the next day, I went and met the Chief Secretary and informed him that I would perhaps not continue to serve in the Health & Family Welfare Department when I come back from leave.

Commissioner of Lower Assam Division, Guwahati from December 1991 to May 1992

After I came back from my leave and as foreseen by me, I was informed that I was posted as Commissioner of Lower Assam Division at Guwahati Headquarters. I was not surprised as the same was expected. Out of sheer curiosity before I left the Department of Health & Family Welfare, in order to join as Commissioner of Lower Assam Division on my next assignment, I spoke to the concerned Deputy Secretary to the government in the Health & Family Welfare Department and ascertained from him what was the development in that particular file and what were the orders given in that file by the Chief Minister. He informed me that the Chief Minister had ordered very briefly the following:

'Consult the LR (Legal Remembrancer) later, but issue the order', as the order was issued by him i.e. cancellation of the posting order which was given to a candidate duly selected by the Assam Public Service Commission (APSC) and issue of a new order to the candidate who was not selected by the APSC but as recommended by the Chief Minister. My successor, who was only 2 years junior to me and had joined a few days before I went on leave, promptly complied with the orders of the Chief Minister.

The consequence of this action was, as noted by me in the file, that such a course of action might involve legal complications. The candidate who was selected by the Assam Public Service Commission and who was issued the original order went and approached the High Court of Guwahati and promptly got a stay order on the appointment of the new person. Before issuing the stay order, the Hon'ble High Court of Guwahati called for the relevant documents and the file regarding the issue of the posting order of the Director of Health Services based on the recommendation of the

Assam Public Service Commission. After examining the file, scrutinising, and, of course, listening to the plea made by the applicant who was the affected party, the Hon'ble High Court of Guwahati issued the stay order in respect of the person recommended by the Chief Minister of Assam and the orders that were issued by my junior colleague. It was a moral victory for the person who was denied justice in the original instance.

In the first week of December 1991, I took over my next assignment, i.e. Commissioner of Lower Assam Division at Guwahati. The reader might understand and appreciate that I worked as the Commissioner and Secretary to the Government of Assam in the Health and Family Welfare Department exactly for one-year, i.e. around 6 months during President's rule and 6 months during popular rule.

There were several districts under my jurisdiction. In other words, I was a supervisory officer of the Deputy Commissioners within my jurisdiction. In those days, the Deputy Commissioner, apart from looking after his primary role as district Magistrate in charge of maintenance of law and order and other issues, was also the Chairman of the district Development Committee (DDC). I had decided that I should undertake tours in all the districts one after another by drawing up a travel programme. I kept the Deputy Commissioners concerned informed a few days before with a request to convene the meetings of the district Development Committee. The very purpose and objective was to understand and appreciate how far the Deputy Commissioner was concerned about the developmental administration within his jurisdiction and whether he was in a position to make effective supervision over the heads of the departments within his district. So when I went to a particular district, of course, the Deputy Commissioner only presided over the district Development Committee (DDC) meeting in the Circuit House as there was a very large number of district-level officers like Heads of Development Departments i.e. Drinking Water Supply, Medical and Health, PWD, Irrigation, Agriculture, etc.

In some of the meetings presided over by the Deputy Commissioner of the district, I could guess that some of them were not fully aware of what was happening on the ground; perhaps, they had not had sufficient time to supervise and intervene or in some cases there was the least amount of interest on their part. Therefore, in such meetings, I started asking too many questions to the officers present, especially the Heads of Development Departments, much to their embarrassment and the discomfiture of the Deputy Commissioner.

I made sure that I would definitely contribute my mite to the best of my abilities in whichever assignment that was given to me during my service period. For instance, if an officer wanted to while away his time, he would easily relax, and once in a while, he could undertake such tours for the sake of conducting tours and meetings of the Deputy Commissioner and other officers concerned. As I took my job very seriously, I visited each and every district within my jurisdiction and advised the Deputy Commissioner concerned to conduct the DDC meeting as per the timetable worked by me, as it would suit me and also give them sufficient time to organise such meetings with the officers of the development departments.

Deputy Commissioners were not used to this kind of intervention by the Commissioner of the Division, though they knew very well that the Commissioner of a Division was their supervisory officer. Perhaps, my predecessors would not have undertaken such tours and conducted such meetings in such a serious and lengthy manner and gone into the depth with regard to the implementation of various schemes for the welfare of the people. During the meetings, though I did not preside over them, the Deputy Commissioner was only the Chairman of the district Development Committee. In my capacity as the supervisory officer of Deputy Commissioners, I had considered that I had every right and responsibility to intervene and pull up the Development Department officers concerned wherever I noticed their lacunae or insincerity or delays, etc., in the matter of implementation of welfare schemes.

Frankly speaking, the district Development Committee meetings were expected to meet periodically, and perhaps, my intervention made such meetings very regular and business-like. Perhaps some of the field-level officers would have found it rather too difficult as they could not afford to relax and execute the schemes according to their sweet will and used to delay the implementation of the schemes. I made it a point that in addition to conducting meetings, I visited various field formations to verify whether the averments made by the district Development officers were true regarding their roles in the implementation of schemes entrusted to them. In a way, it was rather a good augury only to help the Deputy Commissioners exercise their authority with a little more sincerity. But many of the Development Department officers perhaps could not understand and appreciate my direct interference not only during the meetings but also during the field-level inspections concerning their departments. I had an apprehension that some of them might have taken up this issue with the powers that be, suggesting it would be better to get my transfer. I guess, as otherwise, there could be no other reason for me to be transferred within a period of 6 months, i.e., from the first week of December 1991 to the first week of May 1992 as the Commissioner of Lower Assam Division.

Chief Electoral Officer and Commissioner and Secretary to the Government of Assam in the Election Department at Dispur, Guwahati from May 1992 to October 1994

Chief Electoral Officer

I was transferred and posted as the Chief Electoral Officer (CEO) of Assam and Commissioner and Secretary to the Government of Assam in the Election Department. Perhaps, as the Chief Electoral Officer of Assam, I was expected by the State Government to keep myself quiet as there was no immediate chance of conducting elections. So, in a way, I could relax and perhaps the State Government senior officers might have thought that I would not be as active as I was as a Divisional Commissioner. Generally, in the past, the appointment order of the Chief Electoral Officer of the state is issued by the Election Commission of India based on the recommendation of the panel of names sent by the State Government to the office of the Chief Election Commissioner. But in my case, it was not such a simple issue of an order.

Mr. T.N. Seshan was the Chief Election Commissioner (CEC) of India, and he issued a lengthy two-page order appointing me as the Chief Electoral Officer of Assam. The substance of the order briefly stated that as the Chief Electoral Officer of the State of Assam, I had to work under the direct control, superintendence, and directions of the Chief Election Commissioner of India only and none else. In other words, it meant that I should not take any instructions or orders from the State Government concerned on any issues pertaining to my functioning as the then Chief Electoral Officer of Assam.

The Chief Election Commissioner of India issued a very clear-cut direction to me as the Chief Electoral Officer of Assam after I had joined that the intensive revision of electoral rolls should begin within the next few months. The crux of the issue was that door-to-door enumeration was to be organised, and proper verification should be done about each and every voter. As there were lots of allegations in Assam that many foreigners i.e. illegal migrants had been enrolled as electors, he had decided that before the draft publication of electoral rolls, the Chief Electoral Officer's responsibility was to give directions to the district Election Officers to prepare a list of doubtful categories of citizens as well wherever they had suspicion that such persons might not be Indian nationals. The important feature of this process of intensive revision of electoral rolls for the whole state was the appointment of approximately 100 I.A.S. officers as observers at different points of time. The electoral rolls revision work commenced with the door-to-door enumeration of the electors exactly on 14th April 1993, and that was a public holiday, and moreover, it was the popular Bihu festival time. I had brought to the notice of the Chief Election Commissioner that by and large, the people of Assam would not be happy to have this process of door-to-door enumeration done during this festival time, and their own officers were unwilling to work during that important festival time. But Mr. T.N. Seshan, the Chief Election Commissioner, was a difficult personality, and he made it a point that once the decision was announced by him, he would strictly adhere only to it. Since I took over as the Chief Electoral Officer in the month of May 1992, enough time was there to get the enumeration cards and other documents necessary for door-to-door enumeration leading to the intensive revision of rolls in a detailed and meticulous manner. All such documents were prepared and kept ready by that time on 14th April 1993 when the work on the whole intensive revision process throughout Assam commenced. To begin with, 18 I.A.S. officers were posted in the 1st week of April 1993 as observers. The situation was tense, and the Chief Electoral Officer was given very clear instructions that adequate safety and security measures in addition to accommodation arrangements must be made for the observers concerned. As I was the person responsible as the head of the organisation as CEO, I had to ensure that each and every observer was given a Personal Security Officer, a pilot vehicle, and an escort vehicle. It would be pertinent to remind the reader that Assam was a state that had by then suffered almost 15 years of insurgency-driven unrest.

Since it was the first time that 18 senior I.A.S. officers as observers landed at Guwahati airport, I had to organise 18 vehicles separately for the observers in addition to 18 pilot vehicles and 18 escort vehicles. There was a kind of a big procession of vehicles of the officers when all of them were expected to meet me at the secretariat and to get the briefings for their work. If I may say in a lighter vein, one of my senior colleagues called me on the phone to know why and for what purpose so many VIPs were coming with such a display of so many police pilot and escort vehicles.

So at different points of time, the different observers came to visit the districts. They met me on the very first day of arrival before they proceeded to their concerned districts; I gave them a complete set of instructions as had been given by the Chief Electoral Officer to the district Election Officers. I briefly made them understand and ensured that they were happy about the safety and security arrangements made for them. Out of 18 senior I.A.S. observers, some of them turned out to be my own batch mates. When I met them in my office chamber, I informed them that after visiting the different districts and field formations, they were most welcome to bring to my notice any deficiencies or lacunae on the part of the field-level officers under the supervision of the district Election Officers. I also requested them to bring to my notice any modifications that might be required or if they were not happy with the instructions sent to district Election Officers and their subordinates and that they were most welcome to give their comments or suggestions about my functioning as the Chief Electoral Officer, Assam and whether I had faltered in following up the directions of the Chief Election Commissioner of India.

It is a fact that the Chief Election Commissioner did not budge from his stand, and he insisted that the intensive revision of electoral rolls should commence only on the 14th April 1993. For the Assamese people, it was a New Year Day, and it was also *Bohag Bihu* or otherwise called *Rangaali Bihu*. It was the most important festival in Assam; the celebrations and festivities continued for almost a month. Obviously, the officers who were drafted for the enumeration of the voters to begin with were drawn from the district, sub-divisional, and Taluk Administrations only. None of them were very happy to have been drafted for this important work as they were expected to perform door-to-door enumeration of eligible electors in villages, rural areas, semi-urban areas, urban areas, and the cities all over the State of

Assam under the direct supervision of the district Election Officers. The observers, mostly senior I.A.S. Officers, who were drafted for this particular work of supervision, were directed by the Election Commission (EC) of India to visit a day or 2 before and meet me, and also the concerned district Election Officers before proceeding to the field.

As advised by the Chief Election Commissioner and as per the directions of the Election Commission of India (ECI), I had, in my capacity as the Chief Electoral Officer of Assam, sent a series of instructions to all the district Election Officers. The instructions were crystal clear and transparent, and there was nothing more to be explained except in understanding and implementing them. On the very first day when 18 observers landed from Guwahati Airport in my office, along with the requisite paraphernalia of security, etc., I hosted them a proper lunch and gave them a set of instructions. I informed them that from that day onwards for the next few days, there were holidays declared by the government in view of the local, traditional Bihu festival.

I was at pains to inform them that this exercise was undertaken as per the directions of the Election Commission of India (ECI), much to the dislike of the officers and staff in various districts. I wondered if the people would give the requisite co-operation in giving the information whenever the enumerators were deputed to different villages by the officers concerned. However, it was a call of duty to everyone to begin with myself onwards till the last man in the field-level formation in addition to the observers who were deputed in different districts as per the directions of the Election Commission of India.

After lunch and the thorough briefing, each observer went with the complete set of instructions to various allotted destinations. The latter group of observers was advised to proceed to the allotted destinations straight from the Guwahati airport. I had already made arrangements for the personal security officers to carry the set of instructions for each and every observer with whom he would be working during his stay in the state. The whole process of door-to-door enumerations, as per the instructions given by the Election Commission of India, by field-level officers to various houses in the villages, rural areas, urban areas, semi-urban areas, towns, and District Headquarters, took several months.

The observers were originally posted to visit the concerned field formations in a particular district for a week only. After they left, another set of observers was directed to reach the State of Assam by the Election Commission of India. In this process, more than 100 senior I.A.S. officers visited the state at different points of time, and some of them never met me. They would only speak to me on the phone if there were any doubts or if they wished to have any sort of clarifications. Of course, I took excellent care of the observers regarding their accommodation and food arrangements, including that of their personal security officers. The police officers deputed in the pilot and escort vehicles from various districts, along with observers, were also taken good care of in different districts, in addition to their stay and boarding arrangements. To that extent, I had given detailed instructions to all the district Election Officers who happened to be the Deputy Commissioners and Sub-Divisional Officers of the Government of Assam.

As per the directions of the Chief Election Commissioner of India, as the head of the election Department and in my capacity as Chief Electoral Officer of Assam, I had to take various trips and go on tours to different parts of the state. In a way, I had travelled to various District Headquarters and sub-divisional headquarters in a little more than a year and in some places, I went with the observers themselves during the enumeration process. In the very first briefing meeting of the observers, I had given categorical instructions that they were welcome to accompany the enumerators and senior officers during the enumeration process and to visit various homes or houses wherever they were posted to supervise their functioning; but I had also given them very clear instructions that under no circumstances, neither the field-level officers nor enumerators including the observers should enter their houses. They should only stand outside and start collecting the information for the purpose of enumeration of the eligible voters which would ultimately enable the Chief Electoral Officer of Assam to publish the draft electoral rolls. The observers were also observing me whenever I went with them during the enumeration process as to how I conducted myself. I politely refused whenever the villagers or people in the urban areas, out of courtesy and respect, invited me and the observers to come inside for a cup of tea.

After all, I or the enumerator or any field-level officer or the observers had a limited role to play in the whole gigantic exercise of preparation of draft electoral rolls (hereafter called DER) for the state strictly in accordance with the directions of the Election Commission of India. The CEC had given clear and precise instructions that the draft electoral rolls should consist only of Indian citizens based on the documents that were listed in the series of instructions given by the Chief Election Commissioner and communicated by me as the CEO of the state. Wherever there were doubtful cases about citizenship, the enumerators and field-level officers were directed to prepare another set of draft electoral rolls. The whole idea was to ensure that the draft electoral rolls were error-free before publication. When the whole exercise was going on, political representatives belonging to various parties including the ruling, opposition, and other parties were very much interested in meeting me to ascertain whether the entire process was undertaken in a fair, impartial, straightforward, and transparent manner. One such delegation included among its members a former Chief Minister of Assam, a former Minister of Assam, and some MLAs. I was extremely courteous and polite during my conversations with them as the head of the election Department. I informed all of them clearly that the process of door-to-door enumerations and issuing instructions to field-level officers including for the benefit of observers was done in an absolutely transparent manner. I told them that there need be no doubt in anyone's mind that there would be mistakes at the time of the publication of the draft electoral rolls (DER) at the final stage. The entire verification during the enumeration process was strictly done as per the Election Commission's directions only. There was effective supervision at every level in the hierarchy of administration, especially at the level of the Chief Electoral Officer, the Additional Chief Electoral Officers, the Deputy Secretaries to the Government of Assam in the Election Department and of course, the field-level formations like the offices of district Election Officers, and the Sub-Divisional Officers, Taluk officers, and other subordinate formations.

The whole process of intensive revision of electoral rolls took considerable time that went on until October 1994. There were 126 Legislative Assemblies in the State of Assam. During the entire process of the intensive revision of electoral rolls in the state, the exercise was almost through, perhaps to the extent of 90% or so, barring a few constituencies.

Before I could complete the publication of draft electoral rolls (DEC) for the complete set of 126 legislative assembly Constituencies, there was an opportunity for me to go abroad to pursue a one-year Post Graduate degree Programme for the degree of Master of Arts in International Development Studies at the University of Bradford in the United Kingdom.

Thus, by the end of September 1994 with the sincerest efforts of my erstwhile colleagues in the Election Department and field-level formations in the districts and sub-divisions, in addition to the wonderful co-operation extended by the dozens and dozens of I.A.S. officers who had served as observers, we were in a position to complete the exercise of publication of draft electoral rolls for almost all the constituencies except for a few legislative constituencies of the state.

If I remember correctly, we had prepared 2 lists of draft electoral rolls, i.e. one set of the electoral rolls with voters whose citizenship was established beyond doubt and another set of electoral rolls for individuals whose citizenship was in the doubtful category. I completed the publication of the draft electoral rolls and published the same with the approval of the Election Commission of India.

With the completion of the task in hand, the Chief Election Commissioner of India was gracious enough to permit me to proceed to the United Kingdom for the one-year study programme to pursue a Post Graduate degree, i.e. Master of Arts in International Development Studies at the University of Bradford, United Kingdom.

Before I left for overseas, I did have the satisfaction of discharging my duties and responsibilities as the Chief Electoral Officer of Assam in a very challenging role given the circumstances. There was political unrest against the publication of the draft electoral rolls, but as a sincere civil servant, I discharged my duties and responsibilities strictly as per the direction, superintendence and control of the Chief Election Commissioner, scrupulously adhering to the directions of the Election Commission of India. Of course, there was no question of interference from the State Government. Though I had functioned as the senior officer of the State Government and that too, as the head of the election department, I never reported either to the Chief Secretary or to the Minister in charge of Elections, who incidentally happened to be the Chief Minister of Assam.

Indeed, I never called on the Chief Minister of Assam in view of the clear-cut directions to me by the Chief Election Commissioner. Again, on the Chief Election Commissioner's instruction, I rarely went to meet the Chief Secretary.

It was really a very challenging assignment under the direct superintendence, control, and direction of the Chief Election Commission of India, while being an officer of the State cadre of the I.A.S. The reader might not even appreciate how I had spent more than a couple of years without any sort of interference from the State Government, i.e. either the Chief Secretary or the Chief Minister. The style, the manner, and the interactions of the Chief Election Commissioner during the conferences of Chief Electoral Officers were unforgettable. I vividly remember his instructions conveyed in clear-cut and precise language. Of course, he was an excellent speaker and a wonderful orator.

During my Elections Commissioners were appointed by the Government of India. Mr. T. N. Seshan, the CEC, challenged their appointments in the Hon'ble Supreme Court of India, and the case went on through several hearings, etc., and had not concluded until the end of my term in October 1994. There was no doubt that the 2 new Election Commissioners were not allotted any work relating to their roles as Election Commissioners.

Since the then Chief Election Commissioner challenged the appointment of the other 2 Election Commissioners in the Hon'ble Supreme Court of India, the matter was sub-judice. In order to defend his action, the CEC filed a very comprehensive affidavit stating the rationale behind the appointment of the Chief Election Commissioner only as a one-man Election Commission of India since the inception of the office of the CEC. He quoted various discussions made in the Constituent Assembly about the role and functions of the Election Commission of India and narrated in a logical and sequential manner as to why the Election Commission of India should have only one member, the CEC. He sent copies of that very well-drafted affidavit to the Chief Electoral Officers of all the states. I read word by word that particular affidavit, which was not only lengthy but a very well-drafted, admirable document. I wanted to know who exactly prepared that particular affidavit, and so I talked to the Secretary, Election Commission of India, Mr. Kutty. His honest response was that none other than the Chief Election Commissioner himself could have prepared a self-contained, comprehensive, and eminently drafted affidavit.

In the meantime, I got my deputation order from the Government of India to proceed to the United Kingdom to pursue my course, and I was also relieved by the State Government. I left the Election Department after handing over charge to my successor. Of course, the successor was selected by the then CEC as he was aware that I had to proceed abroad for training purposes.

Last but not the least, I would like to record my sincere appreciation about my appointment as the Chief Electoral Officer of Assam for 2 and a half years, my wonderful and memorable interactions with Mr. T.N. Seshan, the CEC, during my meetings with him as well as in the conferences presided over by him during my tenure. I was, of course, an admirer of his ability to speak fluently extempore in a beautiful language, and one could learn a lot about his writing skills, in particular, as I had thoroughly read the affidavit drafted and filed by him in the Hon'ble Supreme Court of India. After all, every human being has his own weakness and strength, and fortunately, Mr. T. N. Seshan never had the occasion to let his anger or harsh words be directed at me during my many interactions with him. He was always very kind to me, maybe due to my own temperament and also undoubtedly due to my style of interactions with him in an absolutely straightforward and transparent manner. I was always well-prepared to attend his meetings, and I could candidly speak in the conferences without any inhibitions, and despite the fact that other colleagues like some of the Chief Electoral Officers of other states were rather hesitant to talk in the manner in which I could interact. I had learnt a lot during my interactions with him as I was more interested in public speaking in a flawless manner and that too, in a style of my own, like Mr. T.N. Seshan's style.

One-year Training Programme at the University of Bradford, U.K. From October 1994 to October 1995

I was selected for the British Council's scholarship for pursuing a one-year Post Graduate degree i.e. MA in International Development studies at the University of Bradford, U.K.

Prior to my departure to the United Kingdom, I had to collect my passport from the office of the Regional Passport Officer, Guwahati. It so happened that the RPO Guwahati once worked with me as a senior supervisory assistant during the troubled days of Assam, especially during the Assam turmoil in the year 1983 when I served as the then Joint Secretary to the Government of Assam, in the Home and Political Departments. Mr. R. C. Malakkar (perhaps, I do not fully recollect his first name or initials) was sincere, hardworking, and a thorough gentleman. During those troubled days when there was so much stress and tension all around, he worked with absolute loyalty, commitment, and dedication to serve the state. It was particularly commendable that he was available at the secretariat during that particular period of turmoil when very few office staff were available to work. He would have been perhaps recommended for the post of Regional Passport Officer of Guwahati at that time, taking into consideration his sincerity of purpose and hard work at a time when the state was witnessing a non-co-operation movement. When I was leaving the State of Assam in October 1994, I had collected the passport not only for me but also for my wife and son. As I was already serving in the super-time scale of I.A.S., Mr. R. C. Malakkar insisted on giving me a red passport, i.e. Diplomatic Passport, and he also jovially informed that my son and wife would also be travelling on the Diplomatic Passports only along with me. Of course, I never asked for this favour from him, and he on his own volunteered to hand over the 3 Diplomatic Passports to me, my wife, and my son. We thanked him profusely and left Guwahati for Delhi on the next day.

I collected the British Airways tickets for myself, my wife, and my son. Here I may like to add that the Government of Assam was kind enough to allow me to draw my salary in advance for the whole year during my one-year of absence abroad. I converted that money into dollars for my expenses during my studies in the U.K. The British Council Office had given clear travel instructions to me. After I landed at Heathrow Airport in London, I had to take a connecting flight to Manchester and then take a train to Bradford. I was told that at Manchester Railway Station, a volunteer from the British Council would meet me and hand over 760 pounds or so as my immediate requirement for settling down once I reached Bradford.

When we reached Manchester Railway Station, a senior British lady met us and handed over the envelope containing an amount of 760 pounds. She was careful enough to count the money in our presence before handing it over. She was also helpful in transferring our luggage onto the train for our onward journey to Bradford. After getting down at the railway station at Bradford Interchange, we had to hire a taxi to go to a nearby hotel. The taxi driver took us to a hotel and left us there. It so happened that the Hotel Manager was a Gujarati gentleman. He gave us a good room, and after that we strolled out and found a Pakistani restaurant where we had a nice late lunch.

We learnt much about the Gujarati community in Bradford during our initial days there. During our initial stay at the hotel, we learnt how the Gujaratis in Bradford celebrated the Navaratri Festival. We had never witnessed Garbha dance until then. The Hotel Manager was kind enough to take all of us one night to a nearby venue where the festival was celebrated by the local Gujaratis. There was much joy and gaiety all around, and ladies and gentlemen went round and round performing the Garbha. I really admired that they were all dancing without any fatigue continuously into the night

After our breakfast on the next day, I left my wife and son at the hotel and went straight to the University of Bradford, which was at a walkable distance. I reported for studies at the faculty like so many new foreign students who had come. In the coming days we all started searching for proper accommodation to stay. There was no question of hostel accommodation for any of us foreign students. I visited the bank also and got my ATM card from Barclays Bank. Again, let me remind the reader that this was 1994 – everything was a novelty for us, whether it was ATM cards, computers all around, or relatively more ubiquitous mobile phones.

After visiting a few housing options, we came to know of a beautiful house in a location called Clayton. It was at the end of a 'cul-de-sac' (i.e. a road that is not a thoroughfare). It was owned by another Gujarati gentleman. We really liked the house. It was slightly expensive for us –287 pounds per month.

Once we moved in, though, we realised that it was a rather foolish mistake made by us. It was away from public transport, and it required us to walk half a kilometre even to get a bottle of milk.

Since I was only getting 519 pounds a month; spending more than half of the stipend on housing was not a great decision. We did not realise at that time that there were other living expenses to be considered as well – water, power, gas, all of which were much more expensive than what we were accustomed to in India. Even regular TV (not satellite or cable) required a licence fee of approximately 90 pounds per year.

I consulted some of my other colleagues, and again, I started searching for rental accommodation closer to the university campus.

Thankfully, we found another accommodation after a month or so, and our landlord, although a bit irritated, understood our situation and even helped us move to the new place.

I was fortunate in getting a two-bedroom flat that was owned by a Pakistani taxi driver. In British parlance, they called it a terraced house. A terraced house means a series of such houses adjacent to each other. I even now remember the door number of that house; it was 144, Wood head Road, Bradford. I had to haggle with the Pakistani taxi driver for a reasonable monthly rent. He was very happy to rent out his accommodation to us and finally agreed to 210 pounds per month as the monthly rent for his flat. In addition to that, the gas, light, and water consumption charges would be around 90 to 100 pounds a month. So we were left with nearly 200 to 230 pounds per month for other expenses. Fortunately, in England at that time, the food items were not costly, and we used to go to the supermarkets nearby and collect the provisions, including vegetables, so that my wife could cook at home for all 3 of us.

The system in the U.K. was that every month, the house owner would come with a notebook, collect the rent, and take our signatures in recognition of our payment. It was a good system in a way that everything was well laid down. It took some time for us to settle down, as we were on our own without any help like servants, staff, or anything like the paraphernalia we had in the State of Assam, where we had been residents earlier. There were 2 supermarkets in our neighbourhood, namely, Haq Halal and Al Halal, owned by immigrant Pakistanis, where all provisions and vegetables were available. At some distance away, we had a departmental store called Morison.

I had to walk to the university every day even though the distance was less than half a kilometre. My son, who happened to be a student, had to go by bus to study in standard 9 at Thornton Grammar School.

After a couple of months, we went to a nearby place called York City, not very far from Bradford and for the first time, we experienced snowfall, which was rather exciting for us. It was a novel experience for us to see the snowfall. During winter, i.e. in the months of December and January, Bradford was subject to severe snowfall, and the road between our residence and the university was full of snow. More than snow, it was ice on pavements that we had to be careful about. It could keep drizzling off and on throughout the day, and by night, with sub-zero temperatures, the rainwater on roads and pavements would freeze, leaving a layer of very thin ice that would not be visible to the human eye. One had to tread very carefully while walking, and I fell down a couple of times as well. This in itself was an unforgettable experience. However, there was the danger of fracturing one's hand or leg due to the fall if one was not fortunate enough.

When I looked back on those days and if I jog my memory, it was quite difficult to study at the age of 44 bereft of government accommodation and transport which were available to me in my various postings and assignments till then in India. This was the first time in October 1994 to October 1995 when I had to stay with my family in a private rental house and had to go everywhere on foot or by taxi if required. I did not feel bad at all that almost after 2 decades of my tenure in the I.A.S., I had to start my life all over again in a foreign country as a Post Graduate (PG) student, more than two decades after I had completed my Post Graduation in the years 1971 to 1973 at my Alma mater, Annamalai University, near Chidambaram.

Though times had changed and the we were living without the perks that an IAS officer would have access to, within India, it was also a memorable experience for me and my family as for the first time we had become tenants of the private rental accommodation, taking into consideration the fact that my wife had only stayed in big government quarters after our marriage. I deliberately mention these details to make the reader aware of adaptability required, which is also a characteristic of the services. One had to adapt to different kinds of situations in different assignments. But after 2 decades of service, if one had become a student, devoid of all facilities as a government Servant, one might go rather depressed, but I literally started liking my student life once again. It was really a pleasant thing to remember that on the very first day of my son's admission into his school at a distance of 2 or 3 kilometres, I had taken him to that school from the City Centre by bus. We both, father and son were students in 2 different institutions at the same time.

Getting a school admission for my son also was a process. Here again, there was a procedure for me to apply for an interview with the district-level educational officer who was taking care of the administration of Public Schools. When I mention the public school, it is nothing but a government school.

All 3 of us were interviewed. Since English was our second language after our mother tongue Tamil, there was absolutely no problem, and within a few minutes, the interview was over, and they decided that my son could join Thornton Grammar School. Of course, it was at a distance from the place where we were residing. I had to guide my son on the very first day to take the bus to the school premises. When he reached the school, we met the Principal, and he advised us to meet the lady at the Reception for filling up the application form for his admission. The lady was a teacher, and she requested me to give the details of wherefrom we had landed in Bradford and the purpose of admission to the school.

I filled in a very simple form in a few minutes. She looked at me with rather delight and could not believe that I had filled in that form within a couple of minutes. She appreciated the style of my writing and immediately admitted my son. The books were given for free. She gave us the correct timings of the schools, and we all came back after some time after going around the school. The reader would be surprised to know that the school was over 350 years old, a government school with a huge set of facilities including multiple outdoor and indoor sports facilities.

It was rather an unusual sight to see how many sports facilities were available to the young kids, especially in a government school.

On the next day, once again I took my son and guided him, and thereafter, it became a regular routine for him to go on his own.

We gradually settled down at Bradford. My wife, though unemployed in the U.K., became a 'housewife' at that time. It is for the benefit of the reader I would like to indicate that though my wife was a highly qualified doctor, she could not take up the medical profession in the United Kingdom as her degree was not recognised by the government of the United Kingdom. In case my wife had to practice or join a hospital, she had to appear in a test called PLAB, i.e. Proficiency in Language and Aptitude Test.

One day my wife was getting bored, as both of us were in our respective institutions she went to the local employment exchange. There she came across an American Gentleman. He told her after knowing that she was a medical graduate that his wife was a doctor and Senior Consultant at Airdale Hospital in Skipton, which was at a distance of 20 km from Bradford. This gentleman was a freelance film producer. He insisted that she should meet his wife even though, as per British rules and regulations, my wife was not supposed to work or practice in any hospital. He advised her to visit Skipton and meet his wife at the hospital as a sort of introduction only. The most interesting thing is that my wife had to spend some money and took a local train from Bradford to Skipton and went on her own and met the doctor. Her name was Dr. Mary Harrington. She was happy to have met my wife and she took her to the Geriatric wards of the hospital and guided her through the hospital and also informed her how they had conducted the tests and treated them with care and caution. This is only to illustrate that everywhere you would come across good people at heart and she had no business to do this but out of a sense of decency for the next human being, she guided her about different functions in the entire hospital and explained about the manner of treatment, etc. Of course, with a clear-cut direction that my wife should not touch any patient. Thereafter, at the invitation of the doctor, my wife went for a couple of hours every week to that hospital just to gain knowledge about the latest innovations and the kind of medicines given to the patients and types of treatment given to the old patients. It was so very nice of Mr. Robert; Dr. Mary Harrington's husband to invite us for dinner as well one day.

In the meanwhile, on one day while I was getting down the stairs at the university faculty, one Assamese officer came and met me. He introduced himself and wanted to check whether it was myself along with my wife who had gone to Jorhat to attend a wedding of one of his relatives in Assam more than a year ago. He was very impressed with my fluency in Assamese. Incidentally we had met before. When we had visited his relative's wedding in Jorhat, my wife was working at the ESI hospital in Guwahati. I forget his name, but he was an officer in the technical department and had come to attend a three-month training programme on some technical issues. He told me that there was an Assamese doctor named Dr. K.K. Das who had his own surgery and would be delighted to meet me and my family as we were also fluent in Assamese. He also informed me that in addition to Dr. K.K. Das, there were many Assamese doctors in Bradford and other nearby places. He added that they would all be delighted to meet us.

He took my address and probably informed Dr. K.K. Das about my meeting with him at the university and also my residence address in Bradford. The very same evening, Dr. K.K. Das landed at my residence and took me, my wife, and son to his house for dinner. They were a wonderful couple, and we became a sort of his family members in our very first meeting. I vividly remember their love and affection and the wonderful hospitality with which he treated myself, my wife, and my son. The only regret for him was that I was only having orange juice and was not taking any hard liquor. He offered me quite a lot of varieties of hard liquor to tempt me. I had told him candidly that as I had made a commitment to my wife after my marriage in November 1979, I never touched liquor thereafter despite many provocations and difficult situations as well. He was a bit upset, otherwise was our very happy and wonderful host. I told him that he was not to worry as I would finish the entire bottle of orange juice.

After I got introduced to Dr. K.K. Das, one after another we had been introduced to so many Assamese doctors and their families living in different places near Bradford. In a way, it was a great opportunity for us to have interacted with so many Assamese doctors who had come from different parts of Assam to serve and settle down in the U.K. The reader may refuse to believe me if I say that the doctors took us around in their own vehicles to Liverpool, Manchester, Stockton, Skipton, and some other cities. Some of them were working in the hospital, and some of them were running their surgeries. There was another Assamese doctor by the name of Dr. M.E. Haque whom I had met in Bradford. He was a visiting doctor to the hospitals, and he was also not staying very far from Bradford, and we had the pleasure of his hospitality on several occasions.

In a way, all of them were very good human beings apart from the fact that they were medical professionals. I had also come across a Bengali doctor gentleman who used to take us for dinner to a very good restaurant. We might have visited their residences many times.

As I had mentioned in the foregoing paragraphs, most of the Assamese doctors whom we had come across were extremely good, kind-hearted doctors and treated us as their own family members. Dr. K.K. Das went a step further. He advised us to vacate the flat where we had lived towards the end of the course for about 4 months and wanted us to shift to his own place above the surgery he used to run. The surgery or clinic was a 3-story building which had 2 rooms on the ground floor for the doctor and the pharmacists, and on the first floor, there were medicines and staff nurses who were present to take care of the visiting patients. On the second floor, the attic, there were 2 rooms, one was like a kitchen, and the other was a hall. What Dr. K.K. Das offered was that we could shift to the second floor where we could use one portion as a kitchen and another portion as a bedroom where he would provide all the necessities for the next 4 months before our departure for home. The very fact he had suggested this course of action was not only to help us in saving the rentals for 4 months but also to help us visit the neighbouring countries on a 15-day trip to Paris, Belgium, Cologne, and Amsterdam. It was so very kind hearted of him to offer this.

While travelling on a 15-day trip during the recess was a wish for us, there was one hitch when we looked at the passports. Generally, in those days after you arrived at the Immigration Counter, the Immigration officer would indicate that you were allowed to stay for a particular period, i.e. this is what actually completed the visa process. However, this was not indicated in all 3 of our passports. This was ascertained when I visited our High Commission Office in London. One of my friends at the High Commission Office looked at the passports and informed me categorically that with this kind of entry by the Immigration officer on our arrival, we would not be able to come back once we went on any foreign trips. So, I was rather perplexed. He advised me to contact the Immigration Officers at both the airports, i.e. Heathrow Airport and Gatwick Airport, on the telephone, adding that they would be able to guide me.

I called the Immigration Officers at both the airports and explained to them who we were, when we exactly landed in the U.K. and what exactly was the purpose for our visiting the neighbouring countries during the college recess for 15 days. The Immigration Officers at both the airports telephonically informed me that under no circumstances would they be able to make any further entries in the passports because the passports were Diplomatic Passports. But one good advice by the Immigration officer at Heathrow Airport was that I should visit Her Majesty's Immigration Office at Leeds and meet the Immigration officer. Probably he would find out a solution for this issue. Leeds was not very far from Bradford and it was perhaps less than 20 km or so from Bradford. Dr. M.E. Haque when he heard about our plight took all 3 of us in his vehicle and to Her Majesty's Immigration Office at Leeds. All 3 of us visited that office and met the Receptionist and wanted to meet the Immigration officer.

So the Immigration officer came out of his chamber and met us in the visitor's hall. He wanted to know what exactly the problem was. Then I explained to him that I had come as a student to pursue a one-year degree programme based on the British Council's scholarship and my wife and son had also accompanied me. As there would be 15 days of holidays in the last term of the course, I wanted to visit nearby destinations in Europe. I showed him all 3 of our Diplomatic Passports with no entries on the day we arrived except the date of arrival. He was rather perplexed and wanted to know how best he could help me. I informed him that I was advised to approach the Immigration Officer at Leeds with a request for him to issue a formal letter allowing us to proceed from Bradford to visit the neighbouring countries during our 15 days' recess and for our return journey back to Bradford at the entry points. Besides, we could show the letter of permission to be given by the Immigration Officer at Leeds at the Immigration counters in other countries. I even explained to him the possible contents of his letter. I also told him that if the letter was given on his own letterhead with his own signature and stamp, it would perhaps help me to re-enter the U.K. after our 15 days of nearby destinations in Europe. I must appreciate that he listened to me very carefully and went back to his room and brought a draft. He asked me to go through the draft to see if it would help me and if I needed to make any suggestions or corrections. So I requested him to give a few minutes to go through his draft and, if necessary, with his permission, I would like to make some corrections or suggestions. He readily agreed with my suggestion and went back to his room. When I carefully read his draft, I noticed there were grammar and spelling mistakes. So I started correcting the draft and wherever necessary made some corrections regarding spelling, grammar mistakes, etc., and went back to him and showed him. I asked him whether it was all right. He just smiled and said he had no problem and requested me to wait for some time. He went back to his room and made the letter ready with his signature and seal after about half an hour or so.

After he had gone into his room, I sarcastically smiled. My son, who was 14 years old, wanted to know why I smiled after the Immigration officer went to his room. I candidly told him that his countrymen, i.e. the Britishers, ruled our country for 200 years and we had been taught English by them when they introduced English education in our country. On that day, it felt so satisfying that I had the liberty to correct an Englishman's draft! However, the fact remained that the Immigration officer took it sportingly, and he did not mind at all. He returned with the proper letter as per my corrections made in his draft and handed over that particular letter in a proper cover. I doubt if any such request at one of our own offices in India would be dealt with in such a manner, and that too with the counter-party having the temerity to point out mistakes to the officer-in-charge!

All 3 of us thanked him profusely, and we left. Throughout our stay in the Immigration office at Leeds, our Dr. Friend Dr. M.E. Haque was patiently waiting for us in the car, and all of us happily came back to Bradford. Thereafter, we commenced our fortnight-long journey to Europe, and we had very interesting episodes and met interesting personalities as well.

Fortunately, one of my dear friends and well-wishers, in view of his contacts and due to his frequent trips abroad, had already informed a French lady in Paris and an Indian officer who was working on deputation assignment at the Indian Embassy in Brussels. He had also booked our accommodation in Amsterdam for a couple of days based on our travel programme. We went by ship when we left the U.K. for Paris. By the time we reached Paris, it was evening. I contacted the French lady after we landed at the Paris Bus station. She took us in her car and literally drove us around like an evening in Paris. She informed us that she would take us to her flat later and, as we were totally new to Paris, we should see the City of Paris in the evening. Though we were tired, we thought that as the French lady and our host offered herself to drive us around the glittering city for an hour or so, we readily accepted her nice gesture. For all 3 of us, it was really a wonderful trip as we were exposed to Paris city for the first time in our lives and that too, in the evening, with colourful lights all over as she drove through important landmarks like the Eiffel Tower, Champs-Elysees and other significant places. It was like a guided city tour.

We came back to her flat and she offered us dinner, and the couple was extremely hospitable. They provided us accommodation for the next 2 days.

For the next couple of days, she offered guidance on how we had to proceed on a city tour through Metro Stations or through city tours conducted by the tourist organisations, etc. We spent a couple of days in Paris and thereafter proceeded to Brussels. We stayed in a three-bedroom flat of a Tamil family, and they were very hospitable and extremely pleasant. We were only introduced to them by our friend and well-wisher who guided us from Madras.

The gentleman who hosted us was a government officer, and he was working at that time on deputation at the Indian Embassy. Based on his guidance, wherever we wanted to go, we took buses and metro trains in Brussels. Of course, on a particular day, he took us in his car to another city called Antwerp.

After we had spent a few days and literally enjoyed his hospitality, we had to proceed to Amsterdam as per our original programme. It was quite interesting to let the reader know that when we visited the Railway station at Brussels for our onward journey to Amsterdam, it was in the evening and all the ticket counters were closed. We were rather perplexed as to how to get onto the train without buying 3 tickets for all of us. Some other passenger at the station informed us that we might buy the tickets inside the train when the ticket examiner conducts the checking of the passengers during our journey. Throughout the journey, nobody came asking for our tickets nor inquired about our ticketless travel. We were totally helpless. By that time, the train had come to Amsterdam and we had to get down. We all felt very guilty as it was our first experience in our life that we had travelled without train tickets like ticketless passengers not out of our own volition but due to circumstances beyond our control. So after we got down from the train, we had to enquire from some other passenger as to how to proceed to the hotel where my friend had booked accommodation for us for 3 nights, including that day's arrival. We were told that we had to take a tram after getting out of the station and that particular hotel was not very far from the last station at which that particular tram would stop. Of course, for this journey, we had paid for our tickets from the place we got in till the last destination after checking with him. While travelling on the train, I checked with the ticket examiner about the location of the hotel accommodation we were supposed to stay for that night and for the next 2 days. It was already around 8 pm by the time we reached the last terminal point. We were the last passengers to get down at that terminal. We had kept our passports, currency, etc., in a small bag as we had to carry a lot of luggage for all 3 of us.

While getting down at that terminal, we all got off the train and collected our luggage and then proceeded to the main road where the hotel was not very far. After we got off the tram with the luggage and had gone some distance, we were supposed to enquire about the route to the hotel. It was rather dark, and at that time, my wife suddenly noticed that the small bag containing our passports, currencies, etc., was not there. We felt that we might have left the bag in the tram itself when we got off in a hurry. Obviously, one had to reach the terminal point where we got off, though the distance might not be very far from the point where we were waiting to proceed to the hotel. However, I did not know how to get back to the terminus. I enquired from a gentleman who was fortunately available at that time and requested him to kindly let us know how to go to the terminus. He gave me some directions on how to proceed to the terminus. My apprehension was that I had to leave my son and wife alone with the luggage and rush back to the terminal point to collect that small bag consisting of our passports, currencies, etc. Literally, I ran faster and mentally made my own route based on the gentleman's guidance. I reached the terminus very fast. Even today, I am unable to comprehend how I reached the terminus based on my own estimation and also as per the guidance of the gentleman who informed us of the location of the terminal point. Of course, this was a foreign country, and only due to God's divine grace, I could reach the terminus with my prayers that the TTE should hopefully be present and I should be able to retrieve my small bag containing our passports, currencies, etc. The moment I had rushed to that particular coach, it was so very nice of the TTE to accost me, and he handed over the bag with a smile on his face. "I think this is yours; Please check it." After thanking him profusely and with my sincere prayers once again, I literally ran back from the terminus to the place where I had left my wife and son on that night in a foreign country.

When I reached there with the small bag, my wife and son were bewildered as to how I could rush back to that particular terminus and collect the bag and rushed back to meet them in the quickest possible time. I told my wife and son that but for God's divine blessings, this would not have been possible for me to first of all reach that train terminus to collect the bag intact without the least difficulty. It was a foreign country, and it was nighttime, i.e. around 9 pm, and there were not many people on the road, and no other transport was possible to reach the hotel. We somehow collected our luggage and walked through to reach the hotel accommodation. This episode had been literally etched in my mind as to how I had the guts to rush to the train terminus based on some vague kind of guidance.

Amsterdam is a beautiful city where we went for a boat ride and also visited The Hague where the International Court of Justice is located. There was another place called Madurodam - it was like an exhibition wherein all kinds of international cities and monuments were kept in miniature forms. Of course, I did not want to take much time in narrating the places of visits in Paris, Brussels and Amsterdam etc., but one place where I visited was near Paris, i.e. Versailles, a beautiful Palace kept in very good condition. We visited Disneyland and spent the whole day there.

One might have heard about the French Revolution and the famous Queen called *Marie Antoinette* who made an unfortunate statement that everyone would have read in history, i.e. if there is no bread, let them eat cake. We saw Marie Antoinette's bedroom, which was decorated with so much paraphernalia.

We also visited Cologne in Germany and spent quite some time visiting the Cathedral, which was very big and impressive, and took a boat ride on the Rhine River.

During our stay in Britain, while I pursued the postgraduate degree course, we also visited London by bus and explored several places and important landmarks, such as the British Museum.

In a nutshell, if I may say, it was only due to God's divine grace that I could pursue a postgraduate degree, i.e. a Master of Arts in International Development Studies at the University of Bradford for exactly one-year, i.e. from October 1994 to October 1995, after about 20 years of joining the I.A.S. Our stay in Britain could also facilitate us not only to visit many places in the U.K., thanks to our friendships established with some Assamese doctors' families, but more so, it was an eye-opener for all 3 of us regarding the educational and health standards that were followed in that country. We were particularly impressed with the health system of the country, which was called the National Health Service.

Since I went as a student, I was also entitled to avail of the facilities of the NHS; by which, I could get a consultation for any kind of ailment with the doctors in the hospitals after prior appointments only, but the system followed was really remarkable. Another important feature that I may like to dwell upon is the social security system that was in vogue in the U.K. at that time. I did not know that if any immigrant, a student or otherwise stayed for more than one hundred and 80 days, he or she was entitled to social security benefits. I got a letter from a particular government Department of the U.K. asking for the details of myself and my studies and the British scholarship I received with my family details. I was pleasantly surprised after 180 days of my stay I could get 10 pounds and 10 pence per week as I was staying in the U.K. with my wife and one son. Automatically every week the money was credited into my bank account.

I was an admirer of the sense of fair play and justice on the part of the British governance system. Though I had initially informed them that I would leave the country by October 1995 i.e. 6 months later than the social security benefits that were extended to me in my bank account, I promptly received a letter at the end of the 6 months' period i.e. the period of social security benefits that were deposited in my account for 6 months after my original stay of 180 days. The letter from that particular Department advised me to let them know whether the social security benefits that were given to me by them should be extended to the place where I should be shifting to after my studies. I candidly informed them that as I would be returning to my own country as a civil servant to take up my place of assignment, there was absolutely no need for them to correspond with me thereafter as there was no such social security benefits scheme prevalent in our country at that time.

During our stay in Great Britain, we had purchased some items which carried VAT. There was a system available in case we had to claim the VAT at the airport at the time of our departure. For certain items, we were welcome to do so. We got the prior information at the airport that we had to carry our bills, etc., where we had paid VAT on certain important items for which a refund was possible. It was then and there given at the airport itself wherever there were no issues. Otherwise, we were informed that after verification, they would send us the requisite payment to our bank account in our country.

In conclusion, I would like to state candidly that fortunately, though I had obtained a postgraduate degree at the University of Bradford in the U.K., my objective was to get exposed to that country's culture and general governance standards, in addition to visiting many places not only for my general knowledge or understanding and appreciation but also for my family. For my son, it was a really good experience, and he could understand the difference in the standard of education between the schools in our country and the schools in the U.K. The school where he studied was called Thornton Grammar School, which was more than 350 years old, and it was a government school only, but the standard of education and the facilities available were far superior when compared to our schools 30 years ago. It was a very good exposure for my son and wife with reference to the various places of interest where we could visit, which enriched our knowledge and exposure in a foreign country. I was particularly happy that I could study in England along with my son as a student as well, though rather belated in my case. As the saying goes, 'Seeing is believing', one really got exposed to the culture, traditions, and institutions of eminence in that country, especially for my son, who was very young and lucky as well. In a way, it was helpful for him to know more about the United Kingdom and its places there than what he could have read otherwise in India or later read about that country, English education, etc.

My family and I spent exactly 366 days in the U.K. after we had left Assam. We never had any kind of feeling that we were treated rather badly as outsiders, as generally people would have come across the comments of racism in the U.K. This kind of development would have perhaps taken place much later.

I narrate below an endearing aspect of life noticed by me in the U.K. which I also advised my wife and son to observe. We had visited many public offices, like the post office or any shop or the grocery store or employment exchange, just to understand how the staff in such places treated any visitor who entered that place. The first and foremost question that would come from the British owner or staff in a shop or an office was, "Good morning to you! How could I help you?" wearing an infectious smile on his or her face. We were rather pleasantly surprised when we noticed this kind of attitude uniformly across the board.

We were particularly impressed with this kind of welcome greeting wherever and whenever we visited any mall, shop, or public office. We felt rather at home, and it was really a very good experience too when the reader knows about our delight in such interactions with those unknown faces even today. That was a pleasant experience, no doubt, but their attitude, behaviour, and conduct were really worthy of emulation.

In a nutshell, we carried back pleasant memories and, of course, very pleasant mementoes from very dear friends and well-wishers, who were not known to us until we landed in the U.K. However, by the time we left the U.K., we could proudly say that we had befriended many of our Assamese doctors, Bengali doctors, a Gujarati gentleman, as well as a Sikh family. It was a fact that we did celebrate Deepawali in the U.K. along with our family of well-wishers, and we also had very pleasant memories of visiting Gurudwaras. Of course, one could write a separate book on our beautiful stay in the U.K. for one-year, but this is not the occasion or place to delve into such thoughts.

Commissioner of Hills and Barak Valley Division and Commissioner of Lower Assam Division, Guwahati from November 1995 to January 1997

Commissioner of Hills and Barak Valley Division.

After I returned in the later part of 1995, I was posted as the Commissioner of Hills and Barak Valley division. When we had left for the U.K., my son was originally studying in Class 9 at Kendriya Vidyalaya, Khanapara, Guwahati. In fact, my residence and the ESI hospital where my doctor wife was working as a Medical Officer and the Central School were all located in the same area.

My wife and I joined our respective new assignments after we had returned to Guwahati from Bradford. We had approached the Principal of Kendriya Vidyalaya, Guwahati for my son's school re-admission in standard 10 after our return from the U.K. as my son had been promoted to standard 10 at his school in Bradford, U.K. The Principal refused to admit him in Class 10 as he did not clear the 9th standard examinations conducted by the CBSE. I found the attitude of the Principal thoroughly unhelpful.

I had to argue with him that the standard of education in U.K. schools was better than the Central School standard available in Kendriya Vidyalaya at that time but to no avail. I finally reported to the Kendriya Vidyalaya Sanghathan Commissioner in New Delhi about the peculiar attitude of the Principal of Kendriya Vidyalaya school in Khanapara, Guwahati.

Fortunately, my own batch mate of Madhya Pradesh cadre happened to be the Special Assistant to the then Union Cabinet Minister of Education, Mr. Madhava Rao Scindia, in New Delhi at that time. When I broached the subject of admission for my son in Class 10, and the odd attitude of the Principal, at Guwahati, he appreciated my stand and advised the Kendriya Vidyalaya Sanghathan Commissioner to intervene. Surprisingly and immediately, after receiving the direction from the Commissioner, Kendriya Vidyalaya Sanghathan, New Delhi, the Principal at Guwahati responded promptly and admitted my son in Class 10. I have deliberately brought this issue up to help the reader understand and appreciate the strange occupational hazards of civil servants. I was not the first civil servant to go and study abroad in this manner, nor was my son the first child of a civil servant to accompany his parents on a government sanctioned and approved programme. Every year, 40-50 personnel would travel as part of such a programme, and most would travel with their families. However, one particular Principal refused to see reason and created an unnecessary hassle. Assam was in the midst of insurgency at that time and that particular school was important from a security perspective, given the proximity of the school near our home, which was a very safe choice that I would not have wanted to change.

After a few months of my joining, I was also posted as Chairman of the Assam Pollution Control Board in Guwahati in addition to my assignment as the Commissioner of Hills and Barak Valley division. With the additional responsibility came a new challenge, the distance between the 2 offices was more than 15 to 20 km. I had to travel between the 2 offices on a daily basis.

When I joined the Assam Pollution Control Board office as Chairman, I was flabbergasted to see the dirty atmosphere of the Chairman's office chamber. Immediately, I went through the entire building and met the officers and staff. Nothing seemed normal in that organisation either in terms of manpower resources or office accommodation. I had noticed that the office of the Pollution Control Board was highly polluted. I was extremely upset and called the senior officers working under my control and gave them strict instructions that pollution control would begin from the Chairman's office itself, then and there. I gave them directions that the entire office should be spruced up, cleaned, whitewashed, and the entire building should appear to be a dignified one within a period of 2 months. I was very rough and tough with them as my predecessor was neither a strict officer nor capable of performing his duties in the best possible manner.

The Minister in charge of the functions of the Pollution Control Board was perhaps very unhappy with my predecessor's performance and hence had transferred him.

Unfortunately, to his dismay, without knowing my background and my work ethics, he agreed to my posting as Chairman of the Pollution Control Board. He regretted it much later. I had to not only ensure the cleanliness of the office building but also cleanse the mindset of officers and staff and ensure effective transfers and postings, in addition to personnel management, in a proper and transparent manner. After going through the records, I made some promotions, transfers, and postings in the larger public interest.

When I did this, the Minister concerned was very much upset and started interfering in my work and started talking to me asking for favours. I told him bluntly to read the Pollution Control Board Act thoroughly; it seemed that he had perhaps never read that Act. Even before effecting transfers, postings, and personnel management in the best possible manner, I had gone through the Assam Pollution Control Board Act thoroughly. As per the provisions of the Act, the Chairman of the Pollution Control Board only was the final authority to effect transfers, postings, or promotions based on the set of rules and regulations, and there was no question of political interference as per the transparent provisions of the Assam Pollution Control Board Act. There were murmurs in the corridors of the secretariat that I was not bothered to listen to the Minister's request and continued to function as the Chairman of the Pollution Control Board in my own style. Actually, I did not do anything wrong; but I did my level best to follow the rules and regulations as per the provisions of the Assam Pollution Control Board Act only.

Some disgruntled elements brought out the note portions of the administrative details regarding transfers, postings, etc., in the local newspapers. They thought that I would earn a bad name in view of my defiance and my 'autocratic style' of functioning according to their viewpoint. I told them candidly that I had never volunteered nor wanted to get posted as the Chairman, Assam Pollution Control Board. The whole thing appeared in the newspapers and some of the junior colleagues and senior colleagues appreciated my guts and style of my functioning. It happened after a year or 2 of this incident.

After a few months, a technocrat from that organisation itself, as per laid down eligibility and qualifications, was posted as the Chairman of the Assam Pollution Control Board. I was greatly relieved. Though I was posted as Commissioner of Hills and Barak Valley division in October 1995, I had hardly been able to spend a few months concentrating on my functioning as the Commissioner of Hills and Barak Valley division, and could not plan visits to the districts within my jurisdiction. Hereafter, I did visit Cachar district and travelled to some areas within the district and interacted with the officials about the development activities in the district. I also visited Karbi Anglong district and North Cachar hills districts and interacted with the Deputy Commissioners and officials of the 2 hills districts in order to understand and ascertain their grievances, if any, for redressal.

As both the hills districts were very familiar to me due to my earlier postings as a Deputy Commissioner of both the hills districts several years ago, I felt at home and tried to ascertain any improvements that were made in both the districts headquarters. I particularly recalled that I had laid foundation stones in the Deputy Commissioner's office for an additional building at Circuit House and also a separate residential office for the Deputy Commissioner at Diphu, in addition to the construction of an additional building within the premises of the Office of the Deputy Commissioner, making a total of 3 additional buildings. Though I hardly stayed for 7 months or so as Deputy Commissioner, I took the initiative to ensure that not only the foundation stones were laid for the construction of these additional buildings mentioned above, but also that the construction work started. I felt delighted to see the completion of these buildings, and I conveyed my sincere appreciation to the Deputy Commissioner concerned when I visited as the Commissioner of the hills Division.

In 1996, I was additionally posted as the Commissioner of Lower Assam Division (LAD) along with my assignment as the Commissioner of Hills and Barak Valley division, as the Commissioner of Lower Assam Division was suffering from some ailment.

Within a couple of months, I had to face a very serious law and order situation in Kokrajhar district of Assam.

It so happened on one fine morning around 8 am, the Private Secretary to the Chief Minister of Assam requested me to visit his residence as all senior officers including the Chief Secretary, Director-General of Police, and senior officers were invited for a discussion. After I reached the Chief Minister's residence, I came to know from the Chief Minister that a very serious law and order problem had arisen in the district of Kokrajhar. Dozens of people had been killed, and more than a lakh of people had taken refuge in the Relief Camps.

According to him, the Deputy Commissioner and Superintendent of Police at that time were unable to control the situation, and therefore, I had to rush immediately along with the Inspector General of Police to Kokrajhar district as quickly as possible. As soon as I reached my residence, I packed my suitcase with clothes and other daily necessities for at least a week to 10 days at the District Headquarters of Kokrajhar for supervising the functioning of the Deputy Commissioner, Superintendent of Police, and other officials of that district. The Inspector General of Police wanted to separately visit Kokrajhar, the headquarter town of the district.

It was a long journey of about 7 hours before I reached the Kokrajhar Circuit House at 4 pm. On the way, before I could reach Kokrajhar, for several kilometres, I could see a very large number of houses burning. Moreover, I saw a large number of people taking their belongings and proceeding to the neighbouring districts. I stopped my vehicle to know from them what had happened. They informed that they were all poor people and their houses were burnt by miscreants. I felt very sad when I looked at their condition. They were scared and some of them were trembling when they spoke to me. I informed them that I was the Commissioner of Division and I was proceeding to Kokrajhar to bring normalcy in the district along with the Deputy Commissioner and Superintendent of Police of the district. I tried to assure them that as far as possible, normalcy would be returned soon and they would be able to come back to their own original places of stay in the next few days and not to panic.

After I left my things at the Circuit House, I immediately rushed to the Office of the Deputy Commissioner and instructed the junior officers to call for the Deputy Commissioner and Superintendent of Police, wherever they were as they were also busy in controlling the situation in the field. Within the next 15 minutes, the Deputy Commissioner and Superintendent of Police of the district rushed to meet me at the Office of the Deputy Commissioner. I told the DC and SP to call immediately a meeting of all the senior political representatives of different parties and the community leaders belonging to various sections of the Society. Within an hour, the meeting started. I firmly informed all present that from that moment, I was taking charge of the entire district administration to ensure proper maintenance of law and order. I had got clear instructions from the government that violence must be put down with a very heavy hand and no more arson, killing and lootings would be allowed.

I made my position very clear to the assembled officers that my topmost priority was to restore confidence in the minds of the people belonging to various communities and to ensure peace and tranquillity. I listened to the grievances of the people assembled there and told them that on the next day all the Peace Committee Members would be travelling in a few vehicles throughout the district to talk to the people and request them to keep absolute peace and avoid violent incidents as otherwise the law would definitely take its course.

I informed them that I would also travel along with the DC and the SP in addition to the Peace Committee Members. The next day, the DC, SP, several political leaders and I travelled together to various places within the district and visited the Relief Camps where the people took refuge with whatever belongings they had. Announcements were made over loudspeakers that the Commissioner of Division along with his colleagues would travel continuously within the district for the next few days and would ruthlessly put down any sort of violence or any sort of mischief if indulged in by the miscreants irrespective of the community they might belong to. Without the least ambiguity, the message given was 'Loud and clear' to everybody in the district that normalcy would be returned within the next few days.

I stayed for a week or so and every day in the evening, I spoke to the Chief Secretary and Chief Minister and informed them of the developments regularly. I advised the Chief Minister to visit only after a week so that the field officers in the district could concentrate on the maintenance of law and order and on the restoration of peace and confidence in the minds of the people belonging to various sections of society. As requested by me, the Chief Minister of Assam visited Kokrajhar after a week only and met the people in addition to the political representatives belonging to various sections. He felt very happy after detailed discussions with the officers and field visits. He requested me to stay for 2 more days before he left Kokrajhar for the State Headquarters.

I visited the Relief Camps during my stay and met the people and enquired about the availability of food, medicines, etc. I also informed them that their security would be ensured, and they need not be afraid of further mischief by miscreants in the Relief Camps. There were approximately one lakh people taking refuge in different Relief Camps. Therefore, it was the duty of the district administration to not only provide food and medicines, etc. for them but also ensure absolute safety and security for the inmates of the Relief Camps.

After making sure that there was absolute peace and tranquillity in the entire district, I thanked the Deputy Commissioner, DIG of Police, Superintendent of Police, and other district officials for their full co-operation in tackling the situation as per my directions. I left Kokrajhar for my home in Guwahati after staying for more than a week.

During my tenure as Commissioner, Lower Assam Division, I was tasked with another important assigned. One day the Chief Minister of Assam called me and requested me to conduct a thorough enquiry about the illegal, irregular appointments of teachers made by the previous regime at Lower Primary Schools, Primary Schools, Middle Schools, High Schools and High Secondary Schools throughout the State of Assam between 1991-96. Somehow, he had great regard for me and he thought that I would do a proper job in eliciting the truth behind such irregular and illegal appointments.

The irregular appointments meant that thoroughly unqualified and disqualified candidates were appointed as teachers of Higher Classes whereas their own qualification was only 7th or 8th standard pass. Illegal appointments implied that there were no vacancies at all as they were only on paper. Poor people were being duped and issued appointment orders as teachers in various schools where there was no vacancy at all. They lost their valuables, land, money, to given bribes to the powers that be during the previous regime on the ostensible presumption that they would all get some suitable appointments within the school system as Teachers. When the government in power came to know about such deliberate cheating and their utter disappointment about such illegal and irregular appointments in view of hue and cry created by such unfortunate citizens in the entire state, it were compelled to constitute an Enquiry Committee and that responsibility fell on me.

While I had to finish this enquiry within a period of a few months as the Chairman of the Enquiry Committee, it took considerable time as I had to call a very large number of officers at the district and sub-divisional levels like district Education officers, Inspectors of Schools, etc. Unfortunately, I had only one stenographer at that time in my office. So I advised the Commissioner and Secretary, Education Department to depute 6 more stenographers for recording the evidence of the officers called by me in addition to the statements to be recorded from the members of the public. For a few months, the Commissioner of Lower Assam Division had received a very large number of complaints. The officers of the Education Department were directed to appear before me for giving their versions based on the specific complaints against them. Towards the end of December 1996, I had the information that I was getting posted as Joint Secretary to the Government of India in the Ministry of Steel, which would be a five-year tenure. Even the orders were issued by the Government of India as well as by the State Government of Assam.

In the meanwhile, I went and called on the Chief Minister of Assam and informed him that I would be completing my enquiry very soon and I would like to leave the day after next once I completed and submitted the report in a sealed cover to the Chief Secretary to the Government of Assam.

I vividly recall the date of my completion of my enquiry after a great deal of effort, engaging more than half a dozen stenographers in giving dictations for the completion of my enquiry report at the office of the Commissioner of Lower Assam Division. I called the Private Secretary to the Chief Secretary and informed him that by 7 pm I would be coming to hand over the enquiry report in a sealed cover to the Chief Secretary, and he should be available in the office. So when I reached the office of the Chief Secretary with a sealed cover and handed over the report, I told him that I would hand over the charge of the office of Commissioner of Lower Assam Division as well as the charge of Commissioner of Hills and Barak Valley division the next day, i.e. on the 22nd January 1997, and proceed to Guwahati airport to board the flight to Delhi in the afternoon.

On 21st January evening when I met the Chief Secretary with the enquiry report, he informed me that it would not be possible for me to leave for Delhi the next day after handing over my charge at the Office of Commissioner of Lower Assam Division and Commissioner of Hills and Barak Valley division. The Chief Secretary explained to me that I would not be able to leave as my successor, who was posted as Commissioner of North Assam Division, would be busy with the reception of the Prime Minister of India, who would come to Tinsukia for laying down the foundation stone of the 5th bridge on the River Brahmaputra. I told him very clearly that there was nothing to hand over in the office of the Commissioner of Lower Assam Division as the permanent advance in that office was only Rs. 150/-. I was even prepared to hand over the money from my pocket if required in a lighter vein. I informed him that I had already categorically informed the Chief Minister a couple of weeks earlier that my appointment order as the Joint Secretary to the Government of India in the Steel Ministry had been issued. The day after I submitted the enquiry report to the government, I would leave for Delhi to board the flight at Guwahati Airport. I categorically told him that nothing would prevent me from boarding the aircraft the next day with my wife and son. After seeing my stubborn attitude, the then Chief Secretary stood up and told me that he would miss someone like me and wondered whether he would meet me at all in the future when I would be back to Assam after my tenure in Delhi for 5 years.

Joint Secretary to the Government of India in the Ministry of Steel, from January 1997 to December 2001

On the 22nd of January 1997 evening, I reached Delhi with my wife and son. On the 23rd of January 1997, when I went and called on the then Secretary to the Government of India in the Ministry of Steel, he told me, 'Mr. Manoharan, would you like to wait for a few more days as the then existing Joint Secretary, who was already transferred to make way for my joining, wanted to avail a visit to Russia.' I told him that I would come back after a week and would not be loitering around in the corridors of the Ministry of Steel until then.

After a week, I reported to the Secretary, Government of India in the Ministry of Steel and formally joined as the Joint Secretary to the Government of India in the Ministry of Steel. I was given the work allocation by the Secretary of Steel. There were 3 Joint secretaries, including myself. In the next 5 years, I held an extremely challenging assignments looking after half a dozen public sector organisations under the Ministry of Steel as well as the policy aspects of growth and development of steel, and other dimensions of the functioning of the Ministry of Steel. For the benefit of the reader, I would like to state that at that particular time, there were about a dozen Public Sector Undertakings (PSUs) under the Ministry of Steel.

One of the PSUs I looked after was the Rashtriya Ispat Nigam Limited (RINL), which owned and operated the Vizag Steel Plant. The Vizag Steel Plant was the only modern steel plant nearer to the seashore in India at that time. It was established with an investment of approximately Rs. 8000 crores, but unfortunately, it was making losses. Another loss-making company, that was also assigned to me in my role was the Hindustan Steel Works Construction Limited (HSCL). The interesting story about this organisation was that this company was originally started for the construction of the steel plants with knowledgeable workers in the Construction of Steel Mills. However, the initial employees' strength of 95 went up to 35,000 or so due to too much political pressure, interference, and nepotism in postings, etc. Consequently, the company was unable to meet the salaries of the workers, and most of the time, either they did not have work or they were not getting salaries.

Within a few days of my joining, the Steel Secretary called me and told me categorically that these were the two most difficult companies and it was my duty and responsibility to take my assignment as a challenge and set them right. There were 4 more companies that were overseen by me, i.e. Manganese Ore India Limited (MOIL), Metallurgical and Engineering Consultations Limited (MECON Ltd), Bharat Refractories Limited (BRL), and Bird Groups of companies. Of all the 6 companies which were under my charge, the only company which was making a profit was MOIL. The Headquarters of MOIL was at Nagpur. The Headquarters of RINL was at Vizagapattinam. MECON Limited had its headquarters in Ranchi, and the Headquarters of BRL was located in Jharkhand. The Headquarters of HSCL and the Bird Group of Companies respectively were at Calcutta. I happened to be the government Director of RINL, MOIL, MECON Ltd, and HSCL. My next officer was designated as Director in the Ministry of Steel, and he was the government Director in the companies called BRL and Bird Group of Companies.

I had to attend many board meetings of all these companies and had to make crucial decisions for their growth and development. For instance, in the case of MECON Ltd, although it was a very good company with excellent managerial skills and very good officers, they were not receiving enough work orders and consequently income growth to cover employees' salaries was being impacted. Given these circumstances, I take pride in being personally responsible for leading the CMD of MECON Limited in discussions with the Chairman of the Indian Space Research Organisation (ISRO), Dr. Kasturi Rangan, to enhance marketing efforts on behalf of the company for the construction of the second Rocket Launch Pad at Sriharikota. MECON Limited was a competitor of L&T. In 1997, India had only one Rocket Launch Pad in Sriharikota. Consequently, ISRO had previously sought assistance from France for launching rockets from their Launching Pads, as we did not have a second Launching Pad Facility at Sriharikota. Therefore, when ISRO issued a tender, MECON Ltd. participated, and the Chairman and Managing Director of MECON Ltd invited me to address the issue with ISRO alongside him. I scheduled a formal appointment with the Chairman of ISRO. Unfortunately, on that particular day when I met the ISRO chairman, he informed me that he had to reduce our meeting time from 30 minutes to 15 minutes as the Chairman of the Russian Space Commission had suddenly arrived. Nevertheless, he graciously discussed the issues with me, the Chairman of MECON Limited, and his colleagues in the presence of senior ISRO officers. Subsequently, he mentioned that the then Additional Secretary of ISRO and Financial Adviser, Mr. Prabhakaran, a very senior I.A.S. officer, along with senior colleagues and scientists at ISRO, would engage in detailed discussions with me, the Chairman of MECON Limited, and his colleagues.

I found Mr. Prabhakaran and his colleagues to be cordial and pleasant. We moved to another room and had detailed discussions. At that time, I argued my level best with Mr. Prabhakaran and his colleagues of ISRO that the advantages of giving the work order for construction of a second Rocket Launch Pad with a government Company, MECON Limited, were greater than that of the Private Limited Company, L&T. I told Mr. Prabhakaran and his colleagues that as the government Director in MECON Limited, I would constantly pursue the Chairman of MECON Limited and his colleagues and get things done wherever and whenever they went wrong and were delayed in their decision-making process once the order was given to them.

Moreover, the price quoted by MECON Limited was lower than that of L&T. In the meantime, Mr. Prabhakaran requested me to visit Sriharikota in the coming weeks to see for myself the existing Rocket Launch Pad Facility at Sriharikota along with CMD MECON Limited. After I returned to Delhi, within a week or 10 days, I went back to Sriharikota along with the Chairman of MECON Limited.

Sriharikota is a high-security zone and no one is generally allowed to enter the site except the scientists and officers working in ISRO apart from the villagers living nearby. It was more or less like an island on the border between Tamil Nadu and Andhra Pradesh. The very first time when I saw the 22-storey building, which is the Rocket Launching Pad Facilities Centre,

I was told by the scientists that at the time of launching of the rocket, the whole launching pad i.e. 22-storey building would slowly move backwards through computerised wheels and the rocket, which was to fly up in the sky, would be separated and kept at a distance. I was fascinated and went right up to the top of the building. On the other side, there was a pristine beach, a very beautiful place which I would never ever forget.

The ISRO officers informed me that at the time of any rocket launch, no one would be allowed to stay within a radius of 5 km or so.

The control room for the operations of the launching of the rocket is at a distance. The entire system is operated through remote control. Unless one visits the place, one may not understand and appreciate the rocket launch mechanism at Sriharikota.

Fortunately, by God's divine grace, I was able to visit Sriharikota for the first time after my meetings with the ISRO chairman and his colleagues.

For the first time when I looked at the building along with the CMD of MECON Ltd, I really wondered whether even with the kind of foreign technology collaboration, our Indian Public Sector Enterprise called MECON Ltd, which has been basically a consulting and project-making company for the construction of the steel mills of Steel Authority of India Limited and Visakhapatnam Steel Ltd, would be able to come up to the expectations of the ISRO scientists in the matter of construction of the second Rocket Launch Pad.

When I heard the whole operations of the technology involved in the launching of the rocket, I took the then CMD MECON Ltd along with me to the top floor of the 22nd storied building and then we came down. With utter disbelief, I had asked the scientists who were there to let us know whether it would be possible for a 22-storied building to get separated from the launching pad and that too, by its slow movement from the existing place of location to a distant location even if it is 100 metres away. They replied that there would be no issues.

Since ISRO had only one Rocket Launch Pad at the time of my visit in the year 1997-98, they were finding it difficult to launch rockets or satellites as per plans from the single available launch pad. Therefore, they used to visit France with which they had long-time tie-ups. So whenever there was any necessity, they used to launch the rocket or satellite from France.

The very purpose of calling for a tender by ISRO for the construction of a second Rocket Launch Pad Facility, for which L&T and MECON Ltd were the primary competitors, was to provide ISRO with the opportunity to successfully complete their plans. We did not have the technical capability in India at that time to construct a Rocket Launch Pad Facility without foreign technology collaboration. I had my own suspicions about whether even with the foreign technology collaboration, MECON Limited would succeed in their job once ISRO agreed to place the orders with them.

L&T was a very resourceful construction company and it had all the wherewithal in addition to foreign technology collaboration as well in this particular work was concerned vis-a-vis the capabilities of MECON Ltd.

I knew the capabilities of MECON Ltd with regard to their consultations on construction matters, especially in the steel industry, in view of the very large number of technical people available within that organisation.

But the construction of the second Rocket Launch Pad Facility was a different cup of tea altogether in which no one had experience in that organisation except, perhaps, through their bookish knowledge or whatever discussion we had with Mr. Prabhakaran, the Additional Secretary and Financial Adviser, and all his scientists and engineers in the conference hall of ISRO.

At that particular time, MECON Ltd was a loss-making company. As a government Director and Joint Secretary in the Ministry of Steel, it was my responsibility to look for jobs that might generate revenue and provide new experience in a different scientific field.

It was a fact that MECON Ltd deliberately quoted the tender price of around Rs. 380 crores, perhaps which was rather less compared to that of L&T.

I came to know later from the Chairman of ISRO Ltd and also his colleagues that they were not confident that MECON Ltd would be competent to perform this particular innovative and very challenging task.

I tried to convince the Chairman ISRO, the Additional Secretary and Financial Adviser, and the scientists and engineers of ISRO during our 3 or four-hour-long meeting that I would try my level best as a senior civil servant and also as a government Director of MECON Ltd. I would take up the challenge and make sure that MECON Ltd would come up to their expectations. I requested them time and again that they might give an opportunity to the Public Sector Enterprise, MECON Limited, in times of their distress and also that would enable them not only to enhance their revenue but also to expand their knowledge and experience in an altogether different yet very innovative and challenging assignment like the construction of the second Rocket Launch Pad Facility.

The difference between the existing Rocket Launch Pad and the new one proposed, for which MECON Limited bid in competition with L&T, was that the building would remain intact in the newly proposed Rocket Launch Pad. Only the Rocket Launch Pad would move away from the main building to its location at the time of launching the Rocket, unlike in the existing one where the building would move, and the Rocket Launch Pad would remain stationary. Later on, the ISRO chairman and his colleagues told me candidly that they knew very well neither L&T nor MECON Ltd would be in a position to complete the construction of the second Rocket Launch Pad within the quoted price. Ultimately, when the work order was given to MECON Ltd with the sole objective of giving that particular work to a PSE, the actual quoted price went up to more than Rs. 500 crores, as it would have been impossible for MECON Limited to construct that second Rocket Launch Pad within the earlier quoted price even with the foreign technology collaboration.

After a month or so, after our negotiations and discussions between ISRO and MECON Ltd's CMD and his colleagues, Mr. Prabhakaran, the Additional Secretary and Financial Adviser, called me and requested me to join them during the agreement signing day in Sriharikota. I gladly accepted his invitation, as he had informed that he would be present along with me and the agreement would be signed by CMD, MECON Ltd, and the Director of ISRO posted at Sriharikota. On the appointed date and time, the agreement was signed by CMD MECON Ltd on behalf of MECON LTD, and the Director of ISRO at Sriharikota signed the agreement on behalf of

ISRO. The agreement was signed in the presence of the Additional Secretary and Financial Adviser, ISRO, Mr. Prabhakaran, and myself.

Thereafter, as per the conditions of the agreement, the construction works were started by MECON Ltd. Of course, it did take a couple of years and by the time the second Rocket Launch Pad was constructed in Sriharikota, I had left the Ministry of Steel as my tenure was over, but in between, I used to go to Sriharikota and visit the place to understand how far the progress of work was being implemented.

I am recording this subject in the book with all humility at my disposal to let the reader know that the PSE, which did not have any kind of experience at all in such technical issues as complicated and as difficult as in the case of the construction of the Rocket Launch Pad, took that crucial decision of participation in the tender process and did succeed in the completion of that complex and significant project. Today it is easier for me to write as to what exactly had happened, but I had my own apprehensions in that year whether MECON Ltd would keep up their words and whether they would throw up their hands due to some difficulties or impediments, etc., later.

Fortunately, by God's divine grace, nothing of that sort happened. I understand that after it was completed, the President of India, Dr. A.P.J. Abdul Kalam, participated in the inaugural function in Sriharikota. The said project was one of the greatest achievements of MECON Ltd. ever since its inception. All credit is certainly due to the excellent execution of the contract by the management, engineers, and other staff of MECON.

Fortunately, the ISRO chairman, who had met me for only 15 minutes, and the Additional Secretary and all his colleagues, especially scientists and engineers, had some kind of confidence in me during the discussions. Everything went off well. It may not be out of place to mention here that the CMD of MECON Ltd, Dr. L. K. Singhal, was a highly qualified and accomplished engineer, and he would have done very well as a Professor in an Academic Institution.

Simultaneously, around the same time, I had to accompany CMD MECON Ltd to the office of the Chairman of Tamil Nadu Electricity Board (TNEB) in Chennai. MECON Ltd had participated in a bid along with some other private companies like L&T for the construction of an external coal handling overhead iron rails transport system. It comprised the construction of a 13 km stretch of overhead iron rails transport system with crisscrossing right from Ennore Harbour to Ennore Thermal Power Station.

In order to make the reader aware of what the external coal handling overhead rails transport system was and how effectively it would be used for quick transportation of coal in large quantities right from the ship up to the thermal power station, I give below some details.

For thermal power stations producing electricity, coal was the main source. In this case, coal was received in large quantities via ships.

So in the normal parlance, when the coal had to be unloaded from the ship, it used to be a combination of manual and mechanical processes of unloading the coal from the ship onto the trucks for its further transportation to the thermal power station at Ennore.

In order to streamline this, the Tamil Nadu Electricity Board floated a tender for the construction of a long stretch of overhead transportation of coal through an iron chain conveyor belt right from the ship up to the thermal power station. In fact, the transportation of coal handling through overhead rails conveyor transport system was not only to supply coal from the ship to the thermal station but also to take one branch of that coal handling system towards the stockyard where the coal was unloaded onto the Goods Wagons for transportation elsewhere in Tamil Nadu for other thermal power plants.

The distance from the ship up to the feeding point of coal in Ennore Thermal Power Station was perhaps of the order of approximately 13 km. Moreover, this kind of a unique coal handling transport system was never attempted in India, and this was the first occasion that the Tamil Nadu Electricity Board took such an important decision to implement the novel idea. For this tender floated by TNEB, L&T was the competitor along with MECON Ltd. The construction of the overhead coal handling transport system was a very complicated and difficult project to construct several pillars, etc., en route that had to bear the strength of the coal handling system, which went up to a 13 km stretch and that too, in a criss-cross manner. In between, they had to construct some other buildings also so that in times of necessity for maintenance, they would have to accommodate the technical people nearer to the thermal power station. If I remember correctly, at that time, the bid value was a little more than Rs. 300 crores.

Mr. Om Kumar was the Chairman of the Tamil Nadu Electricity Board at that time. I took a formal appointment from him for myself and the CMD of MECON Ltd to ensure the award of the tender to MECON Ltd because their quoted price was competitive. Mr. Om Kumar met us along with all his key technical personnel and enquired about MECON's competence and capability for this project, given its very unique nature. He knew that MECON Ltd. was a consultant organisation only and that too, in the steel industry. He informed me in a very frank manner that there were certain complaints about MECON Ltd.

I responded to him very politely and told him that it was a fact that MECON did not have that much experience by itself and would take the assistance of a foreign collaborator not only for designing the overhead coal handling transport system but also for the construction of the same. I informed him that fortunately a construction company called Hindustan Steel Works Construction Ltd (HSCL), a Public Sector Enterprise under the Ministry of Steel, would be assisting them in the construction and handing over of the overhead coal handling transport system to TNEB. I added that once the project was awarded to MECON, the same would be completed with the help of HSCL, with the primary bidder being MECON. I also informed him that I was the government Director for both the companies and it would be my duty and responsibility to ensure that once the job was given to MECON Ltd by TNEB, under no circumstances, would I permit them to have the luxury of time and cost overrun in the implementation of the proposed project.

I requested the Chairman and his colleagues to have a detailed discussion with the CMD of MECON Ltd and his technical colleagues if they had any serious reservations about their competence and capabilities in the matter of construction of the overhead coal handling transport system. I also mentioned to the Chairman that after all, it was a prestigious project for TNEB not only from the point of innovative approach but also from the point of functional utility of that overhead coal handling transport system in the best possible manner by MECON Limited.

I assured the Chairman and all his colleagues present that I would make sure that the CMDs of MECON and HSCL frequently visited the site and oversaw the progress of the project. In addition to that, I myself would also periodically visit Ennore and ascertain the progress from the field-level officers of TNEB, MECON, and HSCL.

With regard to the complaints against MECON, I unequivocally told him that whenever the Public Sector Enterprise competed in such bids, this seemed to be a regular feature to scuttle their sincere efforts. The objective for such issues of false complaints against the Public Sector Enterprise typically was to mislead the client.

In conclusion, I sat with the Chairman of TNEB and his colleagues for a couple of hours and strongly argued as to why MECON should be given this particular work. After all, MECON along with HSCL had constructed several steel plants in this country and therefore, even though the construction of the newly proposed external overhead coal handling transport system was a unique one, it was not such a big task for MECON as it had the fullest support of another sister organisation called HSCL. I had to convince the Chairman of TNEB that he should not bother too much about the false, anonymous, or pseudonymous complaints against MECON as the reason was obvious. I informed him that as I emphasised during the beginning of the discussion, being a government Director of both the companies, it would be my duty and responsibility to help TNEB, which was another public sector organisation, in the best possible manner. Fortunately, the Chairman of TNEB was a very patient gentleman. Even though he was rather senior in service to me, he gave me sufficient time to state my position as to why MECON should be given the work instead of their competitor. Compared to the size of the competitor, MECON was definitely a smaller organisation but it had a dedicated set of technical personnel with very strong qualifications and experience, i.e. consultants and project managers of 3 disciplines, viz., Electrical, Mechanical, and Civil engineering in addition to Metallurgical engineering consultants.

I requested him and rather pleaded with him that he should have confidence in me as the government Director to hand over the work order to MECON. At the end of the conversation, he literally remarked in a lighter vein that as I was extremely competent in my marketing efforts, I should rather take over as CMD of MECON Ltd. I informed him in the presence of the CMD of MECON that the current CMD was extremely knowledgeable and a highly qualified technocrat and he would get the work done with the help of the scientists, engineers, and consultants in undertaking this particular task. I was only acting as a pillar of moral support for them.

Ultimately, TNEB gave this particular work order to MECON Ltd, and this was another significant order worth more than Rs. 300 crores for MECON Ltd.

During that particular time of financial crisis and lack of sufficient work orders, it was a big boost for the organisation of MECON Ltd to get 2 significant work orders, and that too, in and around Madras City.

To be very frank and honest, I would like to state that for MECON Ltd, which has been a consulting organisation under the Ministry of Steel, this was a very rare opportunity to showcase their competence, skills, and implementation of projects and that too, in 2 brand new projects. In a way, it was a dream come true for them.

The success of the entire project was made possible due to the excellent combined teamwork within MECON. My role was that of a catalyst only. The main project proposals, and that too, the very innovative manner in addressing the complicated issues with the organisation of ISRO and TNEB, added to the credit of MECON. Last but not least, MECON approached the entire process with a sense of responsibility, dedication, and determination.

The second Rocket Launch Pad, which was inaugurated by the President of India, Dr. A.P.J. Abdul Kalam, passed the test of mettle. Later on, I came to understand that the construction of the overhead coal handling transport system at Ennore was also completed successfully. I would visit the site frequently and met the officers and staff, encouraging them, to perform their tasks as per the expectations of TNEB during the implementation of that project. Even today, I understand that the external overhead coal handling rail transport system is still in operation at Ennore Thermal Power Station for the transportation of coal from the ship onto the thermal power station.

As I was looking after quite a few loss-making public sector companies in the Ministry of Steel, the Secretary, Steel, had tremendous confidence in me that I would somehow contribute my mite in imbuing a positive mindset to enable them to come back to their original strengths to face further challenges as per the expectations of the government.

As Hindustan Construction Ltd. (HSCL) had been looking for jobs outside the steel sector, such as in the construction sector, due to their vast manpower resources, they somehow secured the work order from the State Government of Tamil Nadu around 1998 for the construction of 4 blocks of a 10-storey building to accommodate the MLAs of the Tamil Nadu Assembly at that time, as the existing MLA hostels were ageing. I also visited the city of Chennai and inspected the ongoing work. It was around the same period when I was regularly visiting Ennore Port to oversee the construction works of the external overhead coal handling transport system by MECON with the help of HSCL. I had a few occasions to visit the new buildings under construction to accommodate MLAs in the government Estate to verify the quality and speed up the construction of the hostels as per the terms and conditions of the work order given by the State Government.

On a later date maybe, after a year or so, I was invited by the CMD and Executive Director and their senior colleagues of HSCL for the inauguration of the 4 blocks of the newly constructed ten-storied buildings for accommodating the people's representatives of the legislative assembly. The function was presided over by the Chief Minister Dr. Kalaignar Karunanidhi. As I happened to be the government Director of the Company, I was also honoured with the presentation of a shawl and a memento by the Chief Minister, in addition to the presentation of shawls and mementoes to the CMD and the Executive Director of HSCL.

I must appreciate that the officers and staff of both the loss-making companies i.e. MECON Ltd and HSCL were aware of their strengths as well as their weaknesses but, in my opinion, needed their morale to be boosted to outperform their implementation aspects when executing such big projects which they never attempted in this country.

Moreover, I would like to inform, for the benefit of the reader, that HSCL was originally conceived after independence for the construction of only steel plants in this country at different places, which were later brought under the ambit of SAIL. But what happened a couple of decades later was that though the company started with only 95 officers and a couple of hundred more highly skilled personnel, the strength of the company unfortunately went ultimately, over a period of time, to 17,000 employees.

Obviously, over a period of time, due to the absence of continuous work orders in the steel sector, at a later date, the company had to forcibly seek jobs in the construction sector. Unfortunately, their incomes were not sufficient at all to pay the salaries of several thousand employees. Most of the employees of HSCL who were located in the states of Bihar and Madhya Pradesh, wherever the steel plants were, were devoid of their salaries for months together. So there was no other way except to take a loan of nearly Rs. 350 crores from the financial institutions backed by government Guarantee for the separation of at least 6,500 employees in one go from the organisation of HSCL. Afterwards, as a consequence of doing that, when the strength of the employees came down, with the new work orders in the construction sector wherever they could get, they could somehow make the payment of salaries. But the big issue at that time was how to separate 6,500 employees in one go without sufficient incomes from the company unless and until the financial institutions agreed to volunteer loans provided the Government of India gave guarantees for such loans.

One could imagine how any financial institution could give a loan to the tune of crores of rupees to a loss-making organisation and that too, with the bloated strength of the organisation. As it was rather difficult to convince my own colleagues at my level in the Ministry of Finance to get the requisite government guarantees, even if I could succeed with my efforts in getting the bank loans to the tune of approximately 350 crores from a few financial institutions, I took the initiative and went along with the Secretary, Ministry of Steel, to meet the Union Minister of Finance to place our argument and request in front of him.

Fortunately for me, the advantage was that the Union Finance Minister was very well aware of the plight of the employees of HSCL as some of their units were located in the state of Bihar. I could thus convince him about the need for separation of a minimum of 6,500 employees through the Voluntary Retirement Scheme (VRS). I went fully prepared on how I would like to proceed in separating 6,500 employees in one go, provided the Union Finance Minister agreed to give the government guarantees if I succeeded in the next couple of weeks in getting the bank loans. I must say that the then Secretary, Steel, was fully supportive of my stand. Thanks to this, the conversation was more or less between me and the Union Finance Minister. It was extremely heartening to see the Union Finance Minister agreeing to my suggestions for the implementation of the Voluntary Retirement Scheme for 6,500 employees of HSCL in one go, at the same time in the largest interests of HSCL in general and for the welfare of the unfortunate employees who were devoid of regular income in particular.

After getting a clear assent from the Union Finance Minister, I proceeded in the next week along with the CMD HSCL and Executive Director to meet the Chairman and Managing Director of state Bank of India and the CMDs of a few more banks in Mumbai. I had to do a lot of canvassing for their help, as they hesitated to give loans to a loss-making company which was in dire straits. Ultimately, if I remember correctly, the company got approximately Rs. 350 crores or so from a couple of banks with the complete support of the requisite government guarantees.

In the next month or so, I was immensely satisfied that we could separate 6500 employees of the company through the VRS system with the requisite financial incentives along with their unpaid wages over some period of time. In fact, they were so happy that at last after several months of waiting, they could get some financial assistance from the government. The reader might be surprised to know that the political leaders who came to put pressure on me originally about the poor plight of the employees who were not paid their wages for months together later on thanked me profusely for helping the company at a very difficult and critical juncture. In this connection, I would like to mention that the Deputy Speaker of the Parliament called me on the telephone and thanked me as well.

After some time, the government decided I should take over as the CMD of HSCL in addition to my duties. The corporate office of HSCL was in Calcutta. So I had to shuttle between Delhi and Calcutta to take care of that company. I was there for 10 months as CMD, also in addition to my duties and responsibilities as Joint Secretary to the Government of India in the Ministry of Steel. The first and foremost thing I did was to shift the corporate headquarters from a rental building to another small rental building as a large amount of monthly rent was unnecessarily being paid to a private organisation for many years. I considered that the corporate office located in the original rental building was too big after the separation of 6,500 employees of that organisation. Therefore, I had the corporate headquarters office shifted to a smaller place where the office staff, including the then Director of Finance and Secretary, could be accommodated in the new premises. I had a detailed talk with all of them and told them that there was no question of insubordination or making unreasonable demands when the company itself was in doldrums. I categorically told them that unless all of them would contribute their mite for the growth and development of the company in a significant manner and obey the orders of the then Director of Finance and the Secretary of the company, I would not hesitate to take the strongest possible disciplinary action against them. As we could separate 6,500 employees in one go with the help of bank loans supported by government guarantees, the employee strength came down sufficiently. Further, with the diversification of works in the construction sector by HSCL and cutting down of wasteful expenditure, the company was somehow able to manage the situation. However, it was rather difficult to control the organisation which had been living in a state of indiscipline.

As the then Joint Secretary, Ministry of Steel, in addition to looking after 6 Public Sector Undertakings, I was also responsible for providing necessary help, support, and guidance to the existing steel mills of SAIL and RINL (VSP) as well as the new steel plants emerging in the private sector.

I would like to state that I was a Government nominee Director on the Board of RINL (Rashtriya Ispat Nigam Ltd) which had only one steel plant, Vizag Steel Plant (VSP), and VSP was not under the ambit of SAIL. VSP was a modern steel plant which was implemented at the cost of Rs. 8000 crores and at that time it was the only shore-based steel plant in this country. When I met the Secretary of Steel, he told me that VSP was making tremendous losses due to the fact that the initial construction cost was too heavy. He added that unless and until the government did physical and financial restructuring of the company, it would be rather difficult for the company to survive. I used to attend the board meetings of RINL at Vishakhapatnam, corporate headquarters and sometimes in the Ministry of Steel.

After I attended a few meetings of the Board, I could understand the strengths and weaknesses of the company. It was decided that the physical and financial restructuring of the company was the need of the hour.

Therefore, we had to call 4 different private sector companies, namely McKinsey, Price Waterhouse Cooper, A.T. Kearney, and another company whose name I do not remember now, who were consultants in the financial sector. I had detailed discussions with my colleagues and all 4 consultant firms before selecting a particular financial firm for giving their suggestions and for implementation.

Ultimately, it was decided that A.T. Kearney would be the business consultancy for us, and we could propose the first physical and financial restructuring of the company, which obviously involved an infusion of a few hundred crores for the growth and development of the company and also to ward off the losses, etc. Before we could convince the Finance Ministry and take up a cabinet note for the said proposal, I had to have detailed discussions again and again with the business consultant. Ultimately, the cabinet note was prepared by the Ministry, and finally, the Ministry of Steel got approval from the government for the proposal for the first physical and financial restructuring of VSP. This could help the plant to continue to survive. Another proposal was also submitted to the government. In fact, the government approved the physical and financial restructuring proposals twice in view of the dire necessity to do so. By that time, my tenure was also coming to an end. I was shifted from the Ministry of Steel as I had to revert to the State cadre.

Subsequently, I was posted as the Principal Resident Commissioner, Government of Assam at Assam Bhavan, New Delhi, in the latter part of December 2001. This was about 50 days short of my tenure as the Joint Secretary in the Ministry of Steel due to the insistence of the Government of Assam for my joining as quickly as possible in my new role at Assam Bhavan, New Delhi.

After I left the Ministry of Steel, in view of the continuous and constant efforts in organising the physical and financial restructuring of RINL and also in view of the steel prices going up by the end of 2001 and also during 2002, I understood that RINL was able to make profits during the year 2003. It was a real job satisfaction for me and ultimately, I could state with a sense of pride in my contribution towards this result.

The only company that was not bothersome for me was Manganese Ore India Ltd, or MOIL, with its headquarters in Nagpur. MOIL had underground mines in the States of Maharashtra and Madhya Pradesh. They were started during the British times. For the first time in my life, I went to the underground mines along with the CMD through a shaft, a kind of lift which went from the ground up to a depth of 200 ft. We descended 150 ft in order to understand how the Manganese Ores were extracted from the earth. The employees were engaged in manually separating Manganese Ores from the earth.

In order to understand and appreciate how the Manganese ore mines were operated, I went to different places in Maharashtra near Nagpur, but most of the mines are located in Madhya Pradesh, i.e. the present state of Chhattisgarh.

In Chhattisgarh, about 6 underground mines are there, and even today the houses that were constructed by the British for the officers and employees are intact and they. They had a very nice Guest Houseguest house in Balaghat for visiting officers.

The company operated from the Corporate Headquarters at corporate headquarters in Nagpur, where I attended a quite a few meetings of their employees as well as those which were held rather in their work placesworkplaces in the State of Chhattisgarh.

During my Steel Ministry days, I also looked after a couple of moreother companies called Bharat RefractorinessRefractories Ltd and Bird Group of Companies.

I was not the Government Nominee Director or nominee director in both of the companies, and the only the Director working with me was the Government nominee Director.

Bird Group of Companies headquarter wasCompanies' headquarters were located in Calcutta, and they had underground iron ore mines in the Statestate of Orissa, whereas the headquarters of Bharat Refractoriness Ltd waswere near Bokaro.

I have narrated below my visits abroad during my stay as Joint Secretary to the Government of India in the Ministry of Steel.

During my stay in the Ministry of Steel for 5 years, I was fortunate in to lead a 5 -member delegation of the Steel Industrysteel industry, including the private sector, for participating in meetings organised by OECD (Organization of Organisation for Economic CooperationCo-operation and Development) headquartered at Paris. The headquarters in Paris were just across the road from the Indian Mission. Continuously for 5 years, from 1997 to 2001, I went to Paris to attend the International Conference of OECD meetings.

OECD was generally by and large represented by more than 85 countries at that time, and India had Observer status. My participation in the meetings enabled me to communicate amongst member countries about the growth and development of the Steel Industry and the contribution of the Government in the development of the steel sector in both the public and private sectors. There were too many representatives representing different countries to participate in the meetings of the Steel Committee. In my very first meeting, I was given 8 minutes, and the first meeting was a fascinating one. The Chairman at the head table had a set of lights in front of him akin to traffic lights. He explained that every speaker would be given exactly 8 minutes to talk and that at the end of the sixth minute or so, the green light would flicker. Once the speaker exceeded the 7th minutes or so, immediately the red light would flicker. That was an indication for the speaker to stop talking. It was a very novel way of stopping the representatives of the different countries notfrom exceeding the time limit given to them.

In my very first meeting, I went fully prepared with my speech. I knew the time constraints exactly; when the green lights started flickering, within a few seconds, I stopped my talk.

In a lighter vein, I informed the Chairman that I did not want him to switch on the red light as there was no need for him to stop my talking and to indicate that I was within my allotted time limit. I could thus impress the audience with the kind of speech I had to deliver in such a conference. Even the private sector representative was flabbergasted. He heard that it was my first conference where I was speaking about the steel sector and the Government'sgovernment's role in the growth and development of the steel industry.

In a way, it was a good gathering where one could understand the state of play from the speeches of representatives of various developed countries and developing countries. In the afternoon, there were very good interactions among the various representatives of the different countries who participated in the conference.

I found that the very first meeting was a very interesting one as I could interact with the senior representatives of the Governments of those countries. As I stated in the foregoing paragraphs that, every year for 5 years I went to Paris with different members of the delegation as the leader of the delegation. It was a fact that the Indian Embassy officials took very good care of my visits, including transport and accommodation. What was more impressive for me to notice was that for such an international conference attended by high officials from different countries in the garb of security, I noticed only one smartly dressed police constable who was outside the building. He quietly observed the movements of the delegates in and out of the building. It was really a wonderful sight to see where such minimal security was only provided, bereft of ostentation.

I had to proceed to China in the year 2000 once as a member of a delegation led by the Chairman and Managing Director, of Manganese Ore India Ltd, with its directors. It was a 5 -member delegation, and we visited Beijing, Shanghai, and one moreanother place in order to explore the possibility of exporting Manganese ore to their companies who were in need of manganese ore. There was a problem of communication as most of them, including the company representatives in China, could speak only in Chinese, and we could speak only in English. Fortunately, they organized an interpreter who was a nice lady and she was deputed to be with us throughout our stay whenever we went to participate in such meetings and for visits to some units beyond Beijing and Shanghai. Moreover, at that time, there was an exhibition related to the development of the steel sector among 9 sectors in China where some countries participated. In India, MOIL's representatives also participated in thea small pavilion and explained to the visitors MOIL's companyvisitor MOIL company's objectives, the products manufactured, and about the company's profitability of the company, visitors, etc.

Within a couple of months of my joining in the Steel Ministry, I had to accompany the CMD, of Kudremukh Iron Ore Company Limited (KIOCL) to visit the mines located in the Western Ghats hills approximately 200 kms from Mangalore Port. At Mangalore, the company had its own factory.

After the iron ore was extracted from the surface mines, it was transhipped in a slurry state to the Mangalore factory of KIOCL. The pellets were manufactured from this iron ore for ultimate transport not only to Japan but also to some other countries.

I was a member of a delegation led by the CMD of KIOCL visiting Tokyo. We spent a few days in Tokyo attending the business meetings across morning and afternoon sessions.

One thing that struck me during the negotiations was how tough and difficult the Japanese representatives were while conducting the negotiations. During the meetings, 7 of the representatives from the Japanese company called Nippon Steel Corporation participated in the negotiations for the purchase of iron ore from KIOCL. Only one person spoke, and of course, in English only. The rest of the members were absolutely tight-lipped. Among them, they were whispering in Japanese language.

On our side also, only the CMD did spoke and interacted with them. But among us, we used to consult about the price reduction or bargaining to be made from the opposite side in the English language, which the Japanese could easily understand

I had noticed one thing especially, in the matter of provision of minimum security in that building of Nippon Steel. During that time, Nippon Steel itself was producing 16 million tonnes of steel, whereas in Japan, there was not a single iron ore mine. They had imported iron ore from different sources, including from various mines fromin our country, and made steel in their factories and exportedto export to other countries.

This is just to give a comparative example, when at that time our country's total steel production was just approximately 10 million tonnes.

Of course, over a period of time in view of the liberalisation and growth of the private sector steel development in our country, the growth and development of the steel industry picked up and perhaps, at a later period, our country managed to produce over 100 million tonnes of steel annually. We are today the world's second -largest steel producer and surpassed Japan a few years back.

In praise of the Japanese negotiators of Nippon Steel, I must say one thing. They were extremely business-like when they conducted the negotiations for the purchase of the iron ore pellets to be exported from India. For instance, the Japanese were not willing to accept an increase of even one penny while conducting their price negotiations. It seemed to bethat their bargaining style was much more than like buying brinjals from a vegetable market. But I found the bargaining power of Japanese company officials in their purchase was far better than our bargaining power in selling our own product.

I must appreciate that even though they were very tough negotiators, they were extremely hospitable. We spent 3 days in Tokyo and all the time we were attending meetings and meetings only except during lunch and dinner. The Japanese officials were very happy with the Indian food and therefore, they took us to different Indian restaurants as hosts for our lunches and dinners for all the 3 days. It was really a welcome change to notice their attitude from that of a tough negotiator to that of an excellent hospitable host.

I only looked after KIOCL for a few months in the beginning as Joint Secretary and attended its board meetings for a limited period. Likewise, I attended the board meetings of National Mineral Development Corporation (NMDC) and looked after the company as Joint Secretary only for a few months. Subsequently, of course, there was another Joint Secretary who was made the Government Nominee Directornominee director for KIOCL and NMDC.

Regarding my role as a Government Nominee Directornominee director, except in the case of KIOCL and MOIL, I did not have any opportunity to visit abroad in respect of promotional efforts of other companies, and there was, in fact, no need to do so.

On the whole, my first deputation assignment at the Joint Secretary level in the Government of India in an important Ministry exposed me to various challenges in the management of difficult Public Sector Undertakings.

I had already in the foregoing paragraphs indicated how difficult it was to turn around RINL, MECON, and HSCL. At the risk of being immodest, I would like to say that I was able to contribute my humble mite to the growth and development of these 3 companies to the extent possible and also to ensure that they got sufficient work orders, especially in respect of MECON and HSCL.

As far as RINL was concerned, I would visit Visakhapatnam and not only attend the board meetings but also went around the organisation and interacted with the employees to boost their morale. For anybody who has not seen a steel plant, it is an eye-opener. Any steel plant is well spread out and looks like a very big township. It would take almost a whole day when I wanted to see the steel production at various stages, especially since I wanted to get acquainted with different types of steel products that were made at VSP.

I considered myself fortunate by God's divine grace that I could land in the Ministry of Steel and face several challenges and also avail the wonderful opportunities to build up the institutions while approaching the officers and staff in an easy manner to understand and appreciate their concerns, their difficulties, and their own suggestions for the organisation's benefits.

In the case of MECON Ltd, the headquarters were at Ranchi, and it was also one of the oldest consultant and projects implementation organisations. It was only MECON Ltd. and HSCL that literally built up the steel plants in the Government sector at the initial stage. Later, they did contribute their mite to the growth and development of the private sector steel plants as well in the years 1998-2000 and onwards. In Ranchi, of course, there were wonderful scientists, engineers, and my interactions with them were a pleasurable exercise. I learnt a lot in that organisation, as they were not building or manufacturing any such products; they were only giving their brainpower as consultants. Later on, they also started implementing projects mostly related to steel industries.

In the foregoing paragraphs, as mentioned by me originally, MECON Ltd and HSCL were conceived for construction of steel projects. Later on, of course, they diversified in the case of TNEB's external overhead coal handling with conveyor belt through rail transport system and construction of the second Rocket Launch Pad at Sriharikota and other construction activities in the Government sector other than the steel sector.

During my 5 years of stay, that is from January 1997 to December 2001, I would like to mention that I was greatly benefitted by my interactions with the Union Ministers and Secretaries as I could understand and appreciate their ways and attitudes in the administration of the Ministry of Steel.

During my tenure in the Ministry of Steel as Joint Secretary to the Government of India, I participated as a member of the Trade Delegation in my capacity as a Government Nominee Director on the Board of Directors of KIOCL Ltd. The delegation was led by the Chairman and Managing Director of KIOCL Ltd to Tokyo, Japan, for trade negotiations on the export of Iron Ore Pellets to Nippon Steel Company Ltd in Tokyo. I led trade delegations to Paris for OECD meetings as Chairman of the delegations consecutively for 5 years from 1997 to 2001.

I visited China as a Member of the 4-member delegation led by the Chairman and Managing Director of Manganese Ore India Ltd (MOIL) in my capacity as a Government Nominee Director on the Board of Directors of MOIL. During our visit to China, we went to Beijing and Shanghai, and I met several prospective buyers of Manganese ore for their plants and visited some units as well in the nearby towns. I also visited Brussels, Belgium as the Leader of the Trade Delegation and conducted negotiations to boost exports promotion measures in the steel sector.

Principal Resident Commissioner, Government of Assam at Assam Bhavan, New Delhi from December 2001 to September 2006

After a five-year tenure as Joint Secretary to the Government of India in the Ministry of Steel, the Chief Minister of Assam wanted me to take over as Principal Resident Commissioner (PRC) of the Government of Assam at Assam Bhavan, New Delhi.

Generally, after a five-year tenure with the Government of India, an All India Service Officer would revert back to the State cadre. But in my case, I continued to reside in Delhi as the Secretary to the Chief Minister. Assam called me and requested that I immediately join as Principal Resident Commissioner of the Government of Assam at Assam Bhavan, New Delhi.

The Principal Resident Commissioner's primary responsibility was to act as the chief representative of the State Government and to attend meetings with the Central Government departments/Ministries wherever there are issues of the state government that required attention at the central level and also to participate along with the senior officers of the State Government in the various meetings of the different Ministries. There was also the necessity on the part of the Principal Resident Commissioner to take care of the guest house at Assam Bhavan with the assistance of officers and staff so deployed. When I joined in the third week of December 2001, there were a lot of problems regarding the ways and means position of the State Government of Assam, and financial resources were not adequate even to make payment of salaries to the employees, including senior officers of the State Government at that time.

Obviously, the role of the Principal Resident Commissioner as the chief representative of the State Government was to negotiate and attend meetings with the senior officers of the Ministry of Finance and to ensure sufficient funds were provided to the State Government to tide over the crisis in view of the difficult financial position of the Government of Assam, even to pay the salaries of employees regularly.

The very objective of my selection and appointment as Principal Resident Commissioner, Government of Assam by the Chief Minister was that having spent quite a number of years at New Delhi as a senior officer of the Government of India, I was in a much better position to interact with the officers of the Finance Ministry, as on a number of occasions, I had interacted with them during my earlier posting. The Chief Minister thought that I would be the best person to conduct the negotiations with the senior officers of the Government of India on behalf of the State Government whenever the State Government officers came to Delhi for taking up such issues. Therefore, I had to take up various issues with senior officers of the Ministry of Finance to get things done to help the State Government departments in times of their need.

Moreover, another important duty and responsibility of the Principal Resident Commissioner, Government of Assam, was to accompany the Chief Minister of Assam during his visits to New Delhi whenever he came to meet the Prime Minister and other Ministers or whenever he came to attend conferences of the Chief Ministers convened by the Government of India from time to time. In other words, I had to be present during his stay in New Delhi and be in attendance at all his meetings with the Union Cabinet Ministers, including the Prime Minister.

My duties as Principal Resident Commissioner also included receiving the Chief Minister and Governor of Assam at the airport whenever they visited New Delhi and seeing them off also on the conclusion of their visits. This was a protocol requirement and, in a way, this was a kind of unavoidable responsibility.

In addition to the successful management of the guest house, I was equally responsible for the proper administration of the office of the Principal Resident Commissioner. At that time, we had 2 buildings, namely, an old Assam House which was in a dilapidated condition and the other one, the Assam Bhavan where my office was located. I tried my level best to convince the then Chief Minister of Assam to demolish the old Assam

House building and to construct a new structure. As requested by the Chief Minister, I got the old Assam House building thoroughly renovated during my time, and a formal function was also held for the inauguration of the newly renovated Assam House building.

In a lighter vein, if I may say so, with great difficulty, I had to put up with less work for more than 4 years, i.e. from January 2002 until September 2006, compared to my various other assignments.

In between, I took a few months of leave as there was nothing much of significance to perform as the Principal Resident Commissioner towards the end of my tenure. In any case, the very objective of my posting as Principal Resident Commissioner was achieved within a couple of years for ensuring regular payment of salaries to officers and staff, and I contributed as a successful negotiator in all our meetings with the Government of India representatives. As I had a Resident Commissioner, who was junior to me, he took care during my absence whenever the Chief Minister and the Governor visited New Delhi at that time, in addition to attending meetings with senior officers of the Central Government. He was taking care of the Assam Bhavan office and guest house as well.

Fortunately, in the months of July to September, I came to know that I was empanelled as an Additional Secretary to the Government of India. Later on, I got my appointment as Additional Secretary to the Government of India in the Ministry of Water Resources at the beginning of October 2006. After a few months of leave in September 2006, I resumed my duties as Principal Resident Commissioner. Later, I informed the Chief Minister of Assam, on the telephone, that I had received my appointment order as the Additional Secretary in the Ministry of Water Resources. He was very happy, wished me all the very best, and requested me to take care of the interests of the State of Assam in the Ministry of Water Resources after joining my new assignment.

Additional Secretary/Special Secretary to the Government of India, Ministry of Water Resources from October 2006 to May 2010

I joined as Additional Secretary in the Ministry of Water Resources, Government of India on October 6, 2006. I continued in that Ministry until my date of superannuation in the month of May 2010 as Special Secretary in the rank and status equivalent to that of Secretary to the Government of India.

In the succeeding paragraphs, I would like to mention about my eventful stay as an Additional Secretary and also my visits to various states as well as abroad in connection with the duties and responsibilities required of this role.

I had a memorable stay for about 4 years in my capacity as Additional Secretary and later towards the end of my tenure as Special Secretary to the Government of India in the Ministry of Water Resources. I worked with 2 Union Ministers for nearly 4 years of my tenure. Both of them were, of course, Members of Parliament for a long-time and had sufficient experience as Union Ministers. They were very decent, pleasant, and wonderful human beings and I vividly cherished my assignment which provided me not only excellent opportunities to work with them as well as various colleagues in the Ministry and several other personnel from institutions under the Ministry of Water Resources.

Hierarchically, there was a Secretary to the Government of India in the Ministry between the Ministers and myself. I was expected to send official files to the Minister through the Secretary to the government. However, I would always be called by the Minister for all meetings addressed by him and they would frequently get in touch with me directly through the intercom and request my presence whenever they wanted any sort of clarifications or suggestions that were felt necessary in several matters of the Ministry. I worked with the first Minister for about 2 years or so and likewise with the second Minister thereafter for almost 2 years.

Immediately after my joining the Ministry of Water Resources, the Union Minister of Water Resources had a detailed meeting with me and ascertained my qualifications and experience, etc., and requested proper guidance in enabling him to make the right decisions on all important issues. I candidly informed him that it was my duty and responsibility to guide him properly in the largest public interest. I also assured him that I would never mislead him on any of the issues.

I had very pleasant memories of visiting Srinagar and also Puducherry on 2 different occasions at different points in time along with the Union Minister. In fact, when I visited Srinagar with him, I took along some of the senior officers of a few organisations within our Ministry for discussions with the State Government Irrigation Department officials. It was felt necessary that we had to discuss with the concerned State Government officials to make certain decisions on pending issues. Throughout the meeting, in addition to our Minister and our own senior colleagues, the local State Government Minister and his officials had a very purposeful meeting. It enabled them to bring to the notice of our officers certain pending matters. Perhaps, this was the first time when senior officers of the Ministry of Water Resources had gone to Srinagar and had detailed discussions with the State Government officers to sort out pending issues directly. They were extremely happy and enthusiastically participated in the process of resolving pending issues. I wished that such a meeting had been organised in the past, which would have made the decision-making process easier and less cumbersome at the level of both the Central and State Governments and in the resolution in an expeditious manner in the interest of time management and in the larger public interest.

I was pleasantly surprised later on when, after the meeting and while I was resting in my room, the local Minister dropped by to thank me for organising such a meeting. It was really gracious of him to have taken the trouble to come and meet me at my place of stay just to express his gratitude.

I may like to say that had the Union Minister of Water Resources not taken the initiative to organise such a meeting at Srinagar itself, the decision-making processes at various levels in the Ministry of Water Resources would have consumed more time as well as a lot of unnecessary and unwarranted correspondence between the State Government and our organisations in the Ministry. As the saying goes, 'all is well that ends well'.

On another occasion, I accompanied the Union Minister of Water Resources to Puducherry to attend a conference of officials of various organisations working under the water resources management both from the local Union Territory administration as well as NGOs. This meeting was attended not only by our Minister but also by the then Chief Minister and other senior officials both from the Government of India as well as that of the Union Territory of Puducherry. Of course, attending meetings was part and parcel of our civil service life, but why I wanted to mention this was that I accompanied the Union Minister of Water Resources from Chennai airport to Puducherry by road. His Private Secretary, being a friendly junior colleague in our civil service, insisted that I should accompany the Minister and guide him thoroughly during this sojourn as I hailed from the state of Tamil Nadu. I must say that the Minister was extremely inquisitive, and he started raising so many questions about the state, the people, and the names of villages on the way. By and large, he wanted to have a feel of what exactly was the importance of the places enroute. But unfortunately, it was rather late in the evening, so we could only talk about the general issues.

On our return journey from Puducherry, it was rather late in the afternoon. On the way back, we visited Mahabalipuram. The Minister went round the Shore Temple and started observing the sculptures, asking several questions about the Pallava temple. He was so happy to have visited the places, though the time was very short, and we had a flight to catch later that day. He had a childlike inquisitiveness about knowing many issues of people who might have lived in the past in those areas. After all, it was an ancient temple stretching back 1600 years. It was perhaps the only Shore Temple which survived the vagaries of nature as 6 more temples built by the Pallava Kings had already been washed by the sea. I informed him that historically it was a belief that there was a tsunami more than 2000 years ago and during the occurrence of that tsunami, all such temples had gone underwater. Fortunately, the only one at Mahabalipuram survived the vagaries of nature even after 1600 years.

The reader must be wondering why I mentioned the Minister's visits and his inquisitive nature. By and large, people have their own perceptions about politicians and civil servants. I deliberately mentioned the way the Minister conducted himself in the meetings at Srinagar and also at Puducherry, where I could understand his humility and a good quality of inquisitiveness about the issues he wanted to know.

In my civil service days, I never had any issues that could not be resolved while dealing with politicians or Ministers. In my experience, it all depends on how you understand their priorities and how you can convince what was possible and not possible within the set of rules by which a civil servant would be able to make decisions in the best interests of the people. Obviously, it does not mean that every politician is a paragon of virtue, or that even the relatively well-meaning politicians are unfailing at all times. But what it does mean is that many had the right intentions and were willing to see reason.

In the succeeding paragraphs, I would like to mention my visits with the second Minister of Water Resources to the state of Kerala and also when I accompanied him to attend the World Water Week in Stockholm, Sweden.

I accompanied the Union Minister of Water Resources to Kumarakom and Alleppey to meet the villagers and also to discuss the issues of agriculture in the Kuttanadu region. We had a very good meeting on a big boat where the public representatives, along with their local MLAs, our Minister, myself, and other senior officials of the Ministry of Water Resources participated. During the meeting, we tried to understand the issues raised by them and assured them that appropriate decisions would be taken to take care of their interests. After all, we had gone there only to listen to them, understand, and interact with them personally so that there were no communication bottlenecks and one could make the right decisions without hesitation. I considered it a wonderful visit not only from the point of satisfaction with our efforts but also a memorable one where we could do something to the satisfaction of the people in whose interest we had gone there.

As regards our participation in the World Water Week at Stockholm during 2009, I met the Minister and informed him that by and large in the past there was a tradition of either the Minister or the Secretary to the government of the Ministry attending the World Water Week every year. No other officials were encouraged to attend such an important event. I felt very bad and rather disappointed to notice that when the Ministry of Water Resources had 17 organisations under its administrative control and especially when we had technical organisations like the Central Water Commission, Central Ground Water Board, National Institute of Hydrology, and Central Soil and Materials Testing and Research Station including the National Water Development Agency in the Ministry, it was never thought that any one of the representatives should have attended such an important event. Therefore, I met the Union Minister of Water Resources, took up the issue with him, and gave my sincere suggestions. I informed him that the Minister might consider a team of 5 or 6 officers to visit the World Water Week at Stockholm and also allow the officers to put up a pavilion in the exhibition organised simultaneously with the World Water Week to depict the activities of at least a few organisations under the Ministry of Water Resources.

I also told the Minister that as far as I understood, other countries did depute their officers for participation in such an important event and also for participation in the exhibition organised simultaneously at that event. I informed the Minister that I was not interested in accompanying him but I would be very happy if he could agree to my suggestion to allow our officers to participate in that important World Water Week and to establish our pavilion depicting our competencies in these organisations. The objective was not just to offer a 'foreign trip' to the officers. The officers handling these highly important organisations needed this exposure. Their networking with counterparts from other countries could hopefully generate new ideas, which could be beneficial to the country. It also allowed us to project to the wider world the work that India was doing.

He readily agreed to my suggestion of our colleagues' participation in the event. At the same time, he was insistent that I should also accompany him.

I visited Stockholm a day before the arrival of the Minister and went around the venue where the World Water Week was expected to begin the next day. Before proceeding to Stockholm, I called a meeting of the officers who had to accompany me and told them to put up an excellent pavilion depicting their areas of work including research, etc., for the benefit of the visitors. I categorically informed them that they should try their level best to put up a good show to make their pavilion attractive.

The next day, I visited the venue along with the Minister and attended the inaugural function. There was a deputation of a few senior officers of the government of Tamil Nadu for participation in the World Water Week. They were very happy to have participated for the first time in an event like this. After the inauguration, there were a few more interactions with the participants from various countries. Of course, all the colleagues who had been deputed by the Ministry representing various organisations did participate. I introduced the State Government officials to our Minister and also took him to our pavilion to interact with the representatives of our Ministry. The Minister was extremely happy with the interaction and very much impressed by the pavilion.

Since a few more days were at hand before the concluding function of the World Water Week at Stockholm, I accompanied the Minister on a visit to Norway during that interval. We reached Oslo from Stockholm by travelling on a train for 6 hours. We stayed in Oslo for 2 days. Fortunately, my batch mate, an Indian Foreign Service officer, happened to be the Indian Ambassador in Oslo, Norway. Likewise, my other dear friend who was junior to me by a year in the Indian Foreign Service happened to be the Indian Ambassador in Stockholm.

At Oslo, Norway, the Indian Ambassador organised meetings for the Minister with the Indian community. It was nice of him to have introduced the people of the Indian community who lived in Oslo to our Minister and also organised a luncheon session. Some of the Indian members also invited us to participate with them later on for a dinner. The next day, we had a very good meeting with senior officials of the Norwegian Geotechnical Institute. We had a detailed discussion for possible collaboration between the Geotechnical Institute and our organisation such as the Central Soil and Materials Testing Research Station (CSMRS) in New Delhi for further research and development activities. The meeting was followed by lunch hosted by the Norwegian side. On our way back from Norway, and after visiting some places in Stockholm, we attended the concluding ceremony of World Water Week. Our Minister participated in the concluding session and addressed the gathering.

Many of the officers belonging to other Ministries and senior officials might not be fully aware that there were 17 organisations reporting to the Ministry of Water Resources. Just for the information of the reader, I would like to mention the following: Central Water Commission (CWC), Central Ground Water Board (CGWB), and Central Soil and Materials Testing Research and Station (CSMRS), etc. They are based in Delhi.

The Central Water Commission has offices spread over different parts of the country. Likewise, the Central Ground Water Board also has different regional centres in various regions of the country. We have only one Research Station under the Ministry of Water Resources, i.e. the National Institute of Hydrology at Roorkee near Haridwar, a very distinguished institute entrusted with the study and research aspects of hydrology. This institution has research scholars and engineers who are devoted to ascertaining the objectives of not only the hydrology of water but also its applications in various formats.

There is another important training institution, i.e. the Central Water Training Institute in Pune, where officers belonging to different State Governments and other organisations dealing with water resources are deputed for training. It has been functioning as a regular training institution with all facilities for academic studies and hostel facilities for trainees to attend the training programmes over different durations.

The Central Water and Power Research Station (CWPRS) in Pune was one of the oldest institutions under the Ministry of Water Resources.

We have another important institution, a government undertaking called Water and Power Consultancy and Services Limited (WAPCOS) and National Project Construction Company Ltd (NPCC). These are Public Sector undertakings with their Board of Directors under the administrative control of the Ministry of Water Resources.

WAPCOS was a profit-making organisation at that time, in view of their admirable work on consulting services on water and power projects in various organisations within the country, and they had helped other State Governments as well during my tenure.

NPCC was a construction company and at that time it was not making a profit. The organisation was dealing with construction activities related to the water sector based on the work orders received at different places. The headquarters of both organisations were in New Delhi.

I interacted with the heads of so many institutions under the Ministry of Water Resources at different points of time, in addition to visiting these offices in Delhi and other places. If I may say so, on the whole, it was an unforgettable and wonderful experience to have worked with the Union Ministry of Water Resources.

This assignment gave me another important opportunity to interact with senior officials of the Water Resources departments of various State Governments whenever they came to meet the Minister or attend meetings convened by the Ministry of Water Resources in connection with various issues relating to the problems faced by the Water Resources Departments of the States. There were, of course, a lot of opportunities available for interactions with the concerned officers not only in the regional headquarters of the Central Government organisations under our Ministry but also in understanding the problems and finding solutions in various organisations of the Ministry in the different states. I had adopted a kind of principle that I was always accessible to the officers not only among the organisations of our own Ministry but also to the officers belonging to other concerned departments of the State Governments.

I also attended international conferences relating to the water sector in different countries, namely Brussels, Tehran, and Kathmandu, in addition to Stockholm in Sweden. I attended meetings for 3 days in Sacramento in the state of California, USA, in connection with an international conference on drainage and irrigation. I also attended a 4-day United Nations Conference in New York on sustainable environment in connection with the agriculture and water sector. I attended the UN Conference as a representative of the Ministry of Water Resources led by the Union Secretary to the Government of India in the Ministry of Environment. I led a delegation of some of our colleagues in the Ministry to represent certain issues in the water sector to be taken up in Europe. Therefore, when a meeting was called, I went with a few officers to Brussels, Belgium.

During my tenure in the Ministry of Water Resources, I led a 5-member Indian delegation to participate in an International Conference of G-15 Group of Countries on Agricultural Development and Water Resources

Management in Tehran, Iran, in the year 2007. The delegation included a couple of representatives from the Union Ministry of Agriculture and also a representative from the Ministry of External Affairs.

Later in the same year, I visited Kathmandu, Nepal for 3 days as the leader of a 5-member official delegation to participate in a conference of all the Member Countries of SAARC on 'Rain Water Harvesting and Ground Water Augmentation'. It was a very useful visit wherein one day was devoted to field visits and 2 days were devoted to interactions with the other participating member States of SAARC Countries.

I again visited Kathmandu, Nepal in 2008, leading an official delegation to negotiate the issue of some pending projects relating to water resources management at the Indo-Nepalese border.

I visited Madrid and Zaragoza in Spain as the Chairman of a 4-member official delegation to discuss and promote water consultancy and management. CMD, WAPCOS, and its directors were members of the delegation. Our delegation also participated in an exhibition relating to water management.

I also attended an International Conference on Irrigation and Drainage of Water Resources in Sacramento, California, USA as a member of the 5-member Indian delegation in the year 2008.

I was a member of the Indian delegation to the 17th session of the United Nations Commission on Sustainable Development in New York, USA. The delegation was led by the Secretary to the Government of India in the Ministry of Environment and Forests in the year 2009.

In addition to my useful and memorable visits abroad connected with my role in the Ministry of Water Resources, I also had the wonderful experience of attending National Conferences and interacting with various organisations not only within the Ministry of Water Resources but also with different Ministries and State Government departments, which had a particular emphasis on the importance of water. For instance, the reader may not know that water as a subject is also dealt with by the Ministry of Agriculture, the Ministry of Drinking Water Supply, and various other organisations under the State Governments. This is a very broad subject as water itself is a vital element for survival. I spent nearly 4 years of my tenure under the leadership of 2 different Union Ministers who were knowledgeable and experienced, and definitely interactive with the officials of our organisation in-depth during our meetings whenever there were issues to be discussed.

Another very important innovation that was introduced during the years 2007 and 2008 was based on the suggestion given by the Union Minister of state for Water Resources. This related to motivating the non-governmental organisations on the proper usage of water not only from the point of view of the availability of water but also from the point of view of the conservation of water in different aspects of our functioning in the urban and rural areas.

For the first time in the country, a National Water Award was instituted, and the first recipient was awarded a sum of Rs. 10 lakhs. In addition to the National Water Award, a few more awards were suggested by the Minister for organisations in the matter of propagation of proper utility and conservation of water, not only from the point of drinking water supply but also from the point of contribution of water for agricultural development in the country. Certain norms were suggested by him. The Minister himself had suggested that a committee might be formed under the Chairmanship of Dr. M.S. Swaminathan. He had also suggested to me the listing criteria after consultations with the senior officials of the Ministry and thereafter call for applications from many non-government organisations. By issuing general notices to the public in newspapers in local vernacular languages and in national newspapers as well, applications were invited with the stipulation of criteria for such awards.

After a huge response was received in the Ministry, the committee, as suggested by the Minister of Water Resources, met and considered all such applications. Apart from the Chairmanship of the Committee headed by Dr. M.S. Swaminathan, the committee included the Member of the Planning Commission, namely, Mr. B N Yugandhar, a retired I.A.S. officer, a representative of a Non-Governmental Organisation called Science and Environment, Ms. Sunitha Narayan, a Professor at a university, and also a scientist from a government Organisation relating to Water and Agriculture. The reader might be interested to know that Mr. Yugandhar is the father of Mr. Satya Nadella, the current CEO of Microsoft Corporation.

The Minister advised me that I should provide the logistic support and other assistance in going through the responses before the committee. So I went to meet Dr. M.S. Swaminathan, a Member of Parliament at that time, in order to organise the meeting at a venue of his choice. As suggested by the Chairman, I organised the meeting with the Committee Members in my office chamber. The committee examined all the responses to the advertisement issued, not only for the National Water Award but also for a few more awards to be given to certain non-government organisations. The responses were very good, and it took some time for the committee to examine all such responses based on the stipulations listed out by the Ministry of Water Resources in the advertisement for obtaining the prescribed awards. The committee patiently went through all such written responses and finally decided who should be the winner of the National Water Award, and a few more awards as well.

It was decided in that Committee Meeting that the President of the Hiware Bazaar Panchayat, Ahmednagar district, Maharashtra, be awarded the National Water Award for his wonderful activities in the matter of not only water conservation but also for motivating the villagers to effectively utilise the water for drinking as well as for agricultural development in an efficient manner.

It was a wonderful experience for me to have worked in the Ministry under the leadership of 2 different Union Ministers under their excellent guidance. I also acquired new domain knowledge and greatly benefitted because of my association with the highly qualified technical officers and scientists in various organisations under the Ministry of Water Resources.

Part-Time Assignments After Superannuation

CHAPTER

20

After my superannuation in the year 2010, I was appointed as Chairman of the Achievements Review Committee (ARC) by the Government of India, Ministry of Water Resources. This was my first part-time assignment. The ARC Committee consisted of technical experts, namely, the Chairman of the Central Ground Water Board, Retired Engineer-in-Chief of the Water Resources Department of the government of Bihar, Retired Professor of the Water Resources Department of I.I.T. Roorkee, and Scientist F of the Institute of Hydrology, Roorkee, as the Member-Secretary. The objective of the committee was to review the performance of the research works undertaken by the National Institute of Hydrology (NIH).

In the beginning of 2011, I settled down with my family in our own home in Chennai. I had the opportunity to serve in different part-time assignments by God's divine grace and, of course, with the guidance of well-wishers. If I may say so, the part-time assignments were of different types.

For instance, within a month of coming back to Chennai, I was appointed as an independent part-time Director in Ennore Port Company Ltd for a period of 3 years. Ennore Port Co Ltd was the only Government of India undertaking under the Ministry of Shipping. For me, it was certainly a novel exposure to work in the field of shipping as I had never had an opportunity to serve in the Ministry of Shipping. In addition to me, 2 more independent directors were also appointed, and we used to attend the board meetings. Fortunately, the CMD and his colleagues were kind-hearted and very helpful during our deliberations on important issues relating to the management of the company. Though their functions were at Ennore Port, the corporate headquarters office was functioning only from the City. Later on, they shifted the corporate office as well to the Ennore Port Office.

One interesting thing I could learn about this particular assignment was about the functioning of the Ennore Port Limited and also the materials that were transhipped by ship, especially the automobiles from Chennai. I visited a ship, and I was particularly interested to know how the automobiles were transported from one country to another.

On board a ship, it was really an interesting experience to know that several dozens of cars manufactured in Chennai were exported to other countries. Ennore Port was meant to handle not so clean cargo like coal etc. It was very interesting to know how the imported coal from other states through ships was offloaded from the ship directly to the overhead conveyor belt at Ennore Thermal station and also to the stockyard there. For me, it is not a new thing as I had visited the place several times in the past and that too when I was the then Joint Secretary to the government in the Ministry of Steel. I had to handle the issue of putting a conveyor belt system and got the work order from TNEB. Of course, I had informed this matter to the CMD and his colleagues of Ennore Port Ltd. I was involved in the project for transhipment of the coal from the ship to the thermal power station through the external overhead conveyor belt transport system. I was in a position to tell the other independent directors and other members of the Ennore Port Ltd that I had contributed my humble mite to their business activities without them knowing who was responsible for this kind of transportation of coal from their port to the nearby thermal power station, which was part and parcel of their activities.

This term of my 3-year assignment as an independent part-time Director of Ennore Port Ltd came to an end in Feb 2014. However, even before I could complete this 3-year assignment, I was also appointed as an Independent Director on the Board of KIOCL with its headquarters in Bengaluru. I could continue in that assignment up to 2017. In 2017, I was appointed as an independent part-time director on the Board of Oil India Ltd, which is a Navaratna Public Sector Undertaking under the Ministry of Petroleum and Natural Gas. I served in that assignment up to September 2020.

During my post-superannuation period, in addition to being an independent director on the Boards of 3 different public sector undertakings under 3 different Ministries of the Government of India, I was also appointed as an independent external monitor for 2 organisations, i.e. Chennai Port Trust and North eastern Electric Power Corporation Ltd., at Shillong. The objective of the appointment of an independent external monitor was to ensure that the contracts entered into between a Governmental organisation and the contractor were executed in a transparent manner so that there would be no conflict of interest.

Incidentally, I had another interesting post-retirement assignment as a Member of the three-member committee formed to select a suitable candidate for the Vice-Chancellorship of India Maritime University at Uthandi, Chennai. The committee was headed by a retired Vice-Chancellor. He was a thorough gentleman, and we had to go through several applications to select a panel of candidates after our meetings and examinations of biodata and other official records. We could select a panel of names and refer the matter to the Ministry of Shipping.

As an independent director on the boards of 3 Public Sector Undertakings, I could contribute to the growth and development of these organisations post-retirement as well. For instance, in Ennore Port Ltd, whenever any important issues were discussed and decisions were to be taken, it was wholeheartedly and effectively discussed in a threadbare manner. The officials of the undertaking, along with the Independent Director, actively participated in several meetings. I noticed at that time that the organisation had only fewer than 130 members right from the CMD to the lowest category of staff. Therefore, sometimes I had noticed that there needed to be a proper work orientation and proper deployment of personnel for different types of assignments. So, based on the company's request, I and other independent directors formed the committee of our own and suggested the reorganisation of several staff units so that with a fewer number of people, the organisation could cater towards the proper and effective functioning of Ennore Port Ltd. I had detailed discussions with the officers and staff, along with the other members of the committee, and earmarked certain functions and staff members so that the ultimate objective of job satisfaction was achieved.

The other 2 Public Sector Undertakings like KIOCL and Oil India Ltd were very old, and decision-making processes were largely focused on the largest interests of growth and development of KIOCL and Oil India Ltd.

I was already associated with KIOCL in my capacity as Joint Secretary to the government in the Ministry of Steel, however, I had no exposure to the Ministry of Petroleum and Natural Gas. For me, it was literally a learning curve to know more about the oil industry. In fact, I was fortunate to get appointed as an independent part-time director on the Board of Oil India Ltd.

Generally, the Annual General Meetings were held only at Duliajan of Dibrugarh district, i.e. the location of Oil India's field headquarters. In that area, only oil was explored several decades ago, and even today, oil is extracted by the company in and around Duliajan and other places. I could interact with the officials and staff of Oil India Ltd at Duliajan and other places, in addition to their corporate headquarters office at Noida. My assignment as an independent part-time non-official director on the Board of Directors of Oil India Ltd was a wonderful opportunity to know more about oil exploration and its exploitation, and of course, other issues connected with the oil industry. For me, it was definitely a very pleasant opportunity to interact with the officers from Assam as originally, when I worked in Assam, I had been to all these places, and I never knew that I would be associated with the company after my retirement. It was perhaps ordained that I would go back to Assam and associate myself with the industry there.

Fortunately for all my post-retirement assignments, without any effort on my part, I was appointed to different assignments due to God's divine grace and the wishes of my well-wishers, as mentioned earlier and now as well.

My Association With Senior I.A.S. Officers

Ever since I joined the Indian Administrative Service on the 13th of July 1975, I have had many occasions to come across a large number of well-meaning, civilised, gentle, and unforgettable senior civil servants from whom I had learnt a lot.

When I entered as a trainee officer for the first time in Assam, I had gone to call on the Chief Secretary of the Government of Assam along with my other fellow trainee officers of the 1975 batch. Mr. Rana KDN Singh was the Chief Secretary in the year 1976. For a very young recruit and that too, for a probationer like me, the Chief Secretary was the ultimate personification of authority and symbol of the government, as he was the head of the administration of the state.

My colleagues and I found him to be a very warm-hearted personality, but also a gentleman who meant business in the strictest sense of the term. He gave us a pep talk over a cup of tea and generally made us comfortable with his delightful interactions. To me, he appeared to have a positive mindset for ensuring the completion of given tasks in a scheduled timeframe.

As we had to pursue a two-month training period on survey and settlement of the land records, which was a must for understanding and appreciation of the revenue administration at the field-level of the district administration, we had to attend classes giving us the technical aspects of survey and settlement processes in addition to clearing examinations after the training period. Therefore, we had to take public transport in the form of old model city buses from our place of stay at Dispur to a distant place at Santipur in Guwahati, at a distance of approximately 18 kilometres one way.

In a nutshell, the whole training period was a very pleasant one, and it was real field training with the revenue officers of the administration as our instructors. The revenue officers who were our teachers did impart theoretical and practical training, which we were expected to undergo as trainee officers devoid of inhibitions or having a mindset of unwarranted superiority complex that on a later day, the said teachers may turn out to be our junior colleagues or our own subordinate officers.

Prior to visiting the State Headquarters, I had spent a few months at the District Headquarters of a district as part of my initial period of district training with the Office of the Deputy Commissioner of Cachar district headquartered at Silchar. The Deputy Commissioner was supposed to be a friend, philosopher, and guide for a young I.A.S. probationer regarding the complete training schedule for a year with varied aspects of the functions of the establishment of the Deputy Commissioner of the district.

After the training schedule was given to me and as I was supposed to undergo different learning processes, I did take a proactive role myself as an eager and willing trainee to understand, appreciate and grasp the nitty-gritty of the functions of various offices under the ambit of the Deputy Commissioner's establishment.

After some months of my joining, of course, another new Deputy Commissioner joined and he took some interest in my training. At least, he exuded a little more warmth. After I joined within a couple of months, there was devastating floods in the entire district. In the district, wherein, I underwent training, in view of the unprecedented floods, with approximately 75 per cent of the District Headquarters town impacted, the situation was very grim. The control and management of floods became a very serious one warranting the presence of the Divisional Commissioner Shri. P. H. Trivedi who literally took reins of the district administration. For a period of 10 days, he presided over the flood control, management and supervision of all the district-level functionaries. I attended the meetings day in and day out and was entrusted with the recording of the proceedings of the meetings. I specifically mentioned this issue at this juncture only to highlight the importance of my first and foremost interactions with the Divisional Commissioner who was pretty senior and had held various important assignments prior to that field-level posting as a Divisional

Commissioner. He was a pretty serious type of a bureaucrat and I didn't see him ever smiling even once during those days. Probably it may be due to the prevailing situation and he meant business and wielded his authority to the hilt.

Coming back to the survey and settlement training period and along with the brief and pleasant interactions with the Chief Secretary of Assam, I may like to state that I and my other fellow trainee officers had a chance meeting with a very senior civil servant who was the Divisional Commissioner based in Guwahati. It so happened that at that time a very big annual conference of a national political party was supposed to be held, and various infrastructural amenities were to be organised by the State Government in view of the impending visits of VIPs, etc.

I understood that the Divisional Commissioner based in Guwahati, with a no-nonsense persona, was entrusted with all kinds of infrastructural development of the state, especially in Guwahati and its suburbs, in a time-bound manner as per the dictates of the highest levels of the State Government. In addition to the participation of many Governments in setting up large pavilions, the Commissioner was entrusted with the functions of a Chief Coordinator so that nothing went wrong and all the planning and implementation of several projects that were undertaken, like widening of the roads, provision of adequate water supply, and other necessary facilities, including the construction of 2 large state guest houses for accommodating VIPs.

The Commissioner, Smt. P. P. Trivedi, allotted certain duties to me and my other fellow trainees, numbering 3, as well as all other departmental heads of field-level officers. She did exhibit admirable and competent leadership qualities of head and heart.

After the completion of my district training and after attending a three-month professional course at the Lalbahadur Shastri National Academy of Administration in Mussoorie, I proceeded to join my first substantial posting as the Sub-Divisional Officer of Golaghat Sub-division in Assam.

Coming back to the narration of my reminiscences of interactions with senior civil servants, I met the Divisional Commissioner Mr. A. K. Palit, under whose jurisdiction the Deputy Commissioner of the district and in turn I, as the Sub-divisional officer, had served. He was a wonderful person and a father figure with a humane approach and helpful attitude. He used to speak less and prefer to listen to the junior colleagues in order to understand and appreciate their points of view.

After a year or so, another respected senior colleague, namely, Mr. S. D. Phene, who was a stickler for decency and transparency in his outlook with a positive mindset, always used to interact in a very congenial and delightful manner. He could easily be described as a friend, philosopher, and guide in the strictest sense of the term.

After about 20 months or so, I was transferred from my field posting i.e. Sub-divisional officer to the secretariat, and I met the Chief Secretary to the State Government. He was one of the brilliant officers of the Assam - Meghalaya cadre. His name was Mr. R. S. Paramasivan. I have learnt one of the fundamental etiquettes of a civil servant, i.e. how one should receive a visitor irrespective of the status of a person who may be the junior-most or a very senior colleague in the official hierarchy. I had learnt from him this unforgettable lesson in my life. When I went to his office chamber for the first time as a young Sub-divisional officer to call on him, the moment I entered after seeking a prior appointment, the Chief Secretary got up from his chair and welcomed me by extending his hands and shook hands with me. It was a very warm welcome from a senior civil servant to his youngest colleague who was more than 2 and a half decades junior to him in the Indian Administrative Service. It was my very first meeting, and he exhibited his affection and warmth. He also conveyed his appreciation of my fluency in learning the local language and for having given a lecture in the Assamese language to the students of the college at my place of posting. He came to know about this perhaps from an acquaintance of his who happened to be at the Circuit House and listened to my address on that occasion. His acquaintance had never met me nor known me. It seems that he only heard my speech thanks to the loudspeaker facility at the college, which was in the neighbourhood of the local Circuit House at Golaghat.

What struck me most, and it was an indelible imprint in my mind, was that the Chief Secretary got up from his chair and went right up to the door of his chamber and opened the door when I took leave of him after my very pleasant interaction with him. He held the door open and took leave of me. It was such a gracious gesture on the part of the head of the state administration to one of his junior-most colleagues.

I have never ever come across a very senior colleague like him getting up from his or her chair to receive a junior colleague on his entry into his or her office chamber and thereafter getting up again to see off the visitor. Mr. R. S. Paramasivan was an exceptionally brilliant, competent, dynamic and a very warm-hearted gentleman and an exceptionally capable officer of the Indian Administrative Service.

Likewise, I have very fond memories of my interactions with Mr. B. S. Sarao, a very large-hearted and kind senior officer. Even today, I vividly cherish my pleasant meeting with Mr. B. S. Sarao when I met him during his assignment as Additional Chief Secretary in charge of the Personnel Department in the latter part of the year 1979 to seek permission to grant me leave for a period of one month to get married in Tamil Nadu.

He enquired about my date of marriage and my future wife's qualifications, etc., and details about the distance to the place of my marriage in Tamil Nadu from Guwahati. Though he was always friendly, I was rather wondering whether I would get sanction for a one month leave period as I had to take long-distance train journeys both ways. He immediately called for the file from his subordinate officer in which my leave application was dealt. He wrote in my presence on that file as follows. I was literally flabbergasted to hear him when he wrote on the file and informed me simultaneously that "Marriage comes once-in-a-lifetime in respect of an individual. I hereby order that Shri. Manoharan may be granted 2 and a half months' leave on account of his marriage. The state can wait for his arrival back. Heavens will not fall down."

What a fine and magnanimous gesture on the part of a very senior officer that made sure that a junior colleague felt at home, bereft of anxiety and anguish.

Of course, that was not the first time I had met him in my service after joining the cadre. I had occasions to meet him at Kaziranga Tourist Lodge when I went to meet him as S. D. O. Golaghat with Mr. S. K. Chakravarthy, Deputy Commissioner of the district. Mr. B. S. Sarao was the Agricultural Production Commissioner of the state, and he had come along with the

Secretary to the Government of India in the Ministry of Agriculture, New Delhi, for a visit and to attend official meetings. In his very first meeting on that day with myself, he made me feel at home. There were absolutely no airs about him or his seniority. I had worked with him briefly as the Joint Secretary to the Government of Assam in Home and Political Departments later while he had served as the then Chief Secretary to the Government of Assam. He later served as the Chief Commissioner of the Union Territory of Chandigarh before retirement.

I would like to state that I worked as Joint Secretary to the Government of Assam in the Home and Political Departments in the year 1983. I had the pleasure of working with Mr. Ramesh Chandra, the then Chief Secretary, for a longer period. Additionally, I worked with Mr. B. S. Sarao as Chief Secretary before that and later with Mr. A. K. Palit as Chief Secretary for a brief period as well.

Throughout my service career in the Indian Administrative Service, I have never come across a senior officer like Mr. Ramesh Chandra at the level of the Chief Secretary who was thoroughly unruffled and maintained his equilibrium despite very serious law and order situations that arose in the entire state due to the agitations galore as well as the fact that in the entire state, the government servants at every level in the hierarchy had literally adopted a non-co-operation movement. The state witnessed so much violence - arsons, killings, and there was a nightmarish situation all over the state with hardly 20 persons working at the secretariat. When the state was on fire and the conduct of general elections to the legislative assembly was thrust on the people, one could imagine how much pressure would have been brought upon the head of the state administration and that too, during the President's rule in the state.

I was more and more tense after receiving so many dozens of wireless telegraphic messages about the violence, arsons, deaths, etc., reported from many parts of the state. But Mr. Ramesh Chandra had kept a cool head, and it was remarkable to see him functioning as the head of the state administration with a calm mind and composure.

He was always very kind to me. Every now and then, he used to call me from his official chamber. I was at his beck and call and also worked very closely with Mr. M. Gopalakrishna, the then Commissioner and Secretary,

Home and Political Departments. I was nicknamed the 'Running Joint Secretary' as I was frequently on the move between my office chamber, the office chamber of the Chief Secretary, and the office chamber of the Home Commissioner. Mr. Ramesh Chandra later got transferred to the G. O. I. and was posted as Secretary, Housing and Urban Development Department of the Government of India.

Mr. A. K. Palit succeeded him. He was an exceptionally honest and ramrod-straight gentleman. Perhaps, if I vividly remember correctly, I could vouchsafe for the fact that he had paid money for the petrol for using the government vehicle from his residence to the office of the Chief Secretary at the secretariat. He was a stickler for norms and an unassuming, very soft-spoken gentleman to the core. He always maintained absolute dignity and interacted with his colleagues and subordinates in a friendly and pleasant manner. Of course, I have had occasions to interact with him as Sub-Divisional Officer of Golaghat Sub-division when he had served as the then Commissioner of Upper Assam Division at Jorhat. He was always considerate, kind-hearted, and had very pleasing manners.

I happened to be the Deputy Commissioner of Karbi Anglong District during the tenure of Mr. A. K. Palit as Chief Secretary to the Government of Assam. I came to know that an appointment order was received for my central deputation assignment (Deputy Secretary Level) under G. O. I. at Madras. I immediately rushed to Dispur, Guwahati and met Mr. A. K. Palit, and requested him to get me relieved from my assignment which would enable me to proceed to Madras for taking up that assignment.

He was extremely reluctant to relieve me and informed me that he would send the file to the Chief Minister with his reluctance to relieve me. Then I informed him candidly that as it was a golden opportunity to work in Madras for 5 years on central deputation in my home state, with his permission, I would meet the Chief Minister with my request to relieve me from my assignment to proceed to Madras to join the central deputation assignment under the Ministry of Commerce, Government of India. Of course, when I met the Chief Minister, I candidly stated that I would like to be relieved even though the Chief Secretary was reluctant in view of his insistence that I should continue to serve in the State of Assam. Fortunately, the Chief Minister heard me patiently and agreed to consider my request.

I was relieved in a week's time and I proceeded to Madras after formal orders were issued relieving me.

During my stay in the State of Assam, I have had opportunities to serve in different assignments at various levels and have interacted with senior officers in the State cadre.

Mr. Sushanta Kumar Chakravarty was exactly 10 years senior to me in service and was my immediate supervisory officer, as Deputy Commissioner of the district of Sibsagar with Jorhat as the District Headquarters. I was the Sub-Divisional Officer of Golaghat Sub-division under his administrative jurisdiction. In a nutshell, I would like to state that he had treated me more like his own younger brother with love, affection and warmth rather than as a senior supervisory officer. I served under his leadership for a period of 20 months. There was never ever a single occasion to say candidly that he neither cautioned me nor reprimanded me. He was an admirable, very friendly, helpful and a thoroughly warm-hearted gentleman to the core.

When I was transferred from Golaghat to the secretariat initially for about a year as Secretary of the Commission of Enquiry meant to inquire into the conduct of several construction works in connection with the AICC session of the ruling party in 1976 by the successor government formed by the erstwhile opposition party later in 1979 and thereafter as Deputy Secretary of the Transport, Tourism, and Co-operation departments for a few months only, I met Mr. K. Sridhar Rao as Secretary of the Tourism Department.

Mr. K. Sridhar Rao was instrumental in training me on how to organise my work as Deputy Secretary and advised me to proceed to Kaziranga and some other places of tourist importance and to give my suggestions for providing the requisite infrastructure and other amenities for the promotion of tourism in the state. I discharged my duties as expected of him and gave my report. Thereafter, I have had occasions to interact with him in my several assignments and especially as the Chief Electoral Officer when he happened to be the Additional Chief Secretary. He always treated me as a well-regarded younger colleague with due respect and always interacted with a positive attitude.

I would like to record that Mr. H. N. Das, the Chief Secretary, never ever interfered during my tenure of assignment as the Chief Electoral Officer of the state. I only used to meet him as and when I felt it necessary to apprise him about my functions as the CEO and the directions and instructions of the Election Commission of India. He always treated me as though I was a member of his own family rather than as his junior colleague. I thought that it was my duty and responsibility to apprise him even though he never ever advised me to meet him nor ever interfered in my functions as the then Chief Electoral Officer for more than 2 and a half years.

During my assignment as the Deputy Commissioner of North Cachar Hills district with headquarters at Haflong between 1980-81, I had the occasion to serve under 2 senior officers as Commissioner of Hills and Barak Valley division, namely Mr. P. N. Rao for a very brief period and Mr. T. K. Kamilla for a longer period. Mr. P. N. Rao was a very strict disciplinarian and very particular about constant and continuous supervision over the law and order situation in the district even though the situation was far better in the district compared to the plains districts in view of the prolonged agitation and bundhs, etc. in the entire state. Mr. T. K. Kamilla was equally a strict disciplinarian, and I had the occasion to work under his supervision later as well when he was the Chief Secretary of the State Government during the years 1996-97. He was business-like and straightforward in his interactions in all matters concerning the welfare of the people and for taking appropriate actions in times of necessity regarding the maintenance of law and order and handling of difficult situations with firmness.

During my central deputation assignments, I have had the occasion to serve under some exceptionally outstanding officers with excellent qualities of head and heart and with impeccable integrity and rectitude.

I would like to mention especially the names of my supervisory officers, namely Mr. Rajiv Lochan Mishra and Mr. Tejinder Khanna as the then Chief Controller of Imports and Exports when I had served under the Ministry of Commerce. In a nutshell, if I may say that in such a sensitive assignment in a licensing organisation, literally when import licences worth several crores of rupees and cash incentives worth several crores of rupees were issued to the importers and exporters of various items day in and day out, one could easily imagine the types of pressures, stress, and tension that were faced by me as the then head of the organisation at Madras.

When I joined in 1985 as the then JCCI&E, Mr. Rajiv Lochan Mishra was the Chief Controller of Imports and Exports, Government of India in New Delhi. He was my immediate supervisory officer for a couple of years. Later on, Mr. Tejinder Khanna succeeded him as the Chief Controller of Imports and Exports for a little more than a couple of years.

If I may say so, I considered myself fortunate to serve under both of them with their genuine attitude of friend, philosopher, and guide as my supervisory officers. This helped me to handle such a challenging and difficult licensing organisation as the South Zone head of the organisation with confidence, commitment, courage of conviction, impeccable integrity, and rectitude in view of their admirable leadership with admirable qualities of head and heart.

During the period of my assignment as the then Joint Secretary in the Ministry of Steel for 5 years, I have had the occasions to serve under the supervision of 4 secretaries. I would like to make special mention of only 2 of them from whom I had learnt the art of management of difficult situations with, of course, proper organisation, confidence, commitment, courage of conviction, missionary zeal, and enthusiasm.

Dr. J. K. Bhachi was the Secretary in the Ministry of Steel when I first joined as Joint Secretary in January 1997. Although I would have loved to serve under him for a longer period, he had reached superannuation 6 months after my joining. He was always very pleasant and a gem of a person during his interactions, with an infectious smile and a sense of humour. He had allocated the supervision of works relating to half a dozen sick public sector undertakings under the Ministry of Steel to me.

I would like to make a mention of the qualities of head and heart of another gentleman, i.e. A. K. Agarwal, as the then Secretary, Ministry of Steel. He was always very kind to me with his polite conduct, and he had interacted with me in a very pleasant manner with due respect and listened to my suggestions regarding the revival and handling of the issues of difficult and loss-making public sector undertakings. I would like to mention briefly his absolute physical and moral support to me as he had agreed in total about my suggestions and plan of actions regarding the revival of one of the utmost difficult undertakings with the separation of 6 thousand employees in one go with financial incentives after getting the requisite loans from financial institutions with, of course, government guarantees on very valid grounds only. For brevity's sake, I didn't like to write in an expansive manner about the issues and concerns regarding the revival of that very sick Public Sector Undertaking and the revival of a couple of more such undertakings of the Ministry of Steel.

I had the occasion to work as an Additional Secretary and Special Secretary in the Ministry of Water Resources, Government of India for nearly 4 years before my superannuation. I would like to briefly mention that Mrs. Gauri Chatterjee was the Secretary when I joined as Additional Secretary in the Ministry of Water Resources in October 2006, and she had served as Secretary for a little more than a year. Later, Mr. U. N. Panjiyar was the Secretary from the first week of February 2008 until my superannuation in May 2010. It is a fact that by the time I had joined as Additional Secretary in October 2006, I had already completed 31 years of public service in many responsible assignments in the State of Assam and in Government of India organisations.

Conclusion

Every beginning is followed by an end. Therefore, towards the end of my narration, I trust that I did attempt to make the reader get a feel of the reminiscences of a civil servant, i.e. myself, with regard to the assignments over a period of time after my entry into the Indian Administrative Service. It was a long-drawn journey of a civil servant that commenced from Lal Bahadur Shastri National Academy of Administration on the 13th of July 1975. The number 13 is generally considered to be an unlucky number, but it turned out to be a lucky number for me, as I had an eventful career in the civil service over a period of 35 years or so and ended happily and peacefully on the 31st of May 2010 in New Delhi.

During the period of approximately 35 years in the civil service, I worked in 3 different states and participated in 2 Post Graduate level programmes. If I may say so, by God's divine grace, I could enter the I.A.S. due to my sheer hard work, dint of merit, and a positive mindset that I developed over a period of time without any let up. Of course, I was rather apprehensive that I did recall the various anecdotes and events in my life spread over more than 3 decades and that too, after more than a decade of my superannuation. Fortunately, due to my good memory, I could recall as far as possible my experiences of an erstwhile civil servant in the state of allotment i.e. Assam and in the state of Tamil Nadu and Delhi on Central Government deputation assignments in different Ministries.

It is with a tremendous sense of pride and indomitable spirit that I would like to record with the same kind of enthusiasm and hard work I had put in for my entry into the I.A.S. immediately after my postgraduation. I had attempted to write this book with, of course, God-ordained memory power even after 48 years of my joining the I.A.S. I had to face several difficult situations in my life dealing with different sections of people, including politicians, civil servants, and members of non-governmental organisations, etc. Moreover, it gave me opportunities to get recognised for the hard work I put in the states where I had worked and, of course, the goodwill I earned from the people whom I had served. I had always believed that in addition to maintaining my utmost integrity, straightforward dealings in a transparent manner in whichever organisations I had contributed my mite for the benefit of the people of this country, certainly as an unservile civil servant to the best of my abilities in the largest public interest.

As the civil service gave me wonderful opportunities to adapt to various situations and in varied milieu of organisations wherein, I could contribute my mite with utmost competence, capability and efficiency as expected of me. When I looked back after completion of the various chapters in this book, I had my own sense of satisfaction that after all I did serve the people in the best possible manner with commitment, compassion, dedication and sincerity. Of course, it is a crystal clear fact that I did come out without any blemish in many assignments in the Central and State Governments at different points of time.

I considered myself fortunate by God's divine grace that I could straightaway join the LBSNAA after my postgraduation in a science subject without doing any other service or without trying to get into the civil service again and again in a few attempts. I did get into I.A.S. in the very first attempt and without any parental civil service background. I could come up on my own to this extent due to sheer good luck and hard work. Last but not least, the reader may find my assertions to be immodest but that was not my intention. My intention was to make the reader aware that with great perseverance and steadfast hard work I made myself fit for the conditions of the civil service despite various adverse situations in different assignments and that too, in a state not of one's own choice. I would like to thank the reader for his or her patience in going through this book comprising the reminiscences of my civil service days.

In conclusion, I would like to mention that if I may sound as though I was rather overconfident, I would be delighted and privileged to ensure a place in the mind, heart, and soul of the reader. In fact, as an erstwhile civil servant, I was certainly unservile but as a humane public servant, I discharged my duties in the largest interests of the public for more than a period of 3 decades.

I thank the reader very much for his kind courtesy and sincere patience with which he would have read my book with abiding interest in my lifelong struggle as an erstwhile civil servant, despite many impediments.

Acknowledgement

Iattempted to write my memoirs as a former civil servant with God's divine grace.

At the very outset, I would like to express my deepest gratitude to all my family members.

I would not have entered the civil services without the support and love showered early in my life by my mother, the late Mrs. K.V. Namagiri Lakshmi, my sister, Mrs. Jamuna, and also by my brother-in-law, Mr. D.K. Meganathan.

I believe I have had a fulfilling career, and these memoirs are a reflection of my time spent working in different places and situations. My family has played a wonderful role in supporting me through this journey.

As such, I would not have put pen to paper, or rather in these times of advancement, finger to keyboard, if it wasn't for the continued encouragement and highly needed prodding by my beloved wife, Dr. Kalarani, as well as my son Rajkumar, daughter-in-law Divya, and my lovable granddaughter Anoushka for their encouragement and moral support.

My sincere thanks also go to my brother-in-law, Mr. G. Chandrasekar, who inspired me with his boundless motivation, encouragement, and continuous persuasion.

My special thanks are certainly due to my former respected colleagues Mr. M. Gopalakrishna I.A.S. (R), Mr. M. Ganapathi IFS (R), and Mr. N. Balabaskar I.A.S. (R) for their insightful analysis, continued encouragement, and honest feedback.

I shall be failing in my duty if I do not mention with regard to the excellent guidance given by Mr. Vivek Harinarain I.A.S.(R) in helping me to undertake my task of writing this book. I convey my sincere gratitude to Mrs. Chella Vaidhyanathan without whose painstaking efforts, it would not have been possible for me to publish this book.

My career would not have been as personally fulfilling as it was to me if it wasn't for the bonds I built with the 1975 batch of the civil services as well as the fine officers of the Assam-Meghalaya cadre, as well as the countless people that I have worked with over the years. The reader will read about many of them in this book.

I do hope and pray that the readers will find at least something of value or interest as they read about my past experiences as an erstwhile civil servant of our great nation.

Mr. S. Manoharan belonged to the 1975 I.A.S. batch. After completing his postgraduate studies in Master of Science from Annamalai University in the year 1973, he appeared in the I.A.S. and allied services combined competitive examinations conducted by the Union Public Service Commission in 1974.

He succeeded in his very first attempt at the UPSC examination and joined the I.A.S. on 13th July 1975. During the first phase of the training period, he was allotted to the Assam-Meghalaya cadre. He held several assignments in the State of Assam and performed his duties and responsibilities on Central Government deputation assignments as well during different spells in the then City of Madras and New Delhi. After approximately 35 years in service, he attained superannuation on the 31st of May 2010 as Special Secretary to the Government of India in the Ministry of Water Resources, New Delhi.

www.ingramcontent.com/pod-product-compliance
Lightning Source LLC
Chambersburg PA
CBHW060525160726
47991CB00001B/182